# THE WORLD'S MOST BIZARRE MURDERS

JAMES MARRISON

# THE WORLD'S MOST BIZARRE MURDERS

TRUE STORIES
THAT WILL SHOCK
AND AMAZE YOU

JOHN BLAKE

Published by John Blake Publishing Ltd,
3 Bramber Court, 2 Bramber Road,
London W14 9PB, England

www.johnblakepublishing.co.uk

First published in hardback in 2008

ISBN: 978 1 84454 667 1

British Library Cataloguing-in-Publication Data:

A catalogue record for this book is available from the British Library.

Design by www.envydesign.co.uk

Printed in Great Britain by Creative Print and Design, Blaina, Wales

1 3 5 7 9 10 8 6 4 2

Papers used by John Blake Publishing are natural, recyclable
products made from wood grown in sustainable forests.
The manufacturing processes conform to the environmental
regulations of the country of origin.

Then – in my childhood, in the dawn
Of a most stormy life – was drawn
From every depth of good and ill
The mystery which binds me still
From the torrent, or the fountain,
From the red cliff of the mountain,
From the sun that round me rolled
In its autumn tint of gold,
From the lightning in the sky
As it passed me flying by,
From the thunder and the storm,
And the cloud that took the form
(When the rest of Heaven was blue)
Of a demon in my view.

From 'Alone' (1829) –
Edgar Allan Poe

# CONTENTS

# CHAPTER ONE

# SANTOS GODINO: ARGENTINA'S JUG-EARED MONSTER

Did child-killer Santos Godino's 'odd' features offer a clue about why he liked to torture toddlers and slaughter infants?

While there have been many cases of children who kill, perhaps none has been as instinctively savage and ferocious as that of Santos Godino. The sixth of seven children, Godino was born on 31 October 1896 in Buenos Aires, Argentina. Deformed at birth, with saucer-sized ears, a short body and overly long arms and legs, he soon became known as the local neighbourhood freak, dubbed 'el Petisu Orejudo', or 'the short big-eared one'.

Godino grew up in the neighbourhood of Parque Patricios. Today, this is a pleasant enough locale of Buenos Aires; trees line the streets among the fairly modest high-rise tenements. A hundred years ago, however, it was a poverty-stricken slum and home to an enormous slaughterhouse; four whole blocks of it were cut off each day as the cattle were driven in and killed on the streets, in plain view of the local residents.

As if the sight of blood and the sound of screaming cattle weren't bad enough in the morning, at night the whole of the city's waste was brought to Parque Patricios, and then burned. Since most of the houses there were made out of salvaged junk, it went by the name of 'the city of tin' or 'the bonfire'; the neighbourhood stank of stale blood and burning rubbish. The majority of people who lived there were Spanish or Italian immigrants who had come to Argentina looking for a new life and found themselves working at starvation wages in the local slaughterhouse. In short, it was the kind of place that would swallow you whole in around five seconds flat if you didn't know your way around. Perhaps nobody would come to know the streets of Parque Patricios better than Argentina's first and most notorious serial killer.

As his home life was utterly dismal, Godino spent most of his time trying to avoid it. School didn't provide much escape: expelled almost instantly from every institution he ever attended, from the age of ten he took to wandering the streets, returning home only when hunger drove him to it. His father had been drunk for as long as Godino could remember and frequently beat his wife and kids senseless. But Godino, uncontrollable from the start, came in for special attention and his father frequently thrashed him around the head with a belt buckle. By the time he was 16, he had 27 scars on his head to prove it.

Most people regarded him as a slightly demented but harmless local pest; in fact, behind his somewhat vacant gaze, Godino was a fairly resourceful killer. At the age of seven, he was busy torturing to death every animal he could get his little hands on, and then keeping them under his bed in a box. What's more, on his daily jaunts about town, he was single-mindedly luring children to abandoned houses and wastelands and murdering them.

It took him a while to get it right.

When he was seven, he beat up 17-month-old Miguel de Paoli and then threw him into a razor-sharp thorn bush, but was spotted by a policeman who had seen the small boy crying and rushed over to see what was happening. The resourceful Santos began caressing the boy, told the policeman he had found him in the bush and insisted that he take him back to his mother. When he got back with the child, he was rewarded with some sweets.

Godino wasn't the brightest boy in the world, but he had a cunning streak. Of the 11 times he tried to kill, he was interrupted five times by nearby adults or police but managed to talk his way out of it every time. Even when he was taken to the police station (which happened three times), his age worked in his favour and he was released soon afterwards. Moreover, in most cases his victims were too young to even talk.

A year after trying to kill De Paoli, he hospitalised toddler Ana Neri for six months after trying to cave her head in with a rock. Believing the girl dead, he found the girl's father and told him that he had found her lying on the ground and that she had fallen over. Shortly after that, he claimed his first fatality. He was never able to remember her name properly and her body was never discovered but he did remember later that she was too young to walk so he had carried her to an abandoned patch of land – where he buried her alive in a ditch.

It was March 1906 and Santos Godino was nine years old.

In the same year, his father gave up on him and took him in to the local police station, complaining that his son was utterly indifferent to any kind of authority whatsoever. As well as hurling rocks at the neighbours and seriously injuring them, by now Godino was also attacking his brothers and sisters. His father told the police that, if they didn't take him into some kind of custody, he would 'kill the little bugger' himself. (He had, so legend has it, on that very morning found a dead bird in his boot – a present from Santos, no doubt.)

According to a statement signed by Francisco Laguarda, the head of the local police station, Godino's father Fiore walked into the station and filed official charges against his own son. The statement reads as follows: 'In the city of Buenos Aires on April 5 1906, a person appeared before me and identified himself as Fiore Godino, a 42-year-old Italian immigrant who has been living in Argentina for 18 years. During his testimony, Fiore Godino said that he had a son called Cayetano Santos who is an Argentine citizen by birth and who is nine years and five months old. Fiore Godino contends that his son is uncontrollable and rebellious and does not respond in any way at all to any discipline of any kind and so he formally requests that the police take charge of his son and place him in whatever institution they see fit and for as long as they see appropriate.'

Godino spent two months in the reform school but was soon back to his usual tricks – and some new ones. At the age of ten, he discovered the wonders of masturbation and started masturbating three times a day. Meanwhile, he continued to attack children.

In 1908, now 12 years old, he tried to burn a girl's eyes out of her sockets by setting light to her eyelashes and also tried to drown 22-month-old Severino González Caló in a water trough. Luckily, the farmer heard screaming and came to her aid. Santos blamed the crime on a short woman dressed in black, explaining that he had actually come to the little girl's assistance and – luckily – arrived just in time to save her.

After another two months had elapsed, his parents simply couldn't stand him any longer and put him into another, much tougher reform school; he would stay there for the next three years, until he was 15. It was on his release that his true reign of terror began.

Reform school had only made Godino worse. He had been able to escape out of there most nights anyway and, along with his only friend, had begun stealing watches and selling them to buy alcohol. He was soon drinking almost as much as his old man and had also discovered another new hobby.

Maybe it was the sight of the rubbish burning constantly on the horizon at night, but Godino was now unable to resist setting fire to something if it looked like it would go up in flames fast enough. Thief, murderer and now pyromaniac, he set alight a wine cellar – creating a conflagration that took firemen three hours to put out – a lumber mill, a shop, a tramway station and two warehouses.

By this time, even the tough residents of Parque Patricios were giving him a wide berth, but children, he soon discovered, could be easily lured away from their protective gaze with sweets. He had also begun carrying a homemade garrotte.

In 1912, he committed three murders. In January, he tempted 13-year-old Arturo Laurora to an empty house, tied him to the floor, removed his trousers and underpants and then strangled him to death. A month later, he crept up behind a five-year-old girl as she was looking in a shoe-shop window and set light to her dress, leaving her to die.

Just before Christmas, he encountered 18-month-year-old

Jesualdo Giordano, asked the boy where the nearest sweetshop was; when the boy told him, Godino said he wanted to reward him for showing him the way. They went together to the sweetshop and Godino told the boy that he would walk him home. He then led him to an abandoned house.

As the boy didn't want to go into the house, Godino dragged him by his leg, stretched the boy out on the floor and tried to strangle him with a rope. But the boy kept on struggling, so Godino tied him up then decided to drive a nail through his skull. While looking for a nail, he left the building and ran into the boy's father who asked him if he had seen his son.

Godino told him that he had not, then helpfully suggested that he should go to the police station. He then went back into the house, finished the job and went home.

The boy's father, meanwhile, carried on looking. He looked all over the area until he entered an abandoned building and there, among the rubble and rubbish, was his son. At first, he thought he had found him hiding, and called his name but received no reply. He moved closer to the toddler, then, according to a report in Argentine tabloid *La Razón*, 'He took him in his arms and with desperation and grief started running with the boy to his house that was a short distance away. To begin with Giordano didn't realise that he was carrying a corpse in his arms, as the body was still warm but once inside his house and surrounded by his wife and neighbours it was confirmed that his son had been horribly murdered.'

That night, the boy's father held a wake for his son. Among those who attended it was Santos Godino, who approached the coffin and touched the skull, curious to know if the nail, which he had driven into the toddler's skull that morning, was still there. He didn't know it, but he was already under police surveillance. A girl who had been playing with Jesualdo when he had been abducted had clearly remembered his murderer and described him to police.

After the wake, Godino returned home for a while then went out to buy the evening edition of the local paper. As he was illiterate, he went to his friend's house and got him to read aloud an article about the murder, then tore it out and put it in his pocket. The press, who were having an absolute field day with the crime, were already hinting that an arrest was imminent, but that didn't bother Godino; he simply went home. He was drinking tea when police arrested him and took him in for questioning.

Using a very limited vocabulary, and with a soft, childlike way of expressing himself, Godino initially gave the impression of being utterly harmless and even vulnerable. Then he confessed to the murder.

As *La Razón* reported at the time, 'The subject said that the boy went with him to the store on Progreso and Jujuy where he bought two cents worth of sweets two of which he gave to the minor... as the boy started to ask for his father he gave the boy three more sweets and so managed to get him as far as the corner of Catamarca and 15 November where he approached a deserted house.'

Then, with an empty expression, he calmly told police that he had killed another three children and tried to kill another seven. He complained to his interrogators that he suffered from terrible headaches and said that, while being in the grip of an overpowering urge to kill, besides the three murders he had committed that year, he had also lured two other girls from their homes and tried beating them to death – in the last week. He also confessed that he had tried to strangle two-year-old

Roberto Russo to death in an abandoned house in November. According to police records, 'Godino confesses that he did all of it for fun and for entertainment, that it was purely the desire to kill that was the motivation to carry out his acts due to the fact that it gave him pleasure.'

And why not? He had been acting well within his rights, he told police. After all, plenty of other people did it too and, he added, 'It would really cheer me up to kill kids from the local hospital.' As well as confessing to all of his crimes against children and his frequent arson attacks, police records reveal that Godino also confessed to having stabbed a horse to death. 'As he recounts these incidents,' the official report reads, 'he does so with the utmost indifference affirming that he found pleasure in harming and killing animals. Indeed he shows not the slightest remorse for his acts, talks lucidly and shows satisfaction while recounting them. He says that he masturbates frequently and that he has had no dealings at all with women but that the sight of them he finds quite agreeable. He drinks strong alcohol on a regular basis and has done so ever since he was 12 when he started drinking four glasses of whisky per day. He has had little or no formal schooling. He is illiterate but is capable of signing his own name. He has a good memory. He has many interesting physical characteristics and would be an interesting subject for further study.'

*La Razón* also managed to interview Godino, shortly after his confession. 'Many mornings,' he told them 'after the usual moaning from my father and brothers and sisters I would leave my house with the idea of finding work and as I never found any I found myself feeling that I wanted to kill someone. So I would look for someone to kill. If I found some kid I would take him somewhere and strangle him.'

The journalist asked if he felt any remorse for his crimes. 'I felt some regret but only for a moment. Last night I went to Jesualdo's house and when I saw the boy in the box I felt like crying then I ran out of there because I was afraid.'

As Godino awaited trial, some of the most eminent doctors and physiatrists in the country examined him. One of their conclusions was that Godino was driven by an almost primeval animal instinct to kill. They declared that he felt absolutely no remorse for his crimes, was extremely dangerous and should spend the rest of his days in a lunatic asylum.

Some argued that his crimes were the result of systematic abuse, while others pointed to numerous physical and mental anomalies about the boy and argued that he was in fact mentally retarded. The two judges overseeing the case agreed that he had not been responsible for his actions and he was therefore transferred to the high-security wing of Las Mercedes hospital. There, his antics continued. Not only did Godino try to escape, but he also attacked a paralytic, tried to strangle one patient in his bed and put poison in another patient's tea.

Meanwhile, the police were trying to find the body of his first victim – the girl he told them that he had buried alive. Godino pointed out exactly where he had killed her, but by that time a two-storey building had been built on top of the site; neither the architect nor any of the builders had found any traces of a body. One detective took it upon himself to investigate all the reports of missing children in the area from March to April 1906, in his free time. He discovered that a three-year-old girl had been reported missing to authorities and had never been found. Her name was Maria Roca Face and she is now officially believed to have been Godino's first victim.

While at the insane asylum, Godino found himself adopted by one of the doctors as his pet project. The doctor was busy developing a crackpot theory – later to be resurrected by the Nazis – that certain physical characteristics could be linked to inborn moral depravity. And what better proof of this than Godino? (See Chapter Twenty-one: How to Spot a Natural Born Killer.) He paraded Godino in front of his students and the story goes that, as he recounted the despicable crimes carried out by the horror now standing before them, he pointed at his subject's big ears. Godino is reported to have said, 'Please excuse me, Doctor, for interrupting, but would you be so kind as to go fuck yourself.'

As Godino continued to raise hell at the mad house, many newspapers were expressing outrage at the perceived lenience of his sentence. 'This disgusting fellow,' one indignant journalist wrote, 'whose crimes horrified the public only a short time ago has just been declared not responsible for his horrible acts. The killer will be placed in a mental institution even though the general public is completely opposed to such a light sentence. This *beast* who heeded his most basic of instincts on innocent creatures. This *beast* whose brutal confession outlining his horrible deeds shocked the most hardened and seasoned of detectives. This *beast* whose account caused a terrible all-pervading sense of fear to creep into households throughout the capital. This *beast* whose accounts of his crimes caused papers to censor the horrible facts of the case so as not to permanently damage the sensibilities of their readers.

'The *boy*,' the journalist continued, 'who apparently lacks the faculties necessary to judge his own acts and take responsibility for them but at the same time is perfectly capable of erasing the traces of his crimes. The *boy* who carefully made sure that his victims were completely unable to defend themselves. The *boy* who revelled in acts of the utmost perversity. The *boy* with subnormal intelligence who somehow managed to avoid capture and repeat his crimes. This little monster I say! Little because of his age perhaps but old in the scope and magnitude of the crimes he committed. He has been forgiven all of this by our legal system!'

As he was only 16, Godino was too young to face the death penalty but the prosecutor, with the public opinion rising against Godino, obtained a retrial and this time the teenager was found guilty and sentenced to life imprisonment.

He went first to a jail in Buenos Aires but in 1923 he was transferred to one of the toughest jails in Latin America: Ushuaia, otherwise known as the 'prison at the end of the world'. Located in Argentina's southernmost tip, it was as good a place as any to banish this national embarrassment.

In 1927, doctors in the jail performed surgery on Godino's ears to try to curb his aggressiveness, but – unsurprisingly – this didn't do any good. After 23 years in jail, Godino applied for parole but was denied on the grounds that he still presented a danger to society. In all, he was punished 13 times for insubordination, spent 30 years of his life in prison without a single visitor or a letter and was refused parole three times. So ashamed of him were his parents that they returned to Italy, along with his brothers and sisters.

Godino died in his cell at the age of 49, on 15 November 1944. His death certificate states that he died in his cell as a result of internal bleeding brought about by an ulcer, but the circumstances around his death remain unclear. Legend has it that he died soon after he'd received a tremendous kicking at the hands of his fellow prisoners. Unrepentant to the end, he just hadn't been able to resist throwing the much-loved prison cat into an oven.

## CHAPTER TWO

# ISSEI SAGAWA: HOW TO EAT PEOPLE AND INFLUENCE THEM

Cannibal Issei Sagawa murdered then ate a young student in Paris in 1981. But instead of being ostracised and hated, fame and stardom beckoned.

One trait that cannibals share the world over is that they very rarely rush their food. They don't like to throw away cuts that can be stored and set aside for later either. While many of us might be too precious to eat sweetmeats or offal, a cannibal has no such reservations, knowing that they can be saved for a tasty snack or starter.

Cannibals are, of course, pioneers in the relatively uncharted area of human cuisine. When faced with a willing audience, they are known to go into details on the subtle change in taste and texture of each body part, while in the kitchen they can prove themselves adept in the ways of pickling and creative and inventive in the use of daring culinary combinations. Eager to provide tried-and-tested recipes (stew being a particular favourite), they wax lyrical on the challenges each limb presents, and many cannibals are even known to put a morsel aside and carry it around for later – just in case they get peckish.

But if the confession made by the so-called Japanese cannibal Issei Sagawa is to be believed, he was different from his peers in many ways. Sagawa told the authorities that he had been waiting for his chance to eat another human being, and when it finally came, he claimed, he consumed as much of his victim as he could stomach in a 24-hour feeding frenzy – and he ate most of her raw.

Sagawa was declared insane and not responsible for his actions by the French courts. Instead of being ostracised and hated, however, he soon found himself catapulted into the surreal world of Japanese show business where, for almost five years, he eagerly cashed in on his own notoriety. While the 'joke' lasted, Sagawa's cult status allowed him to take part in porn films and chat shows, write a bestseller and even appear on the front page of a cooking magazine slurping on sushi.

A bright boy with an exceptionally high IQ, Sagawa was the son of a millionaire and enjoyed a privileged upbringing in his hometown of Tokyo, where he showed a natural talent for languages. But from an early age he was prone to nasty tantrums, and from the age of 12 he suffered violent nocturnal seizures and nightmares.

His cannibal fantasies began at the age of seven and to begin with revolved around boys, but this changed during his teenage years. The shy, retiring Sagawa found himself lusting hopelessly after tall, blonde Western women, whom he found impossibly daunting and out of reach.

While studying English literature at Wako University in Tokyo, Sagawa made his first attempt to eat someone, attacking a German woman. Having stalked her and followed her back to her apartment, he tried to knock her unconscious while she was asleep. She fended him off and Sagawa fled, only to be arrested shortly afterwards. In a taste of things to come, Sagawa served just ten days at Kitazawa police station for the attack.

In 1977, now on prescribed tranquillisers, Sagawa was quietly packed off to the Sorbonne Academy in Paris, ostensibly to further his studies in French literature. In September 1978, aged 28, he bought a .22-calibre rifle.

By 1981, even with the change of scenery, Sagawa's luck with the ladies wasn't improving – he wasn't helped much by the fact that he was less than 5ft tall. He found it hard to make friends at the university, regarded first as an outcast, then a pest, and was described by fellow students variously as 'childish', 'sensitive' and 'embarrassing'. Indeed, Sagawa was more or less friendless save for Dutch student Renée Hartevelt, who took pity on him and agreed to help him with his German. Perhaps unsurprisingly, Sagawa fell head over heels in love with her. Tall, beautiful and intelligent, Hartevelt was just the type of girl he had been drooling over for all those years.

According to his confession to the police after his arrest on 11 June 1981, he invited Hartevelt (then aged 25) over to his apartment to read some German poetry – and promptly declared his love for her. Not one to stand on ceremony, he also asked her to go to bed with him. Hartevelt refused. Sagawa acted as if nothing had happened and asked her to resume her reading, which he was recording. At 5.30 p.m., he fetched the rifle and shot her once in the back of the head.

Sagawa later made a great deal of money by writing about what might have happened next in his bestselling book called *Into the Fog*, which earned him rave reviews from many Japanese critics. Sagawa set the story in Paris, though in the Latin Quarter, not Montmartre (where he had actually lived). The hero of the piece is called Akito Kamura, a 30-year-old Japanese student who is studying literature at the Sorbonne. Because of his vast intellect, Kamura is greatly appreciated by his teachers but less revered by the other students in the class who regard him as distant and arrogant. The lonely Kamura therefore spends most of his free time listening to classical music, reading and working on his thesis. Then, one day, Kamura meets a student from Holland. She is friendly and open and they quickly become friends. One day he invites her to his apartment for dinner. After she turns down his advances, he shoots her.

Sagawa has made varying claims as to how much he remembers after he had shot Hartevelt – and also told one journalist that he wrote the book because he was flat broke and needed the money. It's possible, then, that the acts Sagawa writes about next in the book were exaggerated in order to maximise shock value – and therefore sales. Having said that, many of the details that feature in *Into the Fog* tally with the autopsy that was carried out on Hartevelt's corpse. Whatever the case, the chapter on how the hero of the story eats his victims reads as if Sagawa is wistfully reliving a particularly pleasant and unusually long dinner.

In between declarations of love and gratitude to the lifeless corpse, no part of the body was taboo, and, the way Sagawa tells it in the novel, the more flesh the character eats, the more curious he becomes. Kamura starts off by sinking his teeth into his victim's buttocks. For some reason, this gives him a headache, so he starts to hack at the body with a knife and starts chewing on the tasteless fat, which is, Sagawa writes, reminiscent of tuna.

After engaging in sex with the corpse (for ten seconds), Kamura hugs her and then, after a brief scare as the body seems to let out air, he roasts her hip in a pan and seasons it with salt and mustard. While Kamura eats, he listens to her dead voice, recorded reading German poetry only hours before, and dabs at the corners of his mouth with her panties. He then bakes one of her breasts and eats that too.

Next, Kamura turns in for the night – taking what is left of the corpse with him. With a renewed appetite the next morning, Sagawa's character is relieved to find that his sleeping partner hasn't decomposed too badly and almost immediately he starts chewing on her calf and then her ankle. He then moves on to her foot before deciding to eat her armpit.

By this time, the whole flat smells of what Sagawa describes as 'fried chicken' and there are flies buzzing all over the corpse. Saying a final farewell, Kamura begins to dismember the body, only stopping for the occasional snack. He plays around with her internal organs for a while, then puts the head in one plastic bag and the body in the other and stuffs her remains in a suitcase.

We cannot be sure how closely these actions match the real-life events involving Sagawa himself. We do know that, once Sagawa had finished with Hartevelt's body, he carefully disposed of her clothes and personal belongings in the River Seine and in rubbish bins around Paris. He also disposed of some of her flesh and internal organs in garbage boxes. Back home, Sagawa saved some parts of her body in the freezer in anatomically labelled bags and called a cab. When the cab driver put the suitcases in the boot, he joked to Sagawa that they were so heavy that he must have a body inside them.

Sagawa took the cab to the Bois de Boulogne park in Paris

with the intention of throwing the remains into the Lac Inférieur – one of the Bois' many lakes. But the suitcases were so heavy that he didn't have time to dump them before a middle-aged couple spotted him trying to lug them to the water's edge; realising that he had been spotted, Sagawa immediately fled, leaving the two suitcases under a bush. After he had disappeared, the couple went looking for a policeman who got a very nasty surprise when he opened up those cases. The couple later provided a description of Sagawa and the taxi driver was able to remember the address he'd picked him up from. Three days later, Sagawa was questioned in his apartment and promptly confessed to the hideous crime.

It wasn't long before Sagawa was back sleeping in his own comfy bed at home and walking the Tokyo streets, though. His family employed one of France's top lawyers to argue his case for a rumoured million-dollar fee and Sagawa was deported back to Japan and treated in the Matsuzawa mental institution for a further 16 months. As he had entered the institution voluntarily, he was also, in theory, able to leave it, and with his father pulling the strings Sagawa walked out a free man in September 1985.

On his release, Sagawa kept a fairly low profile, embarking on a short-lived career as a dishwasher and also made an unsuccessful attempt to get work as a French tutor. He did, however, persuade a literary magazine to run instalments of one of his novels and he also found more creative work by writing the subtitles for a film about a man who made handbags out of the skin of corpses. But his really big break into show business was just around the corner.

It was the reign of another Japanese killer, Tsutomu Miyazaki, that paved the way. In 1983, Miyazaki killed four young girls and tormented their families by sending them gleeful accounts of their deaths, along with charred bones and teeth. A painfully shy 26-year-old printer's assistant, Miyazaki was also a cannibal; he had devoured his grandfather's cremated bones and gnawed on his final victim's wrist.

The case provided Sagawa with a highly fortuitous break. He soon found himself appearing on chat shows and writing editorials for highly respected newspapers and magazines, offering his own peculiar insights and first-hand experiences of what it was like to eat another human being. From there, stardom beckoned.

Veteran journalist and photographer Antonio Pagnotta was there to observe the phenomenon first hand and wound up spending six months interviewing and researching Sagawa while living and working in Tokyo. It was 1992 and Sagawa was at the height of his popularity. Pagnotta's story, which was published in France, revealed how adept Sagawa had now become at manipulating the media; protected by a large circle of admirers, he was treated with respect and even awe, happily wallowing in the media spotlight. The report caused shockwaves all over France, where most believed Sagawa to still be locked up in jail.

Sagawa was furious and publicly claimed that the allegations made by Pagnotta were false in an interview published in a monthly magazine called the *Tokyo Journal*. When Pagnotta refuted Sagawa's claims in a letter that was published two months later in the same magazine, Sagawa was livid. 'I will never ever forgive Antonio Pagnotta, this yakuza photographer has followed me for months and has stolen much information,' Sagawa wrote to the editors of the *Tokyo Journal*. 'I want to hang him upside down and smash his skull with a metal bat. I will kill him for sure.' Sagawa also left ominous messages on an answer machine, was seen lurking outside Pagnotta's old apartment and very nearly assaulted him in a restaurant. Indeed, the story took its toll on Pagnotta who suffered recurring nightmares of Sagawa trying to attack him and eat his brain.

'Sagawa is a very cunning man,' Pagnotta told me. 'Way beyond imagination, and I suppose the reason he wanted me dead was because I had exposed him in a crude manner as a sexual pervert, porno actor and a could-be serial killer.'

Pagnotta had first met Sagawa at Tama tube station in 1992. 'Standing one and a half metres in height, wearing a child-sized white ski jacket and thick, tinted glasses, he stood out unmistakably in the busy Tama station,' Pagnotta remembers. 'But everybody ignored him. It was incomprehensible that his child's body would emanate such a powerful aura of menace. To most, he might seem to be a pathetic midget. There was something more to him. As I approached to shake hands, my instinct, beyond understanding, abruptly set off alarms. His sickly acne-scarred face did not suggest any emotion. His skin appeared to have been repeatedly washed in cleansing lotions. He had tried to remove an invisible stain, or perhaps tried to reach under the skin. As we were almost touching, we made eye contact. I felt overwhelmed by nausea.'

Despite Pagnotta's gut feelings, the fact is that Sagawa is well educated and usually well mannered, traits that earned him the nickname of 'The Gentleman Cannibal' in Japan. 'He spoke French passably and his manners were gracious,' Pagnotta concedes. 'He even appeared somewhat modest, the sign of a proper education. No doubt about it, this diminutive man showed good breeding.'

All the same, according to Pagnotta, money was a passion for Sagawa, even though he was still getting a healthy allowance from his millionaire father. If you wanted to interview or take his photo, you invariably had to pay for it. You also had to deal with his many cronies who, Pagnotta says, openly shared Sagawa's obsessions. One wanted to eat a baby, while others wanted to join Sagawa in another killing.

Sagawa himself was open about his past. 'As in a thriller movie script,' Pagnotta observed, 'I had noted that Sagawa did not hide his obsessions, he even wanted to openly share them. Every year, almost ritually, the cannibal gathered friends and admirers for Hanami, a traditional party under the cherry blossoms of a nearby park.

'The main dish was barbecued meat. That year, he wanted me to join in. Reality and fiction had fuzzy borders for him. I was sure Sagawa was reliving permanently his crime in his books. I observed his jubilation when asked about his carving of the cadaver. He preciously kept a collection of horror movies running scenes of cannibalism next to a collection of magazines which carried a story about him, and he permanently updated both.'

Sagawa also kept a busy schedule, regularly filing movie reviews for *Brutus* magazine. So when a movie called *Foam of Light* was released – based on a true story of how Japanese troops in World War II had resorted to cannibalism to survive – a tabloid paid for Sagawa to attend the premiere where, according to Pagnotta, he was treated like Hollywood royalty.

The release of *Silence of the Lambs* inevitably resulted in another surge of interest in the poison dwarf. The *Asian Wall Street Journal* quoted Sagawa as finding Hannibal Lecter 'unrealistic and comical. He was portrayed as a monster and ate everything. Normally a cannibal is delicate and selects his victims carefully.'

Sagawa also made a big impact by appearing on Fuji TV in a show called *Alphabet 2/three*, a popular late-night programme for young adults. Pagnotta recalls how Sagawa was addressed as 'sensei' (honourable master) and described as 'a genius and a gentle person' by the show's director. For the show, Sagawa was filmed in a Japanese loincloth and also as a priest – a role he clearly relished. 'Dressed as a Catholic priest and flanked with two blonde twin sisters in red mini skirts, a sick reminder of his victim's features, he became the first convicted psycho killer to act on TV,' Pagnotta remembers. 'His professionalism was impressive. He fitted into the production like a veteran. In his theatrical TV clergyman's appearance, the lines were: "Believe, believe; only those who believe will be saved!" During the shooting, I could tell… that he was ecstatic.'

Sagawa also dabbled in the weird world of Japanese underground porn. In one film, he appears on the set while a couple is busy having sex and grabs a girl's breast. Also according to Pagnotta, for porn magazine *Takarajima*, Sagawa appeared in a black-leather S&M mask; he also dressed up in bondage gear for *Sniper* magazine, wearing a helmet wrapped with barbed wire. Pagnotta also discovered the most shocking photo of all, which was published in May 1996, where Sagawa appears dressed in a schoolgirl uniform while a half-naked woman urinates on his face.

In his heyday, Sagawa travelled the world over, enjoying all-expenses-paid trips to Germany, Norway, Denmark, Canada, Mexico, Iceland and India. The fact that he had murdered a young woman and eaten her seemed to have been forgotten. He lectured on the nutritive values of human flesh. He featured as a meat expert for a gastronomy column. He planned to open a vegetarian restaurant.

However, Sagawa's popularity soon faded. The media work, which started to peter out in the late nineties, has now all dried up completely apart from a brief interview with *Sixty Minutes* and an interview for an HBO documentary. Nowadays, Sagawa (who is diabetic) spends much of his time belly-aching about his lack of cash and his inability to get a job. There are no family payouts any more – both his parents are dead – and for a while he was even forced to claim welfare.

In fact, according to a recent report in the *Scotsman on Sunday*, Sagawa is now broke and living under an assumed name in a small apartment outside Tokyo. He does still see Western women from time to time, however, and one, according to the same report, even begged him to eat her. On Saturday nights, Sagawa occasionally still haunts Tokyo's red-light zone, Roppongi, where he chats up the Australian nightclub hostesses and strippers and often gets their numbers. According to a recent report, Sagawa even managed to pick up an Australian girl and go on holiday with her to Canada, until she realised who he was.

He still makes the occasional headline. In 2002, Japanese tabloid *Shukan Shincho* reported that Sagawa was spotted attending an anti-war rally in Tokyo. 'People are all beautiful. People shouldn't kill people,' his sign said. Apparently angered by the United States' attack on Afghanistan, the diminutive cannibal told the newspaper that he planned to spend the rest of his days studying what 'life is'. But nobody seemed to take much notice of him and he shuffled off soon afterwards.

In October 2007, for the magazine *Jitsuwa Knuckles*, Sagawa told writer-photographer Noboru Hashimoto, 'When I see a beautiful girl while riding the train, I feel like eating her.' He also referred to the killing of Renée Hartevelt, telling the journalist, 'I invited her to join me for some Japanese food. But Japanese restaurants in Paris were expensive, so I said I'd prepare sukiyaki at home. No one else came along, and usually a girl would be on her guard to be alone with a man at his place, but Renée was completely at ease.

'The sukiyaki got burned and stuck to the pot, and, while she stood at the sink washing it, I got this feeling while looking at her from behind – I don't know why – that she looked like a whore, and I was overcome with this compulsion to eat her.'

The fact still remains that, for years, Sagawa cashed in on the murder of a young woman, reducing his horrible deed to nothing more than a sick joke, and the media was more than happy to play along. Today, his novelty has worn very thin, though. The joke isn't very funny any more, even in Japan.

## CHAPTER THREE

# MARCELO COSTA DE ANDRADE: THE VAMPIRE OF RIO

Ex-rent-boy-turned-religious-maniac Marcelo Costa de Andrade made headlines in Brazil in 1992 when he confessed to a nine-month murder spree. Brazil's most infamous killer said he had raped and slaughtered 14 boys from the slums of Rio so they would 'go to Heaven'.

A million people live in the slums of Rio de Janeiro. The most notorious ghetto is Rocinha, which sprawls down the hillside and overlooks the elegant high-rises of Sao Conrado and some of Brazil's most spectacular beaches. Perhaps nowhere in the world is the disparity between the haves and have-nots more striking than here, and there is no more potent reminder of that imbalance than the thousands of homeless kids who constantly roam its streets.

Rocinha has an estimated population of 150,000. Armies of children maraud their way through its labyrinthine alleyways, and youngsters die in the shantytown in such numbers that Brazil has been compared to a country at war. Between December 1987 and November 2001, 3,937 children died violent deaths – the majority were victims of an ever-escalating drug war that had been raging in the slums since the cocaine trade took hold there in the early 1980s. Employed as 'soldiers' by drug lords to protect and expand their turf, armed teenagers murder each other in pitch battles and innocent bystanders get caught in the crossfire almost every day.

Those who don't run drugs are forced to survive any other way they can. They scavenge for food, sell gum, polish shoes, beg, steal, mug people... and sometimes kill. Blamed for the spiralling crime rate, and for making Rio one of the murder capitals of the world, the children elicit very little sympathy from the citizens of Rio. Universally despised, they are routinely beaten, abused and attacked.

The situation was made even worse in the 1990s, when they were regularly being picked off by roving extermination squads, made up primarily of off-duty policeman and security guards. These squads were on the payroll of normally law-abiding citizens, and their mission was to clean up the streets. In 1991, at least four children were being executed every single day on average.

For a murderer, especially one with a liking for young boys, the conditions on Brazil's streets at that time could not have been more ideal. Such was the daily death toll, the Brazilian authorities didn't even notice that somebody else, acting on their own, was slaughtering young boys in the slums just for fun.

For Marcelo Costa de Andrade, who had spent almost his entire life on the streets, it wasn't difficult to blend in and lure children away from prying eyes to abandoned spots and their slaughter. The children from the Rio slums were wary of the dangers that constantly surrounded them, but De Andrade seemed to be one of the few adults they could trust, with his harmless appearance, a gentle manner and a soft, childlike way of speaking.

The 23-year-old lived with his mother, regularly attended church, had a normal job and made constant allusions to his faith in God when talking to children. Having grown up poor in the Rocinha slum, his childhood was in many ways the same as that of the street kids: no food on the table, no running water, constant abuse and hardly any school. De Andrade spent most of his time on the street hustling, and was just ten when he ran away from home for the first time. At 14, he started selling himself to adults for sex.

On the rare occasions he was at home, De Andrade was beaten senseless by both his step-parents and was sexually abused. At 16, he moved in with an older man, but when he was thrown out he went to live with his mother in another nearby Rio slum. Aged 17, he tried to rape his ten-year-old brother and started listening obsessively to tapes he had made of his brother crying.

But it was only after he had left hustling for good and was attending church regularly with his mother that his killing spree began. According to De Andrade, it was an encounter with a young transvestite that was the trigger. And once he'd begun there was no stopping him.

'One day when I was walking I met a 14-year-old boy. A transvestite,' De Andrade recalled in an interview with *Epoca* magazine in 2003. 'He propositioned me to go to a hotel with him. I had sex with him and kissed him on the mouth. I paid him 50 Reais [£12]. I never got to see him again. But it sparked the desire for new boys. As I didn't find another one like him I ended up forcing myself on others. I always took them to a deserted spot.

'The sadism went to my head. I ended up killing some of them… I do not remember their faces very well. The first one I caught was in Niterói. I only know that his name was Anderson. I offered him money. I said he could help me light candles in the church. I took him to a deserted place. When we got there I raped him. I then strangled him with his own shirt. I returned to the spot where the body was three times, to see if anyone had discovered anything. Nobody ever suspected me.'

De Andrade went on to murder 13 other street kids, following the same pattern as the first. He lured them with sweets and money to secluded spots, raped them, strangled them or beat them to death and had sex with their corpses. He then buried them in shallow graves.

De Andrade targeted the 'prettiest boys' he could find, always hunting for 'smooth legs, and a pretty face and body' and later declared that he had killed them so they would 'go to Heaven'. (He also removed his victims' shorts and kept them as trophies.) In two instances, he drank his victims' blood. After sexually abusing them, often for an entire night, he would crack their heads open and collect the blood in a bowl to drink – allegedly so that he would be 'as young and cute as them'. The majority of his victims were found in the Niterói, just outside the capital of Rio across Guanabara Bay, and as this was the site of his first victim it earned Andrade the nickname in Brazil of 'the Vampire of Rio'.

But there was also a religious motive for his murders. The church De Andrade attended was the controversial Universal Church of the Kingdom of God. Founded by Edir Macedo, a state-lottery employee turned American-style evangelist, it is the fastest-growing religion in Brazil and now has branches in 172 countries. From its beginnings in 1977, the church has often received fierce criticism from more established religious groups. Part of the criticism levelled against it has been the emphasis on the payment of tithes. These can often constitute upwards of 10% of a congregation member's income, an amount that many believers are quite happy to pay in the belief that this money will be paid back in full and with interest – not on the Day of Reckoning, but in the church member's lifetime. The church has particular appeal among the impoverished who, of course, take comfort from its message of guaranteed future remuneration.

In fact, De Andrade seemed far more interested in another aspect of the church – namely the casting out of demons, something that happens quite regularly during services in the Church of the Kingdom of God. As well as offering protection from voodoo and witchcraft, the church claims that 'demons' are responsible for people's problems (including homosexuality, which is viewed by the church as a disease). De Andrade's church would cast out these 'demons', and to this day the murderer claims he was possessed by evil spirits who forced him to kill because 'they like children's blood'.

In the midst of his killing spree, the devout De Andrade still attended church four times a week, for up to five hours at a time. He later declared that a priest had told him that boys who died under the age of 13 automatically went to heaven. He misunderstood the priest's message, he claimed, interpreting it as meaning that by killing the boys he was not only ending their awful existence in the slums but also ensuring them a one-way ticket to paradise. It was for this reason that De Andrade never targeted girls. Girls, he claimed, were different from boys because they didn't go to heaven – and, of course, boys were 'prettier'.

Dr Helen Morrison, a forensic psychiatrist and well-known serial-killer profiler, went to interview De Andrade in Brazil in November 2001. Dr Morrison interviews murderers for hours and hours at a time, believing that they are only able to copy normal behaviour until the mask cracks. She believes that serial killers are born, not made, and are genetically prone to kill. Morrison has interviewed at least 80 serial killers during her career, including John Wayne Gacy, the convicted killer of 33 young men and boys. (In fact, Morrison actually took possession of John Wayne Gacy's brain after he was executed and donated his body to science. She keeps it in the basement of her house.)

She recounts the experience of her interviews with De Andrade in her fascinating book *My Life Amongst The Serial Killers: Inside the Minds of The World's Most Notorious Murderers*. Through an interpreter, De Andrade reiterated to Dr Morrison his claim that he had been doing his victims a favour by killing them. 'The children have bad lives here,' he told her. 'If they are children when they die, they go to heaven. A better place.'

But De Andrade went much further than gently sending them on their way. After raping and killing 11-year-old Odair Jose Muniz, whom he had met near a football pitch, he returned later in the night with a machete, which he told his mother he was taking to cut some bananas. Back at the scene of the crime, he hacked the boy's head off. 'Why?' asked Morrison. In order, De Andrade told her, that the other children in heaven would make fun of him because he wouldn't have a head. After all, the kids used to make fun of him at school.

De Andrade's killing spree was prolific but mercifully short-lived. On 11 December 1991, brothers Altair (aged ten) and

Ivan Abreu (aged six) were picked up by De Andrade, who offered them $20 if they both accompanied him while he lit candles in a nearby church. The boys readily agreed. But as soon as they were away from public view, De Andrade turned on Altair and made to kiss him. Altair tried to run, but his molester was too quick for him, grabbing the boy and throwing him to the ground.

Then he turned his attention to Ivan and started strangling him. 'I was so paralysed by fear I could not run away,' Altair later recalled. 'I watched in horror, tears streaming down my cheeks, as he killed and then raped my brother.'

When it was all over, De Andrade moved towards Altair, opening his arms wide. According to Morrison, the terrified boy could smell his dead brother all over De Andrade's clothes and was convinced the monster looming above him was going to kill him. Instead, De Andrade embraced him. 'I have sent Ivan to heaven,' the killer told him. 'I love you.'

Too terrified to try to make a run for it, Altair agreed to spend the night with De Andrade, sleeping rough in the bushes behind a petrol station. The next morning, De Andrade even took the boy to work with him in the tourist district of Copacabana, where he handed out fliers for a jewellery shop. However, Altair managed to escape and find his way home. He told his mother what had happened and a warrant was issued for De Andrade's arrest.

In the meantime, the killer, who often revisited the scene of his crimes and left trays of food and other offerings to his victims, had returned to Ivan's corpse to tuck the tiny boy's hands into his pockets so the rats wouldn't chew on his fingers.

Instead of making a run for it, De Andrade carried on as if nothing had happened, and was arrested at work in

Copacabana. Initially, he confessed to only the murder of Ivan, but, when his mother was called in for questioning two months later, she reluctantly told police that her son had once asked for the use of her machete and had come back the next morning with it smeared in blood.

De Andrade finally confessed to 13 other murders and led police to the burial sites. Found insane by psychiatrists on 26 April 1993, he was formally declared to be mad and incapable of understanding his acts by a judge two months later and placed in a psychiatric hospital in Rio. He is evaluated annually; each year since then, he has been declared insane.

I managed to track down Ilana Casoy, a well-known expert on Brazilian serial killers, to ask her about De Andrade, whom she had met and interviewed in the Henrique Roxo hospital in Rio de Janeiro. Casoy found herself in the media spotlight a few years ago for her work as a profiler in the investigation into another famous Brazilian murderer, Francisco das Chagas Rodrigues de Brito otherwise known as 'Chagas', who is believed to have killed a number of young boys over a 12-year period in the Brazilian states of Para and Maranhao. Casoy and her profiling team were able to help lead police to Chagas, a 42-year-old bicycle mechanic. When the police interviewed him, he confessed to a slew of further murders and when the authorities searched his home they found the remains of two bodies buried under the floor of his shack and the remains of another young boy buried in the jungle near his home. In fact, Chagas has superseded De Andrade in the annals of Brazilian crime as the most prolific serial killer in its history. Although he has only been formally convicted of one murder, he faces further charges in the future for the disappearances and murder of 40 boys, some of whom he is believed to have castrated and decapitated in a satanic-style ritual. In 2004, Chagas told an interviewer from the BBC that he had killed them because 'Something was guiding me, directing me. It was like a voice in my head. And it was that thing – the voice – that determined what happened.

'Sometimes I'm revolted by what I did but you must understand that something was using me to do this. Good people will understand that.'

In some ways, De Andrade was not so different to Chagas, in that he believed that by killing young boys he was in some ways being manipulated by a force that was higher than himself, a force that he was helpless to control.

'Many serial killers in Brazil kill children, but each one has their own way of doing it,' Casoy told me. 'Each one of them has his own fantasies and symbolism, his own ritual way of killing someone. But my meeting with De Andrade was different to my meetings with other killers like Chagas, in many ways, because by meeting De Andrade I could really understand what it is to be an insane person. De Andrade has this mental illness and you get the feeling he doesn't know the true scale of what he did, the difference between right and wrong. There is no cure. Nobody knows what treatment he should receive, so they give him drugs to keep him under control, and that's about all they can do.'

In her chapter on De Andrade in *Serial Killers Made in Brazil*, Casoy changed the names of his victims to biblical names, so the mothers who read it would never know which child was their own. Casoy has interviewed and met some of Brazil's worst killers and helped investigate their crimes, but what was it like to meet someone like De Andrade, a monster who had shown such terrible and sickening cruelty to innocent children? Her encounter with De Andrade is something Casoy says she will never forget. 'Meeting someone like Marcelo Costa de Andrade is very hard for any human being. I was sick in bed for four days after I talked to him. He is like a wolf dressed in sheep's clothing. Look at him and you would never for a single second imagine what he is capable of doing with children.'

De Andrade even played a sick joke on the veteran profiler. 'As soon as he told me that he took the shorts off every child he killed and kept them as trophies he asked me to bring him a gift – a pair of new shorts,' she said. 'I'd never give them to him. I hope he stays in the lunatic asylum for his entire life.'

Unbelievable as it may sound, despite the fact that De Andrade was known to be a merciless killer of children and would in all likelihood kill again if he ever got the chance, security in the first mental institution he was placed in was so lax that he managed to walk out though the front door. In January 1997, a guard accidentally left a door open; De Andrade absconded and was on the run for 12 days straight. The press went ballistic while police held their breath and prayed that he wouldn't get his hands on another child.

Thankfully, there were no reports of children found dead and drained of their blood during the time of his escape and frantic police finally managed to track him down to the town of Guaraciaba do Norte in the north-eastern state of Ceara. When he was picked up, De Andrade was carrying a Bible, having managed to hitchhike his way for more than 3,000km to visit his father. He was on his way to the Holy Land, he told police. Still clearly deranged, he also told police that by killing the children he was now purified and so had not felt the urge to kill again.

## MARCELO COSTA DE ANDRADE: THE VAMPIRE OF RIO

De Andrade now resides in the high-security wing of Henrique Roxo hospital. He still claims to be an evangelist and expresses his hope that one day he will be back on the streets. All he needs, he says, is the love of a good woman to keep him on the straight and narrow. He asks God to light the way. But, according to Casoy, his so-called religious convictions are a lie and always have been. 'De Andrade is not a religious guy and he never was,' she told me vehemently. 'He just heard a priest who said that a child under 13 years old goes straight to paradise if he dies without sins. He chose to believe it literally.'

As one of Brazil's sickest criminals, De Andrade relishes his moments in the spotlight and has been known to demand Hollywood-level fees for interviews. 'The Vampire of Rio even phoned up Dr Morrison in her hotel room in Sao Paulo in 2001 and demanded $10,000 for an interview, a request Morrison flatly refused.'

According to Casoy, now that De Andrade's fame is fading, and his exploits have been outdone, he loves talking with anyone who simply pays him attention. His mother is the only relative who visits him, and that's only once a year. He shows absolutely no remorse for his sickening crimes. 'His mind is more or less the same as that of a 12-year-old,' says Casoy. 'He dreams of going to Disneyland or Moscow, winning a million dollars and having plastic surgery on his face so he would never be recognised by anyone. He never feels bad about what did, just worried that it screwed up his life. He wasn't happy telling me what he did, but he wasn't exactly all that sad about it either. It's something that doesn't make any difference to him either way.

'He believes he was utterly tender to the children he killed and saved them from hell. He doesn't know it was really wrong or awful. He told me all of it as if he was talking about simple everyday things, but with specific and cruel details, and the tone in his voice never changed – it never changed for a single moment.'

## CHAPTER FOUR

# RANDY KRAFT: THE SCORECARD KILLER

Mild-mannered computer programmer by
day, murder junkie by night. Meet Randy
Kraft, one of America's most prolific
serial killers.

In his cell in San Quentin, Randy Kraft enjoys watching *Desperate Housewives* and listening to music, especially to Elton John, The Carpenters and Stevie Wonder. He hasn't had the chance to do it for quite a while but he used to enjoy being on the beach with friends too, roasting hot dogs as the sun went down beyond the Pacific Ocean.

Now he spends his time playing bridge, working out, reading and writing and would describe himself as a giving and sharing person. You can write to him if you like, as Randy is looking for a pen-friend, or maybe you might like to send him a book, or even a CD. They are quite difficult to get hold of on Death Row.

He has been there since 30 November 1989 after he was charged and convicted of 16 counts of murder and sentenced to death. Kraft fiercely defends his innocence to this day. But, when he was pulled over for suspected drink driving on 14 May 1983, police found a dead marine slumped in the front seat of his car. They also found 47 pictures of naked men (many of whom were dead) under the car mat, blood on the cushion in the front seat and in the boot of his car a coded piece of paper listing all his kills.

At his home, which he shared with his lover Jeff Seelig, police also found a whole stash of souvenirs that could be directly traced to many of his victims and more photos of dead men, some of them taken in Kraft's own living room. It turned out that he had been driving around California with corpses for almost 12 years.

At the time of his arrest, Kraft was a successful computer programmer with a well-paying job in the corporate computer services department at Lear Seigler. At his trial, co-workers described him as 'pleasant', 'reserved' and 'friendly'. Friends and family recalled how attentive he was to their problems – his niece described him as a shoulder to cry on – while others remembered shared holidays and pleasant evening meals with Kraft and his boyfriend in their home. The general consensus was one of utter disbelief that the affable, gentle Kraft, a successful employee dedicated to his work, could also be one of America's most sadistic serial killers.

But that's exactly what he was. From 1971 to May 1983, Kraft roamed the streets in his car, picked up hitchhikers and men in gay bars, drugged them, raped them, strangled them with their own shoelaces or belts and then mutilated their dead bodies. In many instances, he sliced off their genitals or spent the night dismembering the bodies entirely.

When he was finished with the bodies, Kraft left them in different cities and counties in the state by dumping them from a moving car along California's labyrinthine highway system. Matters were made worse by the fact that Californian police were also contending with two other suspected 'freeway killers' operating in the same area and at the same time. Deranged Vietnam vet William Bonin was busy raping young boys, strangling them or caving in their skulls with a tyre iron and leaving their bodies at the side of the road. Also active at this time was Patrick Kearney, who shot his victims in the back of the head, engaged in sex with the corpses and then dismembered the bodies with a hacksaw. Once he had finished with the bodies he put the remains in bin bags and dumped them along the side of the Californian highways.

Ken Goddard was chief criminalist and supervisor of the Scientific Investigation Bureau at the Huntington Beach Police Department at the time Kraft's victims first started to show up. Later, he attended Kraft's trial, appearing as an expert witness. He still has vivid memories of the murderer to this day. 'I remember Kraft thumbing avidly through one of the photo "albums" we'd put together showing all of the located bodies or parts,' he told me. 'I was sitting on the witnesses' stand at the time, waiting for court to resume, and I remember him suddenly looking up at me and the funny, oddly familiar look on his face. It took me a few minutes to realise where I'd seen that look before. It was when I was out on patrol with a San Bernardino Sheriff's deputy driving around behind a 7/11 and happened upon a couple of young boys reading some kind of porno magazines. In retrospect, I'm sure that for him that album represented the ultimate in porn mags, especially given that the "scenes" were his own creation.'

Goddard had learned much earlier in his CSI career to disconnect his emotions from the crime scenes. As such, he says the sight of the dead and maimed bodies were more of a frustration to him than a 'horror' because of the lack of any evidence that might have helped the authorities focus on a specific suspect. 'Normally, during the CSI process, you tend to get a pretty vivid sense of what the victim went through by figuratively putting yourself "in the skins" of the victims and suspects as you work your way through the scene... But the lack of "place of attack" evidence with the Kraft bodies made it very difficult to imagine the sequence of events, other than the obvious fact that the victims were probably tortured in addition to being tied down and raped... but it got a lot worse in terms of the body parts, and a growing awareness of what the victims were going through.'

The first 'Kraft body' was found in the middle of a back road in Huntington Beach. 'When the patrol officers turned the body over, they discovered the crotch of his pants was bloody... and that his penis and gonads had been cut off with something sharp,' Goddard revealed. 'We examined the body carefully at the morgue for trace evidence, but only observed what appeared to be ligature bruises or handcuff bruises on the wrists... The only significant bit of evidence turned out to be the anal swabs taken by the pathologist and turned over to me for analysis.

'The swabs screened positive for seminal fluids and I was able to locate intact sperm in the swabs. So we knew the killing was part of a sexual assault, but not much more than that. There were other bodies too. I remember being at a morgue and seeing severed body parts such as arms and legs that they were trying to match to torsos, all in varying states of decay.'

It wasn't hard for Kraft to sweet-talk men into his car. Unlike many serial killers, he did not suffer the usual nightmarish childhood of constant abuse and poverty, nor was he a hated misfit. Softly spoken and socially adept, he seemed to have got on well with just about everyone.

Randy Kraft was born in Long Beach, California, the youngest of four children and the only boy. When he was three, his family moved to nearby Orange County; his father worked in the machine shop in nearby Douglas Aircraft and had built the family home on the cheap out of surplus supplies from a nearby military base. Sitting by the side of the highway, it still resembled a barracks with small rooms and it was impossible to see outside unless you stood right by the window and peered over the sill. The young Randy Kraft had to stand on a chair to see outside.

Kraft did well at school and almost skipped a year because of his high grades. Although flat-footed, he also did well at sports, playing on the varsity tennis team and regularly going bowling with his father. He played the tenor sax, took part in debates and was liked by fellow students and teachers, many of whom were later called upon as character witnesses at his trial. The family weren't rich but they weren't poor either, and there was enough money for the occasional holiday and weekend outing.

There was even enough to send Kraft to college. Again he did well and was elected president of a fraternity; among other tasks, he arranged fundraisers for charities. As the Vietnam War loomed, Kraft enlisted in the air force rather than getting drafted into the army, starting his training on 14 June 1968. He was sent to Texas, where he excelled again, becoming platoon leader and earning the American Spirit of Honor medal as an 'outstanding example to comrades in arms'.

But his auspicious military beginnings had a rather muted

end. The air force saw Kraft as someone who was not likely to make a career in the military, due to his education and high IQ, and decided that the extra money used to train him would be wasted. As a result, he wound up as a painter, painting crossroads and on base barracks near his home and back in Orange County.

Kraft had a degree in economics, but, instead of pursuing a steady and lucrative career after leaving the military, he chose to work as a bartender in a succession of gay bars in California. At night he would head mostly to Ripples, previously known as Slithery House, or he spent night after night driving in his Toyota Celica looking for kicks along the Californian highways. Later, when he left the state for his work as a computer programmer, the body count in his new locality inevitably rose. During his trial, the prosecution presented evidence that Kraft had committed eight additional murders in Oregon and Michigan.

After he had committed a murder, Kraft would note the details of his crime down in code. Written in two columns on a sheet of notebook paper, the final list bore 61 cryptic entries in Kraft's meticulous hand. Police believed that each entry on the list referred to one of his victims, earning him the name of the 'scorecard killer'. Four of the entries included the number '2', which according to the prosecution referred to a double hit. So, '2 IN 1 BEACH', the prosecution argued, referred to both Rodger DeVaul and Geoffrey Nelson. Police believed that Kraft met both men on the beach (after leaving his bridge group) and he rendered them helpless with beer spiked with a cocktail of prescription drugs. He cut off Nelson's penis and scrotum, possibly while he was still alive, strangled him and then threw him out of his car. DeVaul suffered a similar fate.

Kraft plied him with so many pills and so much booze that he would have been in a mild coma while he was being strangled. Kraft then started taking snapshots of his corpse. Police found photographs underneath the floor mat of Kraft's car that showed a dead DeVaul in various poses including one of him holding his own penis.

Another item on the list was 'jail out', a reference to Roland Young. Young had been put in jail for public drunkenness and on his release was hitching his way home when Kraft picked him up. In a change from his usual method, this time Kraft stabbed Young four times in the chest and removed one testicle. As with DeVaul, Young had imbibed a large amount of alcohol and drugs, and would have been comatose as he was being killed.

Kraft was an adept murderer; he was only ever seen by witnesses once, and that was very early on in his killing spree. In March 1975, Kraft struck up a conversation with Keith Crotwell and Kent May in a parking lot in Long Beach. They agreed to come with him to his new car, a white Mustang, where he offered them pills and beer. May almost immediately passed out and the last thing he remembered was Kraft driving off with both of them still in the car. Kraft then returned to the parking lot and threw May out.

Two of their friends, who had come out looking for them, saw Kraft throwing May out of his car and then speeding off with Crotwell in the front passenger seat unconscious. Two months later, two young boys discovered Crotwell's skull floating near a marina. In October, other children found what was left of him wrapped in a rug in a large pipe. In court, the prosecutor argued to the jury that 'PARKING LOT' on the defendant's list referred to Crotwell's murder.

Kraft continued to get away unpunished and the atrocities of his crimes worsened. On 3 January 1976, an off-duty policeman found the body of Mark Hall in the sand dunes in the area of Saddleback Mountain. This time Kraft had surpassed himself. The cause of Hall's death was found to be a combination of suffocation and acute alcohol intoxication. Kraft had removed Hall's genitals and filled his mouth and throat with dirt so that he choked. A print unearthed on a broken beer bottle near the scene of the crime was Kraft's. Hall had last been seen alive on 31 December; Kraft had written on his list 'NEW YEARS EVE'.

According to author Dennis McDougal, who wrote the bestselling book *Angel of Darkness* about Kraft, the killer may well have also had an accomplice: a seriously disturbed drifter. He certainly confessed to McDougal that he had been involved in some of Kraft's most heinous crimes. Kraft wasn't a strong man physically and it would have been tough to move those bodies by himself; what's more, McDougal says, Kraft didn't have access to a photo lab, nor did he know how to develop photos. It was also claimed that Kraft only listed his more memorable kills and hinted that the final tally could well have been as much as a hundred. McDougal further speculated that Kraft might have practised his drink-spiking technique by drugging an ex-girlfriend. In an article published in *Long Beach* magazine, she told McDougal that she would sometimes have a beer while Kraft drove and would wake up with a splitting headache and no recollection of what had happened.

Kraft's body count is up there with some of America's most infamous killers, yet, strangely, he doesn't enjoy their celebrity status. He absolutely refuses to acknowledge any guilt and offers no glimpses whatsoever into the darker side of his nature. I talked to a long-term pen-pal of Kraft. Like many people who have got to know him over the years, she still finds it hard at times to believe that he is a killer.

'Randy,' she told me, 'is intelligent, well read, has an excellent general knowledge, and is extremely literate; his letters are a pleasure to read. He is polite, considerate and respectful. He is also charming, but in a gentle, understated kind of way, and there's a sweetness and warmth too in Randy that makes him very likeable, which causes you to start to think that maybe he really did not commit those dreadful crimes, and you want so much to believe that he didn't. But I see too, at times, a certain tendency towards having high expectations, perhaps even a demand for perfection, but rather in himself, than in others.

'I do believe, though, that, in many ways, Randy lives in a romanticised world, where families are perfect, loving, supportive and nurturing, almost like the early TV family sitcoms with the strong, morally upright, but caring father, the devoted domesticated mother and the happy, doted-upon younger children and fun-loving teenagers. Perhaps Randy's own family was like this, but I think that it is more likely that this is how he wants to remember his past, rather than the way it actually was.'

This idealised version of events is reflected in Kraft's childhood memoirs, recently posted up on his website, which is sponsored by an anti-death-penalty organisation. Kraft earnestly paints a picture of the all-American family and – ludicrously – comes across rather like a modern-day version of John Boy from *The Waltons*. It makes for tough reading. There is a whole story about the time his sister couldn't cook pie crust properly and another gripping tale about going to the local shop and buying chicken feed (literally). There is also one story about whether he should buy a Christian Endeavours tie clip for himself or if he should save his hard-earned quarters and buy a nice new white Bible for his mom. Apparently, as a child Kraft was a paragon of virtue and most of his memoirs are littered with expressions such as 'Neat O' and 'Oh Boy' and even sometimes 'Gee Thanks!'

In those memoirs, Kraft also gives his own explanation for the scorecard hit list that earned him his nickname. He says that the words on the list were related to his computer-programming job and that the police had cut and pasted the list to make him take the blame for 65 unsolved crimes.

The memoirs jump abruptly to a day in 1983, when Kraft remembers sitting out on the sun deck with a cold beer with his dog, Max. It was actually Friday, 13 May, and his last day as a free man. Kraft remembers that a sudden chill and feeling of impending doom descended on him and writes that he knew things wouldn't be the same afterwards. Hours later he would kill again, but for the last time. At last the 12-year-long murder binge was drawing to a close.

His last victim was Terry Gambrel, a 25-year-old marine. Kraft was pulled over for suspected drink driving by the California Highway Patrol when they spotted someone in the front seat. Kraft claimed that he was a hitchhiker. According to court records, one of the officers 'observed that Gambrel's trousers were unbuttoned and pulled down between his waist and his knees so that his penis and testicles were supported by the crotch of the pants. The crotch area was wet. There were indentations on Gambrel's wrists similar to those a wide rubber band would make.'

According to the autopsy, Gambrel's death resulted from asphyxia due to ligature strangulation. Again, according to court transcripts, 'The ligature consisted of a strap that had been tightened around Gambrel's neck. There were also ligature marks on both of Gambrel's wrists. Petechial haemorrhages in the neck organs indicated the killer had repeatedly tightened and loosened the ligature."

Gambrel was 25 years old and engaged to be married. It is believed that he was hitchhiking his way to a party when he was picked up by Kraft.

It took five years before Kraft was sent to court. The trial lasted 13 months and cost the American taxpayer $10 million, making it one of the longest and most expensive trials in the history of the American judiciary system. Throughout the trial, Kraft maintained his innocence and even served as co-counsellor. After both sides had argued their case, the jury decided on the death penalty – a decision that was upheld by the judge – and Kraft was sentenced to die in the gas chamber in San Quentin on 29 November 1989. Referring to Kraft's crimes, Judge A McCartin summed up: 'I can't imagine doing these things in scientific experiments on a dead person, much less to someone alive.'

But, incredible as it may seem, the bodies keep on showing up. As recently as 2006, the remains of a 17-year-old marine, James Cox, thought to have gone AWOL on 30 September 1974, were found buried by the side of the road and identified thanks to DNA testing. Authorities think that he could well be another Kraft victim.

Meanwhile, Kraft, who shows not the slightest remorse for his crimes, fights against his sentence and for his life. According to his appeal, there were 20 serious errors in his trial and he maintains the search warrants obtained for a search of his car, office and home after he was pulled over for drink driving were illegal. He also contends that he should have been allowed a separate trial for each murder. But his call for a mistrial hinges mainly around the death list. He argues that the list 'lacked value' because any connection between the entries on the list and particular victims was 'speculative'. Kraft also holds the view that any relevancy of the list is outweighed by its prejudicial impact and should have been omitted as inadmissible hearsay.

His latest appeal was unanimously rejected by the Californian Supreme Court in 2000 on all counts. For most families wanting closure, it was good news, but it is unlikely that Kraft will go to the gas chamber any time soon. He has already been on Death Row for 19 years and is likely to remain there for a good while yet. Kraft plans to appeal yet again to the federal courts, a process that will in all likelihood tie up the process for years and years to come.

## CHAPTER FIVE

# DANNY ROLLING: THE GAINESVILLE RIPPER

In his quest for fame at any price and possessed by an evil spirit he called Gemini, Danny Rolling slaughtered his way into infamy during a three-day murder binge on a university campus. Sixteen years later, he died singing at his own execution.

At 6 p.m. on 25 October 2006, Danny Rolling became the 63rd prisoner to be executed in Florida since the state reintroduced the death penalty in 1979. Rolling had turned to God during his last years on Death Row, but there were no pleas for forgiveness from the relatives of his victims who had come to watch him die.

During his final moments, Rolling, who'd once broken into song during his murder trial, stunned onlookers by crooning a hymn he'd composed himself. As the sodium penthonal, the first of the three fatal injections, began to take hold, he kept singing the line, 'None greater than Thee, oh Lord.' Thirteen minutes later, he was dead.

Sadist, murderer, rapist and necrophiliac, Rolling will go down in history as one of America's most savage and unrepentant killers of all time – which is exactly what he wanted. He had craved fame and wallowed in his celebrity status while awaiting execution on Death Row; indeed, by sentencing him to death the judicial system had played right into his hands.

'It's true that Rolling was guilty of terrible crimes,' David Elliot, Communications Director for the National Coalition to Abolish the Death Penalty, told me. 'It's equally true that, as the years wore on after the killings, the memory of his victims faded in the public's mind. So, when it came to the execution, Florida residents knew Rolling's name, but not the names of his victims. That's one thing wrong with the death penalty – the names of the victims are forgotten while the criminals become rock stars.'

In the end, it was a quick and painless death for Rolling, who had eaten every crumb of his last meal: lobster tail and strawberry cheesecake. He would undoubtedly be happy to know a film is now being made about his life.

Josh Townsend's *The Gainesville Ripper* recounts three days when terror struck the town of Gainesville, Florida, and the 33-year-old director vividly recalls what it was like when Rolling embarked on his murder spree. 'I have lived through it all,' Townsend says. 'I'm from Gainesville – it's my hometown. I was born here. I was in tenth grade when he killed those five students, the weekend before school started. I remember it all like yesterday. There was a mass exodus of students and you weren't even able to make a simple phone call because so many parents were desperately calling to check up on their kids.

'While the killings were happening, local stores ran out of pepper spray and all the gun shops ran out. Everyone had a weapon of some sort. But the weirdest thing is that every rumour we heard – like the one about the murderer severing Christa Hoyt's head and leaving it on a shelf – turned out to be true. It's such a small college town that news travelled quickly.'

On 24 August 1990, first-year students Sonya Larson (aged 18) and Christina Powell (aged 17) moved into their new apartment in the university town of Gainesville, Florida. Their apartment was on the second floor of a four-floor building in the Williamsburg Village, a cosy cul-de-sac with a view of the nearby woods. Larson was a science and pre-engineering major and Powell was studying architecture. They were just two of the thousands of students fast filling up the town.

The two girls were unaware of the fact that, while they were busy shopping in Wal-Mart, they had caught the attention of deranged drifter Danny Rolling (then aged 36), who was shoplifting at the store. Rolling had arrived a few days before and had set up camp in the nearby woods. Six foot two and powerfully built with brown hair and hazel eyes, Rolling was already a hardened criminal who had spent much of the last ten years of his life in jail, with previous convictions in three separate states for armed robbery. Rolling had sworn to himself that he would kill eight people – later, he stated this was part of a pact he had made with Lucifer: eight souls for every year he'd done in prison. So far he had killed three.

Rolling hadn't been to college and had very little in common with all the students preparing for the upcoming semester. His father, a policeman, had beaten him literally before he could even walk and the constant physical abuse had continued all the way through Rolling's teenage years. By the time he arrived in Gainesville, Rolling was an alcoholic with a long criminal record and a failed marriage behind him.

He blamed his list of failures on what he claimed was his violent treatment as a child and his anger at this had spilled over into violence only a few weeks before, when Rolling had shot his father twice, nearly killing him. He was now on the run from his hometown Shreveport, Louisiana, and had finally ended up in Gainesville.

Mental illness ran in his family and, by the time he arrived in Gainesville on a Greyhound bus, Rolling had become convinced that he was in the grip of demonic possession. On the way, he had robbed two supermarkets, burgled a handful of houses, stolen a car and raped a woman at knifepoint in her own home.

Rolling followed Sonya and Christina as they left the shop to their home, returned to his tent in the woods and then waited until the sun dipped beyond the darkening trees. He killed time by playing his guitar and singing county and western songs. He also spoke to himself incessantly and recorded his obscure ramblings into a tape cassette recorder. During part of the tape, Rolling left a message for his brother, Kevin, about how it was important when bow hunting deer to 'aim for the lungs straight through the rib cage'. He also left a message for his father: 'Well, Dad, I hope you're doing better. You know, it's probable you don't even wanna hear from me. Well, you know, Pop, I don't think you was really concerned about the way I felt anyway. Nope, I really don't. You never would take time to listen to me, never cared about what I thought or felt. I never had a daddy that I could go to and confide in with my problems. You just pushed me away at a young age, Pops. I guess you and I both missed out on a lot. I wanted to make you proud of me. I let you down. I'm sorry for that. Maybe, in the hereafter, perhaps you'll understand this. I'm going to sign off now. There's something I got to do.'

Rolling stole a bike from outside a trailer park and headed back to the girls' apartment. He then watched them from the edge of the woods until they went to bed at around midnight. At 3.30 a.m., he climbed the outside stairs.

Rolling later wrote an account of that night in a book called *The Making of a Serial Killer*, which he co-authored with the help of true-crime writer Sondra London, whom he later proposed to in jail (see Chapter Nineteen: Serial-killer Groupies). According to the book, on the night of the murder Rolling found himself possessed by a malignant spirit, which he called Gemini, an 'evil puppet master born long ago in a sewage-filled cell in a Mississippi prison'. His account is written in the third person, and begins when he arrives in Gainesville on a Greyhound bus.

'The Grim Reaper,' runs the text, 'came calling on the little college town, not on the wings of some terrible strange bird but on the conventional wheels of man's invention. The silver and black Greyhound swung into the station like a rolling coffin. A fugitive from justice stepped lightly off, carrying a navy-blue sports bag filled with tomorrow's pain.'

Standing on the doorstep of the girls' apartment, Rolling tried to prise the wooden door frame open with a screwdriver, but it wouldn't budge. So he called upon Gemini for assistance. Gemini, according to Rolling's account, promptly obliged. When he tried the door handle, he now found that the door was unlocked.

Wearing a black ski mask, black clothes and gloves, Rolling was equipped with an automatic pistol and a military-style K Bar knife. He saw Christina Powell who was sleeping on the downstairs sofa but he moved past her out of the living room and through the hall and up the stairs. There he pushed open the door leading to Sonya Larson's room. She was asleep; her room was full of unpacked boxes.

In less than a minute, he had covered Sonya's mouth with duct tape and stabbed her to death. As she died, Rolling promised her that he would come back for her later. These were in all likelihood the last words she ever heard. (The neighbours would later recall how they'd heard George Michael's 'Faith' playing loudly at around that time, accompanied by bangs, and had assumed the girls were hanging pictures on the walls.)

Rolling then went downstairs where Powell was still fast asleep; he raped and killed her then returned upstairs to Larson. He tore off her clothes, spread her legs wide open on the bed and put her arms over her head. But she was 'too bloody to rape', in his words, so he went back downstairs and had sex with Powell's corpse instead, chewing on her breasts like 'a mad dog gnaws a bone'. That finished, he went and helped himself to some of the contents of the fridge.

Rolling claimed that the next thing he knew it was eleven o'clock the following morning and he was riding his bike. Suddenly, he felt the urge to check his bag. In it he found a clear plastic sandwich bag containing one of Christina Powell's nipples. He couldn't remember taking it and he threw it in the gutter.

In the next 48 hours, Rolling would kill three more people, all of them students. Their bodies would be found within hours of each other, creating utter panic in the small university town. Nine hours after police officers discovered the corpses of Powell and Larson, they were called to another apartment just nine miles away where they discovered the mutilated body of 19-year-old Christa Hoyt. This time, the attack was even more frenzied. In a rage, he cut off her head and placed it on the bookshelf at eye level in her bedroom. After slicing off her nipples, which he laid on the bed beside her, he carefully propped up her body on the bed and bent her over at the waist. He then 'gutted' her by cutting her open from her chest to her pubic bone. He later said that Hoyt reminded him of his estranged wife and mother to his child, Omatha Ann Halko.

The first victims had been found on Sunday. By Tuesday afternoon, police had discovered Christa's body. Later that day police, also discovered two more bodies, those of roommates Tracey Paules and Manuel Taboada. Rolling had overpowered Manuel while he slept, then raped and murdered Tracey Paules before posing her nude body in a doorway.

Within 48 hours, Rolling had killed five students. There was panic in the small university town. Many students fled the campus for good and nobody in Gainesville slept alone. 'I'm scared to death,' one female student told a local news crew at the time. 'I think someone's going to jump through my window.'

After his Gainesville killing spree, Rolling fled to Tampa in a stolen car. Now in the grip of another demon – this time a freewheeling, gun-toting outlaw Rolling named Jesse Lang – he embarked on a series of robberies. However, he was soon arrested while trying to hold up a supermarket, less than two weeks after the first murder. To begin with, Rolling was just another bank robber awaiting trial, not a suspect in one of the widest murder hunts in US history. But police were already beginning to feel he might be tied to a triple murder committed ten months earlier in Shreveport, Louisiana, Rolling's hometown.

On 4 November 1989, at around 6 p.m., someone had broken into the Grissom family home and stabbed Tom Grissom, his daughter Julie and her eight-year-old son Sean to death. The killer had used duct tape, which he later removed, and raped Julie before killing her. He'd then arranged her carefully on the bed with her legs parted in a sexually provocative manner, before fanning her hair lovingly on the pillow. Rolling had been seen by many witnesses in the town on the day of the murder, and the similarities between the manner in which Julie Grissom had been posed and the way the corpses had been arranged in the recent Gainesville slayings were too much to ignore.

When Rolling went to the prison dentist, investigators were able to get a sample of his DNA, which matched that in traces of semen found in three of the Gainesville slayings. But, despite the compelling evidence against him, Rolling initially denied all the charges – it turned out that, despite the frenzied nature of his attacks, he'd actually been fairly careful. He had removed all the pieces of duct tape from his victims, save one, and carefully scrubbed two of his Gainesville victims with detergent. However, in addition to the DNA evidence, police had found Rolling's tent in the woods, and with it his homemade cassettes, the screwdriver he'd used to try to break into Larson and Powell's apartment, and a pair of jeans stained with Manuel Taboada's blood.

Despite his predicament, Rolling could not resist boasting of his exploits to his fellow prisoners. Apart from his desire to kill eight people to represent his time spent in jail, he also craved fame. He was, he told his cellmates, in reality a country and western singer but that career had failed so the only way he could think to achieve celebrity status was to rape and murder his way to notoriety. His stunned cellmates were quick to rat him out to authorities. One even appeared at his trial and testified against him. 'He was trying to terrorise the city of Gainesville. He was trying to make himself infamous or famous. He wanted to be a superstar amongst criminals,' fellow Death Row inmate Bobby Lewis testified during Rolling's trial.

Exhibit 172 A in the evidence presented against Rolling was a poem that he had written, called 'Gemini':

The moan... the groan...
The silver moon shown...
The whisper... the cry...
Dead leaves fly...
Through the haze it sweeps your fears...
Then... it appears...
Your nightmare come to life...
A maniac... with a knife... The man... the groan...
The silver moon shown...
The whisper... the cry...
Dead leaves fly...
Tonight... in the arms of Gemini...
A captured butterfly will die...
Burned red with fever...
Then turned gold forever...
Forever my dear...
No more pain... no more fear...
Close your eyes my dear...
And sleep...
The moan... the groan...

The silver moon shown…
The whisper…
The whisper… the cry…
Into the night comes Gemini…
And tonight… You die…

The crime scenes were so shocking that many photos had to be censored at the trial in case they prejudiced the court. 'I've got to get out of here,' Rolling was heard to whisper at one point, but overall he seemed resigned to his fate.

Faced with the evidence against him, Rolling confessed to investigators in January 1993. On the eve of his trial, he told Circuit Judge Stan R Morris, 'I've been running from first one thing and then another all my life. Whether from problems at home or with the law or from myself. But there are some things you just can't run from – this being one of them.' He pleaded guilty.

The jury unanimously recommended the death sentence. Judge Morris agreed. However, like many killers in the United States, Rolling had a long wait between his sentencing and his actual execution. Twelve years, in fact, to relish his role as a Death Row celeb. During that time, he wrote and published his memoirs, got engaged and fielded off other offers of marriage from the hordes of serial-killer groupies vying for his attention. As well as becoming a published author, he also became a commercially successful artist. That said, Rolling made no money from the sales of his book *The Making of a Serial Killer*. This was because the State of Florida won a court case against Rolling and his co-author London, which ruled that neither should be able to earn any royalties from the book under the Florida version of the 'Son of Sam Law', a law that was passed in 1977 in New York. The 'Son of Sam Law' rules that killers may not financially benefit by selling their stories to the press and thereby profit from the notoriety of their crimes.

The 'Son of Sam Law' came about after the conviction of David Richard Berkowitz in 1977. Berkowitz was found guilty of six murders and seven woundings after a one-year-long killing spree in which he shot his victims with a 44-calibre handgun.

In notes he sent to the press and one note he left at one of the crime scenes, he referred to himself as the 'Son of Sam'. The reference was to his neighbour's dog. His neighbour was called Mr Sam Carr and Berkowitz claimed Mr Sam Carr's dog was possessed by the devil and was ordering him to kill. Hence the name 'Son of Sam'.

The 'Son of Sam Law' was put into place to stop Berkowitz from signing a book deal amid press speculation at the time that he was about to sell his life story to a publisher for a huge fee.

The law has yet to be applied to serial-killer collector websites and Rolling certainly cashed in on his notoriety in order to sell his paintings. In fact, his artwork is still today avidly collected the world over by serial-killer art collectors. One of the collector websites I contacted told me that a Rolling sketch sold recently for over $1,000.

Finally, after Rolling's last-ditch appeal – which argued that execution by lethal injection constituted cruel and unusual punishment – was deemed without merit by a Florida Supreme Court, Danny Rolling's execution date was set. He had been on Death Row since 20 April 1994, but in October 2006 Rolling finally went to his well-deserved death. Singing all the way.

## CHAPTER SIX
# THE WASP WOMAN MURDER

Twenty years ago, Hollywood actress Susan
Cabot was found bludgeoned to death in her
Los Angeles home. But had the murderer
really been a Latin American ninja, as her son
claimed? Or had the baby-faced mummy's boy
done it himself, driven insane by an infected
batch of hormones from a dead man?

Among the many murderers and psychotics portrayed in
the movies there is one type of deranged lunatic
particularly close to Hollywood's heart and that is the faded
actress-turned-recluse. The Hollywood classics Billy Wilder's
film noir *Sunset Boulevard* (1950) and Robert Aldrich's gothic
horror *What Ever Happened to Baby Jane?* (1962) were set in
decaying Hollywood mansions and both tell the story of
actresses driven mad by their sudden loss of fame. Both movies
end in murder.

So, when in 1986 a real Hollywood recluse was found
bludgeoned to death in her dilapidated home, it made
headlines all over America. Throw in a Latin American ninja
and a dwarf on a strange experimental drug and the 'Wasp
Woman murder', as it was known, became a Hollywood legend
almost overnight.

The murder victim was Susan Cabot, who had been a household name in the 1950s. Cabot had appeared in 20 films, acting alongside Hollywood legends such as Humphrey Bogart, Charles Bronson and Lee Marvin. Her films were usually low-budget westerns, in which Cabot was invariably typecast as the smouldering female temptress. Apart from the steady work in the movies, she also had regular offers of work from Broadway, television and radio and was under contract with Universal International Pictures.

But Cabot abruptly terminated her contract with Universal and after a brief stint on Broadway started working with maverick director Roger Corman. For Corman, Cabot appeared in *Carnival Rock* (1957), *Sorority Girl* (1957), the wonderfully titled but ultimately disappointing *The Saga of the Viking Women and Their Voyage to the Waters of the Great Sea Serpent* (1957), sci-fi flick *War of the Satellites* (1958), *Machine-Gun Kelly* (1958) and last of all the horror movie *The Wasp Woman* (1959).

Cabot was 40 when she starred in *The Wasp Woman* and excelled in what was to be her final role – and the one for which she is best remembered – as Janice Starlin, a character who unwisely tests out a rejuvenating beauty product derived from wasp enzymes. Extracted from royal jelly, these enzymes make her young again but ultimately, in a typically bizarre Corman premise, turn Cabot's character into a lustful, murderous queen wasp.

At the peak of her abilities, Cabot quit acting altogether and soon afterwards disappeared into obscurity. Apart from the very occasional interview, nothing was heard about her for another 20 years. It was known that she had had a son named Timothy, who was afflicted with dwarfism, and it was rumoured, but never confirmed, that the son's father was the

# THE WASP WOMAN MURDER

then King Hussein of Jordan, with whom Cabot had been romantically linked. Cabot and her son lived in a large property in an exclusive neighbourhood in Encino in Los Angeles but were very rarely seen by neighbours. To all intents and purposes, Cabot had vanished.

On the night of 10 December 1986, emergency services received a call from Susan Cabot's home on 4601 Charmion Lane. The caller breathlessly identified himself as Timothy Cabot and he reported the entry of a burglar at the house that he shared with his mother. A fire department paramedic unit responded to the call and arrived just four minutes later, by which time Timothy was waiting for them, now quite calmly, outside the front door. He told the two paramedics that he had been attacked, that his mother was in the bedroom and that he believed she was also injured.

Their house was a prime piece of real estate perched on top of a hill with a view of the lights of Los Angeles below, though it seemed a bit dilapidated from the outside and shabbier than the other impeccably maintained properties on the street. Nothing, however, could have prepared paramedics for the chaos that met them when they pushed open the door.

Inside, rubbish bags lay strewn in every room, newspapers and magazines were stacked in toppling piles along the corridors and trash and rotting food was everywhere. The house also appeared to have been ransacked: furniture was overturned, drawers were open and their contents strewn about the house. The sudden eeriness was made worse by the sound of Timothy's four pet Attika dogs. Usually a docile breed, these four were in an absolute frenzy, and Timothy, in order to protect the paramedics, had locked them up in his room.

The paramedics found Susan Cabot lying dead on her bed dressed only in a purple V-neck nightgown. There was blood everywhere: a large arc of it was sprayed on the bedroom mirror near her bed, there were large splatter stains on the ceiling above her prone body and further bloodstains on the floor and the bed. For some reason, the killer had covered Cabot's face and head with a piece of bed linen before bludgeoning her remorselessly to death. Under the blood-soaked material, Cabot's face was all but unrecognisable. There were human hairs and brain matter smeared on the linen, and shards and splinters of bone protruding from the back of her shattered skull.

By now police had arrived on the scene and were busy checking all of the other rooms to check for signs of forced entry and to make sure that the intruder was no longer on the premises. But the dogs were deemed too vicious and dangerous to remove without the help of animal control and so there was one room they could not enter. Investigators were, however, able to glimpse weight-training equipment and barbells on the floor. On the walls were pictures of Timothy's idol, Bruce Lee.

There was something rather unnerving about Susan Cabot's son. With soft brown eyes and straight chestnut hair, to begin with Timothy looked just like a teenage boy. But on closer inspection his face seemed older, as if a wizened adult were somehow peering from out of a young boy's face. He didn't act and talk like a teenager either.

In fact, Timothy was 22 years old. Born with a form of dwarfism caused by a defective pituitary gland, he should have stood at only just four foot. But due to an experimental growth hormone, which he had been taking for 15 years, he had grown by almost a foot and a half. What he said next stunned investigators. He told police that he had woken up at around nine-thirty, when he had heard his mother being attacked in her room. He had gone into the kitchen, where he confronted a burglar. The burglar, he told police, was a tall Latino man with curly hair, and he had been dressed like a Japanese ninja warrior. Timothy was a practising martial-arts enthusiast, but despite this he proved no match for the masked intruder, who had knocked him out cold.

Over the next few hours, the police began to have their suspicions about his story. According to the initial incident report obtained by this author, Timothy's statements became 'increasingly inconsistent'. The doubts increased when the paramedics examined his injuries. According to the investigator's report, Timothy only had superficial wounds to the arm, torso and head. Paramedics reported to police, 'The trauma to his head did not appear serious enough to cause unconsciousness.'

Timothy was immediately taken in for questioning at LAPD West Valley station, where he held his own during a three-hour grilling. When asked about his relationship with his mother, he described it as 'very close'. His mother and he talked about everything, he told investigators, including 'intimate sexual matters'.

When the questioning was over, Timothy was formally charged with his mother's murder. He demanded that he be taken home to collect some medication that he said he needed, and there, without any prompting at all, Timothy led detectives to the murder weapon.

By this time, it was the early hours of the morning. It had taken animal-control officers six hours to finally remove the dogs and Timothy now led police to a hamper in the room where they had been. Inside the hamper was a box of soap powder and in the box was a bloody barbell and a scalpel. His fingerprints were on one end of the barbell and his mother's blood was on the other. Timothy said that he had hidden the barbell because he was sure that no one would have believed his story.

And, of course, nobody did. Apart from the forensic evidence stacked against him, his story just didn't make any sense. Yet it wasn't going to be a straightforward matter for the prosecution team, even when later he confessed to lawyers that he had made up the whole ninja story and killed his own mother. When he stood trial in May 1989, his legal defence initially put in a plea of not guilty by reason of insanity. In arguably one of the strangest defence strategies of all time, Timothy's lawyers argued that he could not be held responsible for his actions because their client was 'a human experiment gone wrong'.

The experiment in question had first begun in 1958, and Timothy had been one of many test subjects. As a possible cure for dwarfism, the National Institute of Health had started to offer a supply of cadaver-derived pituitary free of charge to children diagnosed with growth hormone deficiency (GHD); the batch of hormones had been extracted from the pituitary glands of around 80,000 dead human bodies. The experiment lasted eight years and around 700 children with GHD received the treatment. Timothy, who had been diagnosed with pituitary dwarfism as a child, was one of them and had been taking the injections since he was six years old.

But, for some, the wonder cure was to have tragic results. Due to a contaminated batch of growth hormones, the supply had been infected with a fatal neurological illness. Over the years, an unusually high percentage of the test subjects had developed Creutzfeldt Jakob disease (more commonly known today as 'mad cow disease'). The incubation period for CJD is long, in some cases 20 years, and as there was no way to diagnose for CJD there was no way of knowing if Timothy had CJD or would one day contract it. All the same, his lawyers used it as a cornerstone of his defence. His mother, they argued, had warped his poor fragile mind by bombing it for decades with potent chemicals, harvested from the genetic material of hundreds of thousands of dead bodies.

This all fitted in perfectly with Timothy's insanity plea, because the psychological symptoms of CJD include extreme changes in personality, dementia, the loss of the ability to think clearly and memory loss. Then, it was sensationally revealed that Cabot, wrongly believing that it would help her look younger, had been helping herself to her son's drugs for years too. So had the frequent injections affected Susan Cabot's mental stability as well? Had she become deranged and attacked Timothy and if so had he simply been acting in self-defence? It was just another bizarre twist to the death of Susan Cabot and inevitably recalled one of her most famous roles as The Wasp Woman, a character who had taken an experimental anti-ageing drug only to become a crazed and violent killer.

Timothy's lawyers were busy painting a disturbing profile of Susan Cabot as a woman unable to cope with her loss of fame, a faded Hollywood has-been who had shut herself up and away from the lights of Hollywood and slowly driven both herself and her son insane. It was straight out of the movies – one movie in particular.

It wasn't long before the reclusive, unhappy existence that Timothy and his mother had shared for 11 years on Charmion

Lane was being compared in the press to the one of Billy Wilder's most famous movies. In *Sunset Boulevard*, Gloria Swanson plays Norma Desmond, a once-famous Hollywood silent-movie star who dreams of the day when she can make her long-awaited comeback. By the end of the film, however, it is clear that Desmond is a dangerous, delusional psychopath.

Actually, very little is known about what really happened behind the walls of 4601 Charmion Lane, or indeed the kind of life Timothy had to endure under his mother's roof. One of the very few people to actually be invited into Susan Cabot's home and interview her before she died was famous film historian Tom Weaver. He had long been a fan of Susan Cabot's work and visited her in her home on several occasions up to her death in 1986. Tom Weaver specialises in the history of B-movies and low-budget horror movies and is the author of such books as *Attack of the Monster Movie Makers* and *Science Fiction and Fantasy Film Flashbacks*.

'It was on my first-ever trip to California, around 1984, that I first met Susan, who had been at or near the top of my find-and-interview list almost since Day One,' he wrote in a recent article on Susan Cabot. 'I not only thought she was a knockout looks-wise in movies like *The Wasp Woman*, *Machine Gun Kelly* and others, but acting-wise too, and it frustrated me that no one knew where she'd ended up. Roger Corman told me, wrongly, that she was living happily in Washington, DC; that bum steer was the closest thing I had to a lead. So I was bowled over when, on that first California trip, Lori "Revenge of the Creature" Nelson mentioned casually that she'd seen Susan just the other day, at some sort of reunion of Universal Pictures veterans.

'To make a long story short, my brother Jon and I were soon

very friendly with Susan, the fun of knowing her only slightly spoiled by her aggressively oddball son Tim. The kid was pleasant but... strange. He struck me as looking like about 12 years old (facially and height-wise) but he was obviously much older, because he had his own car. Too often he did "little things" that would drive his mom nuts, like wearing sunglasses when we'd go out at night and clamming up and ignoring her requests to take them off, refusing to watch some of her movies with us even though she was practically begging him to. Things that seemed to me to be designed to get her worked up.

'A swift kick in the ass would have solved a lot of her problems with Tim, I always thought, but being a star-struck twenty-something kid from upstate New York, getting to visit on various trips with one of my favourite B-movie stars, it certainly wasn't my place to say so.

'Susan's house was also strange. A mini-mansion, walled and gated, including a kennel full of vicious-sounding dogs – a lot fancier than you'd think a single mom, whose long ago credits were mostly B-movies, could afford. There were rumours that, back in the day, she and King Hussein was an item; when I'd bring that up, she was the one who did the clamming up. Eventually I began to think that was where the money was apparently still coming from.

'Inside, it got weirder. The place was a wreck and apparently always had been. There was junk piled everywhere, to the point that finding a place where three or four people could sit down was a major project involving lots of moving-of-stacks-of-junk. The dust was piled almost as high as the junk; I still remember picking up a chessman from a dust-covered chessboard practically in the middle of the room, uncovering a round, perfectly clean spot in the deep dust that indicated that the board had been set up many years before, there in the middle of the room, and then never once touched.

'I couldn't help but think of, say, *Thriller* episodes [an American series of short horror stories that aired in the 1960s] where unsuspecting folks ventured into creepy old mansions unoccupied for decades. I was once with Susan when she needed something out of the trunk of her car; she unlocked and lifted the trunk hatch but, looking at the car, it was as if nothing had been opened. Clothes were crammed so tightly into the trunk that they held the shape of the underside of the trunk hatch!'

Another person who had been allowed to set foot inside the house was Timothy's tutor, who was called as a witness at his trial. She stated that his mother frequently screamed at her son, apparently for no reason. The image of an overbearing, hysterical mother whose mental deterioration was rapidly spinning out of control was further borne out in testimony by Cabot's long-term psychologist, Carl Faber. His patient, he told the court, had spent time in 14 separate foster homes, where she had been sexually abused. As an adult, she had been plagued by bouts of irrational terror and despair and had talked about suicide on the very day she had been murdered. Although she was reasonably well off, Cabot still lived in constant fear that she would lose her home for lack of money and she had learned not long ago that her son could have contracted CJD. Her son, she had told her psychologist many times, was the only reason she kept on living.

According to a paediatric report presented as evidence for the defence, Susan Cabot's degenerating mental illness had already taken its toll on Timothy by the time he was just 11 years old. The report described Cabot as overly dramatic and overly protective and Timothy as emotionally immature and disturbed. But the state of disrepair of the house was perhaps the most shocking indicator as to just how mentally unbalanced Susan Cabot was and filmed footage of the house was shown in court.

In September, Timothy changed his plea from not guilty for reasons of insanity to not guilty. He finally took the stand on 6 October 1989. There, he quickly broke into tears and recalled that his mother, moments before her death, had started screaming at him and had seemed to have had no idea of who he was. Fearful of her worsening state, he had tried to call paramedics, at which point she had attacked him with the barbell. Timothy had taken the barbell off her but she had come at him again – this time with a scalpel. Timothy, in self-defence, had beaten her to death.

On 10 October 1989, Judge Darlene E Schempp announced her decision. She could see no evidence of malice or premeditation. She found Timothy guilty of involuntary manslaughter – a sentence that carried a sentence of six years in jail; he had already spent two-and-a-half years in jail while awaiting trial. He was given just three years' probation. The judge concluded her summation by saying that that there was no doubt in her mind that he had 'loved his mother very much'.

Throughout his trial, the press had described Timothy as resembling a lost, somewhat forlorn-looking little boy. Yet Timothy wasn't a child when he had caved in his mother's skull with such force and repetition that the walls and even the ceiling had been covered in blood.

'The house became his,' recalls Tom Weaver. 'I later heard that it was sometimes used for filming, and that one group of movie-makers, without even knowing about the house's history of murder, became so creeped out by the atmosphere of the place that at least one of them, a woman, wanted to flee... A few years ago I started getting occasional emails from a complete stranger, a Cabot family friend, who said that Tim was hospitalised and suffering from some weird irreversible disease that was slowly making his brain disappear within his skull.'

According to Weaver, the emails abruptly stopped and in fact nothing at all is known about the fate of Susan Cabot's son or where he is now. Meanwhile, the house he once shared with his mother on Charmion Lane has since been demolished and in its place stands a newer, more luxurious property more in keeping with the other elegant houses on the street. What really happened that night over 20 years ago remains a mystery.

## CHAPTER SEVEN

# JEROME BRUDOS: THE SHOE FETISH SLAYER

Hedonistic serial killer and family man
Jerome Brudos killed four young women in
his own backyard and dumped their remains in
a nearby river. But how did he keep his
murderous nature a secret and could it really
have been his love of women's shoes that
made him a killer?

When opportunity came knocking on his door on a late afternoon in January 1968, Jerome Brudos didn't hesitate – not even for a second. Her name was Linda Kay Slawson. She was 19 years old and pretty and was selling encyclopaedias in order to save up money for college.

Jerome Brudos, unlike many of the people Slawson encountered in her line of work, seemed affable enough and in fact appeared genuinely interested in what she had to sell. His wife, mother and children were all in the house, so he led her out back towards his garage so she could show him the encyclopaedias in peace. Slawson must have thought for a moment that it was her lucky day.

Brudos led her around towards the back of his house and past the children's toys littered on the path. As soon as Slawson entered the garage, Brudos snatched up a thick plank of wood and cracked her over the head with it. After a furtive look back to the house, Brudos dragged her unconscious body further into the darkness, where he strangled her to death.

Brudos had physically assaulted women in the past but he had never actually killed before. He now found that he had in his possession something he had craved for all his life: a human doll. Something he could dress up at leisure in his secret stash of women's clothing, underwear and – more importantly – the huge collection of women's shoes that he had stolen.

He calmly walked back into his house and suggested that his family go out and get something to eat. Brudos then returned to the garage, where he stripped Slawson's body, dressed her up in his women's underwear and arranged her body in sexually provocative poses. He then cut off her left foot with a hacksaw and put the foot in the freezer so that he could use it to model his collection of high-heel shoes later on. That done, he put the body in the boot of his car, drove to Interstate 5 and threw it into the Willamette River.

Brudos would spend the next two years seeking out victims – all of them pretty and young, like Slawson – but to begin with he did not seem in any particular hurry to kill again. In fact, he waited 11 months before committing his next murder, and once again the attack was opportunistic.

His next victim was 23-year-old Jan Susan Whitney and her car had broken down on Interstate 5 between Salem and Albany. Brudos – who was blond and chubby with freckles, giving him a slightly youthful air – stopped and offered Whitney a ride to his house, where he told her he would phone a pick-up truck. Once there, Brudos got into the back of the car and strangled Whitney to death with a leather strap. He then had sex with her body in the car.

Brudos carried the body to his garage and hung it by the neck via a pulley, which he had fixed to the ceiling. He kept it hanging there for several days so he could dress it up, have repeated sex with it and take photos. He finally disposed of it in the same spot where he had dumped Slawson: the Willamette River. Again, Brudos had kept a keepsake: a breast, which he made a mould of in resin and used as a paperweight. By this time Slawson's foot had rotted, having been taken out of the freezer so many times to model his shoe collection, and so that had to go into the river too.

Why was Jerome Brudos so obsessed with women's shoes? Much of what is known about him, especially his childhood and growing love of ladies' footwear, has emerged from the extensive research carried out by famous crime writer Anna Rule, whose book *Lust Killer* (1983) is the definitive account of the case.

According to Rule's research, Brudos's obsession began when he was just five years old. She writes that at that age he found a pair of high-heel shoes at a rubbish dump. He went home, put them on and paraded himself in them in front of his mother, who was furious – much to his surprise – and ordered him to take them back to the dump. But, instead of putting Brudos off, the incident had the reverse effect. Women's footwear became an obsession, one that escalated over time; by the time he reached his twenties, he was stalking women, knocking them unconscious and then stealing their shoes for his collection.

I talked to Dr Cameron Kippen, perhaps the world's foremost expert on foot fetishism, to try to understand Brudos's obsession with shoes and how it might have led to his impulse to kill. According to Kippen, exactly why someone becomes sexually aroused by an inanimate object is still unknown. It is likely, however, that Brudos's obsession began during his infant sexual development. 'Something goes wrong in the individual's developing conceptual thought processes and the person is left with a response which triggers their sexual desires when they see or interact with the object,' Kippen told me. 'This secretive behaviour becomes progressively more intense as they go through puberty. Stealing knickers and shoes would be common enough and forms part of a graduation where crimes becomes incrementally more serious.

'I would think by the time Brudos experienced his mother's reprimand, he had a full-blown sexual fascination with women's shoes. Often the "buzz" comes from being caught and this negatively reinforces the behaviour. That would be the thrill he sought to re-create. Being caught and chastised would be more thrilling and negatively reinforce the deviant behaviour. He would seek that out at every opportunity.

'Brudos would love his shoe collection literally and pay the object of his desire the ultimate compliment by presenting them with a foot. Victims may have been chosen because they had a specific foot size, but not necessarily because he was turned on by feet. Lust murderers will revisit the site of their crimes if they can to relive the excitement. They enjoy doing what they do and will experience high orgasms, so any opportunity to relive the experience brings it all back to them. Taking a keepsake would satisfy some, and, in Brudos's case, paying the ultimate compliment to his beloved shoe collection would be essential. So off comes the foot.'

Brudos, according to Kippen, is what is known as a 'retifist', someone who is obsessed with an inanimate object – in Brudos's case, shoes. Although he is often mistakenly labelled as a foot fetishist, he wasn't obsessed with feet at all. One killer who did have a real foot fetish was Dayton Lee Rogers. Rogers – also from Oregon, like Brudos – has been on Death Row since June 1989, having been convicted of murdering six women over a period of ten years. Rogers dumped the bodies of his victims, all of them prostitutes, in a wood overlooking the Molalla River, earning himself the nickname the 'Molalla Forest Killer'.

Rogers, who was a married mechanic, bound and tortured his victims before dumping them and in one case actually gutted one of his victims. According to crime writer Gary King in his account of the case, *Blood Lust: Portrait of a Serial Killer* (1992), Rogers was particularly obsessed with the arches of women's feet. Of the seven corpses found in the forest, one of them had had her foot removed with a hacksaw while another one had her foot cut two-thirds of the way through and then snapped off. According to King's research, this was almost certainly done while the victim was still alive.

According to Dr Kippen, Brudos had what he calls a 'reversed Cinderella fixation'. Instead of presenting the shoe to the foot, Brudos presented the foot to the shoe. Dr Kippen argues that Brudos may indeed have chosen his victims because of the size of their feet. 'He brought the foot to the object of his greatest desire – his shoe collection.'

Four months after killing Slawson, and this time disguised as a woman, Brudos abducted 19-year-old Karen Sprinkler at gunpoint in a car park outside a department store. He brought her to his garage, forced her to pose in his collection of women's clothes and lingerie, again took photographs, raped her, then choked her to death by suspending her in the air with the pulley.

He had repeated sex with the body before cutting off both of her breasts to make plastic moulds. He then tied her body to a six-cylinder car engine with nylon cord and threw her in the river.

Although his killing spree continued, Brudos, in common with many serial killers, was able to completely separate his domestic life from his murderous activities; no one in his family suspected that anything was amiss. But how did he manage to maintain and lead a normal life while at the same time ensuring that his real nature remained a secret?

I talked to Dr Joe Davis – Director of the Department of Forensic Science, Criminal Justice and Criminology at the National University, San Diego, California – about the way Brudos managed to place the different areas of his life into compartments. Dr Davis specialises in forensic psychology and forensic mental health and has studied Brudos's case in depth. He defines him as a 'hedonistic serial killer'. 'Jerry or Jerome Brudos, like so many others – like Bundy, Gacy – had so much to hide but was invigorated by the hedonistic excitement that came from his acts that brought so much sexual and ego-gratification called "ego-syntonic" thinking,' he informed me. 'Driven by pure sexual and physical hedonism, Brudos quickly adapted, and equipped mentally, a persona of a "double life" that could (and did) provide an intellectualised, rationalised and compartmentalised cover or covert life.

'Brudos, like so many others, was able to "protect" via these mental defences his otherwise fragile ego by splitting off and compartmentalising his real self from his imagined fantasised one. This blur was indistinguishable by Brudos demonstrating the ability to turn this on or off at will.'

A spilt personality?

## JEROME BRUDOS: THE SHOE FETISH SLAYER

'No, not a split personality by diagnosis, but one of a life-long malignant personality style, adjustable to fit his pathological needs anchored to narcissism and anti-social traits and behaviours. Each kill or act he performed further reinforced, solidified and galvanised this persona of evil with NO moral consciousness available to him to counteract it.'

Between his third and fourth murders, Brudos also attacked two other women, both of whom were able to escape. On 21 April 1969, Brudos approached 24-year-old Sharon Wood on the basement floor of a car park in Portland.

Ms Wood still lives in Oregon and is now a writer with ten grandchildren. She told me that her brief encounter with Brudos in that car park almost 40 years ago has given her 'a lifetime to ponder survival's mysteries'. Asked what happened that day, she sent me a poem called 'Battle in the Bunker of an Everyday Parking Structure', which tells the story of her chance encounter with Brudos that afternoon in 1969. The poem, Mrs Wood told me, is 'as brief as the encounter that's given me a lifetime, 38 Aprils since and 456 months, to ponder survival's whys and maybes.'

'I was in my forties when I read Ann Rule's book *Lust Killer*,' she says, 'and found out how hopeless it had been for the others. There is a photo of me in the book back in 1969, hair like a painted waterfall, and, though you can't see them, purple suede go-go boots. Now I have ten grandchildren, four of whom could have been someone else's but not mine, because their parents – my twins – were born 1 August 1970, 16 months post the car park attack. My parking garage, unchanged in every way, is still there on Southwest Broadway, the main street of my hometown.' I drive or walk by my memories there two or three times a week, every time just so grateful I survived.'

**Battle in the Bunker of an Everyday Parking Structure**
Daylight surrounded those corner stairs,
But I descended into closed basement air.
It was April, no rain, a light breeze,
The maples new again at hanging leaves.
Both of us in his six-storey lair,
I didn't see him hidden there:
Making his selection, floor by floor
Tracking my lone distraction.
I'd misplaced my keys, spaced my car,
Oblivious, I searched those oil-stained rows.
I was dressed in linen red,
Didn't know he'd fashioned paper weights
Of the last one's breasts –
Thrown into the Long Tom River what was left.
I hadn't yet seen her or all the rest:
Photographs of their waiting eyes,
Options frozen as his camera stalked and pried.
He came at me from behind my left shoulder,
The gun of his body cocked
Like a hair-trigger soldier.
So much we can't know: whether
We will survive if we fight or die if we do.
What I knew was he whispered into my ear:
Don't scream and I won't shoot you.

Brudos was indeed armed with a gun, but Wood fought back and, after a brief but violent struggle, which left Wood unconscious and lying on the floor, Brudos fled. Wood had been extremely lucky. The next day brought another failed attack: Brudos attempted to abduct 15-year-old Gloria Gene Smith in his mother's green Volkswagen but drove off after Smith ran to a passer-by for help. The day after that, Brudos tried again and this time was successful. His next victim was 22-year-old Linda Salee, whom he abducted in a shopping mall car park. Like the others, she was brought to his garage where he raped her and at the same time strangled her to death. Again she was pulled up by the hook in the air while Brudos had fun with her corpse.

This time, he didn't take a keepsake; her breasts were 'too pink', he later told police. Brudos, a trained electrician, did, however, run a current through the body to see if it would jump. It didn't. Later, he tied her body to a car transmission with nylon cord and copper wire and dumped her in the river, just like the rest.

Brudos had also been busy searching for more victims at the nearby Oregon State University campus. According to Brent Turvey, a forensic scientist and criminal profiler, he picked up directories of students on the campus. They had photos in them, so he picked out the girls he liked, 'cold called them and asked them for a date'.

Thankfully, Brudos's murder spree was nearing an end. Less than 20 days after his fourth murder, a fisherman called Sam Wallace spotted a body floating in the Long Tom River and called the police. It was Linda Salee. Just 50ft away, police also found Karen Sprinkler's body.

As part of the murder inquiry that followed, police asked students at the nearby university campus if they had noticed any strange men hanging around. One of them told them that someone had been pestering her for a blind date on the phone. Police persuaded her to accept and were waiting when Brudos showed up. They asked him a few questions, which he answered co-operatively enough, but when he gave them a false address he immediately became a suspect.

Detectives went around to his house and Brudos foolhardily invited them into the garage. One of the officers, Detective Miller, noticed a piece of rope with a strange knot in it, and some copper wire; he pocketed the wire and had it examined. It was determined that the tool used to cut it matched the one that had been used to tie the bodies to the engine parts in the river. Brudos was arrested and soon afterwards made a full confession.

On Saturday, 28 June 1969, press around the country reported that a 30-year-old Salem Oregon electrician named Jerome Brudos had pleaded guilty to three first-degree murders in the slayings of three young women. 'I did it,' Brudos told the jury as he admitted to the murders of Karen Sprinkler, Jan Susan Whitney and Linda Salee.

Brudos told the court that he had killed Miss Whitney with 'a leather strap' after she was abducted on 26 November 1968 and said he used a leather strap 'with a knot in it' to murder Salee. According to newspaper reports at the time, Brudos said he had held Sprinkler for 'about an hour' before he killed her with a rope. He told the court that all three murders had been done with premeditation and deliberation.

There was no death sentence at the time in the state, so Judge Val D Sloper sentenced Brudos to three consecutive life sentences in the Oregon State Penitentiary. At the time of Brudos's conviction, the body of Jan Susan Whitney, his second victim, had still to be recovered. It was found a month later, around a mile downstream from the Independence Bridge, where Brudos told police he had thrown it. The body had been there since November and was tied to a piece of railroad iron.

The story, as it was covered in the pages of the press at the time, was low key across the board. As some writers have observed, serial killers were a relatively unknown phenomenon at time and absent were the lurid details that would almost certainly have been revealed had Brudos begun his killing spree today. Also omitted from the press at the time, and this time for legal reasons, was the fact that while in custody Brudos had admitted to a psychologist that he had killed a fourth girl who was in fact his first victim – 19-year-old Linda Kay Slawson. Tragically for her family, her body was never found.

In theory, Brudos was eligible for parole in ten years' time. Whether he would ever be paroled, though, was 'contingent upon the adjustment he makes during the interim' according to a statement made at the time by Jack Wiseman, then chairman of the Board of Parole and Probation.

In 1995, Brudos was informed by the parole board that he would never be released. There seemed to have been little 'adjustment' in his attitude to his crimes; when he did talk about what he'd done, he sometimes became flippant. According to Anne Rule, when asked by radio host Lars Larson about the murders, he replied, 'It was a slow Saturday night.'

One person who actually met Brudos in jail was Brent Turvey, who was an undergraduate psychology student at Portland State University when he met Brudos in 1991. Turvey told me that Brudos lied constantly to him but was also affable and utterly disarming when he met him in jail.

All the same, Brudos was a constant target for other inmates and there had even been a couple of attempts on his life by the time Turvey and Brudos met. According to Turvey, Brudos was far more popular with the guards than his fellow prisoners, and was a trustee. He had even helped install the cable and computer system in the jail. 'They all loved him,' Turvey stated.

Although Brudos knew he would never be released, he was allowed an interview with the parole board every two years, which was a regular source of anguish to the victims' families. But finally they got some good news: at 5 a.m. on 28 March 2006, Brudos died of cancer, aged 66. He had been in jail for 35 years. It was a relatively merciful end for a killer who had murdered four young women solely for his own personal pleasure.

## CHAPTER EIGHT

# BAR-JONAH: SOMETHING WICKED THIS WAY COMES

Serial sex offender Nathaniel Bar-Jonah
rigged up a pulley system in his kitchen so he
could hang children by their necks and watch
them choke. But had the one-time fast-food
worker really killed and served up a young
boy to his friends and neighbours?

Early on a cold December morning in the small town of Great Falls, Montana, Detective Robert Burton was on his way to work when he saw something that made him very worried indeed. Hanging around the local elementary school was a man whom Burton recognised as Nathaniel Bar-Jonah. Weighing over 230lb, the hulking shadow of Bar-Jonah wasn't hard to miss, even in the early-morning gloom. With a doughy, innocent-looking face, he looked out at the world out of two mismatched eyes – one blue, the other brown.

Bar-Jonah was popular with kids in Great Falls because of his frequent garage sales, where he sold *Star Wars* figures at rock-bottom prices. Parents trusted him and often invited him to babysit their children. But Detective Burton knew better: he knew that, in 1994, Bar-Jonah had been arrested for sexual assault on an eight-year-old boy. Police had not been able to make the case stick, though, and three years later the charges had been dropped. Burton also knew that Bar-Jonah was a known felon in the State of Massachusetts, where he had been convicted of the kidnapping and attempted murder of two young boys while posing as a police officer. What's more, this wasn't the first time Burton had seen Bar-Jonah lurking outside the school. In fact, he had seen him twice in the same spot just the week before. This time, Bar-Jonah was wearing a dark-blue police-style jacket.

Burton immediately contacted dispatch and a patrol unit in the area responded to the call. As it was still dark outside, the squad car turned on the spotlight and shone it on the suspect's face. The police officer told the hulking figure to approach the car and remove his hands from his pockets – a request that Bar-Jonah initially refused. The officer then asked him if he had something in his pocket and Bar-Jonah responded that he had 'a stun gun'. When the police searched him they found that he was carrying two cans of pepper spray, a realistic-looking toy gun and a badge. He was arrested for impersonating a police officer and for carrying a concealed weapon. Two days later, police searched his home for the very first time.

Bar-Jonah had been living in Montana since moving there from his home state of Massachusetts ten years earlier. He had left behind him a string of convictions for offences against children – a record that Montana authorities were mostly unaware of. To begin with, it looked like a relatively straightforward arrest and police were just looking for anything in his house that could incriminate him further on the charge of impersonating a police officer. What they found there, however, would make headlines all over the world and change the small close-knit community of Great Falls forever.

## BAR-JONAH: SOMETHING WICKED THIS WAY COMES

Among the items found in Bar-Jonah's squalid ground-floor apartment were a staggering 14,000 pictures of children, culled mainly from newspapers and year books. Hundreds of others were arranged in two binders. They were all meticulously arranged like baseball cards with the names of the children written underneath, among them many photos of children Bar-Jonah had clearly taken himself. According to court records, police also found 'a blue police coat, a silver toy revolver, a silver badge, a Stunmaster stun gun, a cap with the logo "security enforcement", two disposable cameras, two albums with cut-outs of children, one coat with a badge in the pocket and numerous photos and negatives'.

Beside the photo albums was a list of children written in Bar-Jonah's own handwriting. The list was entitled 'Lake Webster' – a place where Bar-Jonah had spent most of his teenage years. On the list were 27 names written in chronological order dating from 1963 to 1977. The list opened up hideous possibilities, as Lake Webster had been the scene of Bar-Jonah's first convicted attack on a child. Equally worrying was the discovery that on the list were the names of Billy Benoit and Al Enrickias – two other children Bar-Jonah had been convicted of kidnapping and attempting to kill in Massachusetts.

Bar-Jonah – born David Brown – had lived in Lake Webster before moving to Montana in 1991, and as a result of his many attacks on children there he had a long criminal record. When he was just 14 years old, he attempted to lure two young brothers from a neighbouring family with a note in which he offered them '$20 a piece' to meet him at the local cemetery at six o'clock. Thankfully, the note was intercepted by the boys' parents, who contacted the police. They found Bar-Jonah lurking behind a gravestone, waiting anxiously for the boys' arrival. He got off with just a warning that time, but it wasn't long before he tried again.

Three years later, Bar-Jonah struck once more, using a method of attack that he was to improve upon over the years that followed. This time he pretended he was a police officer and showed a fake police badge to eight-year-old Richard O'Connor, whom he drove to a remote spot near Lake Webster. There, he forced O'Connor to remove all his clothes before strangling him with the seat belt of his car. Thankfully, Bar-Jonah took pity on his victim and let him go before driving him home and two weeks later even wrote a letter to the boy's mother and said he was sorry for what he'd done. Again he got off lightly, this time with probation.

When he was 20 years old, in 1977, Bar-Jonah dressed as a policeman and picked up 13-year-old Billy Benoit and 14-year-old Al Enrickias outside the White City Cinemas in Shrewsbury. Armed with a hunting knife, Bar-Jonah handcuffed them both and then drove them to the nearby Charlton woods, where he had earlier set up a tent. Once there he began to choke Enrickias. But the boy, showing a maturity beyond his years, feigned death and then ran to get help. When police caught up with Bar-Jonah after a short pursuit on Route 20, they found Benoit in the trunk of the car. He had been beaten, handcuffed and was severely bruised; Bar-Jonah had half-choked him to death.

After the attempted murder on the two boys near Lake Webster, Bar-Jonah had served just two years in a maximum-security prison before being sent to the relatively cushy confines of Bridgewater Treatment Centre for the sexually dangerous. There, he had taken classes in journalism, worked in the canteen and quickly found God. It was during this period that he changed his name from David Brown to the more Jewish-sounding Nathaniel Benjamin Levi Bar-Jonah – apparently, so he would know 'what it was like to be persecuted'.

In prison, he had expressed perverse sexual fantasies of rape and torture to psychologists, revealing that he had once tried to choke a female classmate when he was just six years old. He also told psychologists about his bizarre fantasies, which revolved around torture, and also expressed a curiosity about the taste of human flesh. After ten long years of intensive therapy, he was still, according to one psychologist report, 'A borderline personality with marked passive-dependent and psychopathic features'.

That didn't stop Bar-Jonah from appealing against his sentence. Two psychologists who submitted reports to the appeal hearing argued that the 'vulnerable', 'honest' Bar-Jonah had 'benefited from therapy' and felt that it was safe to finally let him go. On 12 February 1991, the now Christian child molester, who had openly confessed to fantasising about eating another human being, had been deemed safe to release back into the community.

Three weeks later, he attacked another child – a seven-year-old boy who was waiting for his mother in her car. The obese child molester opened the door of the car, squeezed inside and then sat on top of the boy, though he fled when the boy's mother (the aptly named Nancy Surprise) came back and saw him. Arrested shortly afterwards, Bar-Jonah ludicrously claimed that he had simply been looking for a place to get out of the rain. Incredibly, instead of being sent to prison or being taken back to the mental facility of Bridgewater, Bar-Jonah was given yet *another* lucky break. His lawyers sought a plea-bargain agreement and the boy's mother, believing that the case against Bar-Jonah was much weaker than it actually was (he had actually made a confession), agreed. The direst consequence of this was that his record was not shown in court. He was given just two years' probation for breaking and entering and assault and battery on the condition that he go to live with his mother in Great Falls, Montana. The judge had ordered a psychological evaluation too, but it never took place; in fact, Bar-Jonah was never formally placed on probation. Worse still, the State of Montana was not even warned that he was on his way.

Back in Montana, detectives were trying to figure out what the other names on the Lake Webster list meant. Were they other victims who had fallen prey to the fat teenage child molester? Searching through his notebooks, police saw the name of another boy they recognised, and this one was local: ten-year-old Zachary Ramsay, a Great Falls child who had disappeared early one morning five years previously while taking a shortcut through an alley on his way to school. So was the list of names a victim list after all? Could any connection be established between Bar-Jonah and Zachary Ramsay? And, if Bar-Jonah had indeed killed him, what had he done with the body?

There was one horrifying clue. Among the 28 boxes of papers, police found a series of coded messages. They believed that the code was a device through which Bar-Jonah had relived some of his happiest memories as he had worked on it alone in his room. By taking every second or third letter out of certain sentences, shocking messages began to appear. Police soon became convinced that these messages were reminders of past meals – with Zachary Ramsay as the main ingredient. They read: 'Barbecue bee sum young guy.' 'Little boy stew.'

'Christmas dinner for two.' 'Lunch is served on the patio with roasted child.' 'Little boy pot pies.' 'Sex a la carte.' And 'Barbequed kid.'

Police discovered that a few pages had been ripped out of the notebook, although they were able to re-create what had been written there from the impressions left on other pages. These proved particularly worrying reading as, according to the prosecutor in the case, they concerned various methods of torture. They also provided three other names that were added to the growing list of children that Bar-Jonah may have attacked.

To begin with, though, police did not charge Bar-Jonah with the disappearance of Zachary Ramsay, or make any revelations about his alleged cannibalism. It was a young local crime reporter called Kim Skornogoski who broke the story. She revealed that Bar-Jonah was a suspect eight months before he was actually charged with the murder and it was through her stories that Great Falls learned they had been living with a monster for over ten years. 'In those months between police naming him as a suspect and charging him, I wrote about officers digging up Bar-Jonah's garage, finding a child's bones, and I did extensive research into his criminal background in Massachusetts,' Skornogoski told me. 'So you can imagine that, with each story, there were waves of reaction from the community. The most common feeling was frustration and anger – that Massachusetts would release Bar-Jonah and, when caught jumping into a car with a young boy, instead of sending him back to jail, he was sent to join his family in Great Falls, Montana.

'In talking with investigators, I knew that they suspected Bar-Jonah cannibalised Zach early on. But we didn't report that fact until it was part of the affidavit charging him. That, of course, was quite a shock to the community. There are several sick allegations that he cooked these meals for neighbours and church groups. Many were angry that we would report that part of the case at all.'

Report them they did, though. The 83-page affidavit outlined prosecutor's belief that Bar-Jonah had indeed killed Zachary Ramsay and then served him up to unknowing friends and neighbours, and possibly even to Bar-Jonah's own mother, during a two-week stretch. As police gathered evidence and interviewed friends and neighbours, many of them started to recall that some of the food served up by Bar-Jonah soon after Zachary's disappearance had rather an odd taste.

On one occasion, Bar-Jonah told neighbours that he was serving them deer burgers that he had hunted himself, though he had no hunting licence and didn't even own a gun. In addition, he served up chilli, stews, pies and spaghetti, all of which had a strange aftertaste. After eating some of his 'deer meat', one female friend promptly told him that it must have gone off and Bar-Jonah, in a sulk, threw it away.

If this wasn't all bad enough, some of the negatives police took from a disposable camera were shots of Bar-Jonah lying on the bed in various states of arousal, along with pictures of children who were known to live in the upstairs apartment. Police interviewed the two brothers upstairs and then later their cousin, all of whom told them that they had been abused at his hands. Bar-Jonah was charged with three counts of sexual assault, one count of aggravated kidnapping and one count of assault with a weapon for the attacks on the boys upstairs, and while awaiting trial he was also formally charged with the murder of Zachary Ramsay.

At this point, Bar-Jonah filed a 'Motion for Change of Venue' arguing that, as he was currently linked to a very well-publicised murder case in Great Falls (i.e. the murder of Zachary Ramsay), he could not receive a fair trial for the charges of abuse. The motion was granted and the trial moved 150 miles away to Silver Bow County. There began the largest jury selection in the state's history, as lawyers sifted through 200 potential jurors.

As the abuse case unfolded, jurors were shown the thousands of photos of children found in Bar-Jonah's house, including the photos that he had taken of the alleged victims. Particularly damaging to the defence was Exhibit 91, an article entitled 'The Right Ropes, The Top Knots', which contained instructions on how to tie knots. Then there was Exhibit 92-A, a pamphlet entitled 'Autoerotic Asphyxia'. This helped corroborate the harrowing story of the 11-year-old boy known only as 'SJ' from court records. The boy, who had been eight years old at the time of the attack, told the court that Bar-Jonah had one day asked him if he wanted to play a game called the 'rope game'. Bar-Jonah had then put a tan-coloured rope around his neck and pulled him up on a pulley attached to his kitchen ceiling, to watch him choke. 'It was like a pulley, and he would just start pulling it,' the boy told the court. 'I started choking and I went up – I was scared, I thought I might die.' Thankfully Bar-Jonah let him go.

He was sentenced to ten years for aggravated kidnapping, 100 years for sexual assault and 20 years for felony assault, all of the sentences to run consecutively with no possibility of parole. Since the discovery of the list in Bar-Jonah's house, FBI investigators have compiled a computer database of names or locations connected in some way to the overweight ogre. As the FBI goes about the massive task of establishing exactly where Bar-Jonah was on any given day for the last 15 years, he has become a suspect in many other disappearances, including that of a seven-year-old girl called Janice Pockett.

Janice Pockett was last seen leaving her home in Tolland, Connecticut, on 26 July 1973, riding her green bicycle. The bike was recovered later in the day, but tragically Janice Pockett has never been seen since. Lake Webster is only 20 miles away from Tolland and, although Bar-Jonah would have only been 14 at the time, in light of his attacks against children, which authorities know began at a very early age, he remains a possible suspect in the case.

Forensic scientists also unearthed a collection of tiny pieces of crushed bones buried beneath the garage of Bar-Jonah's previous home in Great Falls. There were 21 bone fragments in all, but only one was big enough to allow for DNA testing. While the DNA did not match that of Zachary Ramsay or Janice Pockett, scientists were able to confirm that the bones belonged to a child aged 8 to 13 years old.

The garage did open up another possibility. When police examined it, they discovered a word written on the wall. That word was 'TITA'. In August 1973, a 15-year-old Massachusetts boy called James Teta went missing and his naked body was later found ditched along a roadside. No definite connection, however, has been made between the disappearance of James Teta and Bar-Jonah.

Police still planned to go ahead and use the 83-page affidavit to support their murder charge against Bar-Jonah in his upcoming trial for the death of Zachary Ramsay, but ultimately they still had no body, no crime scene and no forensic evidence. The final devastating blow came when Ramsay's mother came forward and declared that she would refuse to testify at Bar-Jonah's trial, believing that her son was still alive.

Her belief stemmed from a videotape of a boy who bears a remarkable likeness to her son. Although dental records show otherwise, Ramsay's mother refuses to face the terrible possibility that her son may be dead.

So the murder charges were dropped and Bar-Jonah no longer faces execution. Meanwhile, authorities are still trying to work out whose bones were buried beneath his garage and are still sifting through over 3,000 other names that Bar-Jonah had written in his many notebooks. It is a monumental task as law-enforcement agencies try to track down any children unfortunate enough to have crossed Bar-Jonah's path.

Worse still, it emerged that he had spent time in at least three other states besides Montana and Massachusetts. The search has even gone as far as Canada, which Bar-Jonah is known to have visited on several occasions. The database set up by the FBI to track his movements as far as possible has quickly grown to more than 14,000 names and places. And there are still many unanswered questions. What about those bones under his garage? What about the lists of children? What about his coded recipes? Bar-Jonah won't say.

Instead, he claims he is innocent of all charges against him, even though his conviction was recently upheld by the State Supreme Court on every single count. In the rare interviews he gives from his prison cell in Montana State Prison in Deer Lodge, he now sees fit to warn parents to watch out for child molesters, claiming at the same time that he would never dream of hurting a child. As Nathaniel Bar-Jonah serves out his 130-year sentence, the true fate of Zachary Ramsay – and possibly many, many more missing boys like him – will probably never be known for sure.

## CHAPTER NINE

# NAZIS AND MURDER IN SITCOM LAND: THE DOUBLE LIFE OF BOB CRANE

When faded sitcom star Bob Crane was found murdered in his rented apartment, his dirty little secret was soon out of the bag. Twenty years after his death, his murder remains one of Hollywood's biggest mysteries. But did Bob Crane really get what was coming to him?

I n the UK, Bob Crane isn't all that well known, but for generations of Americans he will always be Colonel Robert E Hogan, star of the smash sitcom *Hogan's Heroes*. Set in Nazi Germany, the show revolved around the exploits of a group of GIs housed in a prisoner of war camp. Playing the title lead – a street-smart soldier outwitting his Nazi guards at every turn – to perfection, Crane's performance made him a household name.

Bob Crane's career had initially taken off in radio, as host to the most widely listened-to radio show in Los Angeles. As the so-called 'King of the Los Angeles Airways', he regularly interviewed big stars such as Marilyn Monroe, Bob Hope and Frank Sinatra and it wasn't long before television started knocking on his door. Crane quickly landed parts on both *The Dick Van Dyke Show* and *The Mary Tyler Moore Show* and soon captured the attention of CBS executives, who asked him to try out for the lead role in their newest primetime sitcom, *Hogan's Heroes*. In due course he was offered the part, but very nearly didn't accept it. Like many of the future cast members of *Hogan's Heroes*, when Crane first read the script, he thought that the show's creators had gone out of their minds.

Then again, *Hogan's Heroes* was never your standard all-American sitcom. According to Brenda Scott Royce's book *Hogan's Heroes: Behind the Scenes at Stalag 13*, the President of CBS found the idea 'reprehensible' and its slogan – 'If you liked World War II, you'll love *Hogan's Heroes*' – hardly endeared critics to the already sensitive subject matter. The obvious parallels to a concentration camp – and, remember, this was only 20 years after the Second World War – were all there: Gestapo agents, barbed wire and guard dogs. And, as a great many GIs had learned, prisoner of war camps were no laughing matter. Indeed, before the show even aired many critics were already berating its writers for their flagrant disregard for the millions who had genuinely suffered at the hands of the Nazis during World War II.

What's more, the premise behind *Hogan's Heroes* was more akin to an action series than a comedy, causing further doubt among television executives and crew members. In the pilot, we learn that Hogan and his crew are all members of the so-called 'Underground Unit', a team made up of men who have willingly given up their own freedom so that they can cause maximum disruption behind enemy lines. As head of this group, the wily Hogan manipulates the bungling camp wardens, helping disrupt the German war effort by sabotaging factories and other Axis operations.

During all this, Hogan, described by radio adverts for the programme as a 'glib and impudent ringleader of a zany band of Allied captives', also somehow finds time to romance Fräulein Hilda, the sultry camp secretary, played by actress Sigrid Valdis. Crane would later marry Valdis on the set of the show and the couple would have a son called Scotty.

Somehow the mixture of comedy and high adventure seemed to work, though. And, although *Hogan's Heroes* did have its fair share of slapstick and often childish humour, there was a darker undercurrent to it too. As a result, it appealed to children and adults alike and was a huge smash at the time, despite all the early criticism. It also went on to enjoy a very long run. First screened in September 1965, in all 168 episodes were made and the show ran for over six years. In fact, it is still hugely popular the world over and when it finally left the air, in 1971, it became one of the most successful syndicated shows of all time. Just a year after the show was cancelled, re-runs were being shown in 45 other countries besides the United States, where it was still being broadcast in every single state.

After the show was cancelled, Crane had hoped, not unreasonably, that his career on television would continue to thrive. But unfortunately he had been too strongly typecast and his career now took a spectacular nose-dive. There were a few promising breaks, such as landing the lead role in the 1973 Disney flick *Superdad*, in which Crane played Charlie McCready, the overpossessive father of his teenage daughter. The film was shelved for a year by The Disney Studio, though, and flopped at the box office when it was finally released. Crane spent the next five years in faded-television-star hell, reduced to playing special-guest-star roles in standard Seventies fare such as *Quincy*, *The Love Boat* and *The Invaders* and appearing with increasing regularity on celebrity game shows – a veritable Death Row for TV has-beens.

In 1976, Crane was hired again by Disney for a film called *Gus*. In the same vein as other slightly surreal Seventies Disney films like *The Cat From Outer Space* and *The Million Dollar Duck*, *Gus* told the bizarre tale of a field-goal-kicking mule on an American football team; Crane only got a small role, as a sports journalist commentating on the eponymous Gus's games. With two Emmy nominations under his belt, earned for his work in *Hogan's Heroes*, it was in many ways a sad spectacle to see Crane taking a bit part in a relatively low-key Walt Disney release.

It wasn't all bad news. Crane was still getting $100,000 a year for those *Hogan's Heroes* re-runs and, of course, as the dashing Colonel Hogan was still recognised wherever he went. The role in the Disney film, although a small one, was promising too, and Crane hoped that the picture would help catapult him into the spotlight once again.

It didn't.

Two years later, the television and film work had dried up completely and Crane was on the road working the unglamorous dinner-show circuit with his show *Beginner's Luck*, which would eventually take Crane to Scottsdale, Arizona. It was a long way from Hollywood.

'My father was not unlike most performers; he needed public adulation, attention and validation,' Bob Crane's son Scotty told me. 'He needed to be loved and wanted, and it really hurt his self-esteem when Hollywood started to turn its back on "Bob Crane". After the Disney fiasco and toward the end of his life he'd take gigs like ribbon-cutting ceremonies for a new Safeway in El Segundo. He'd do anything to be in the public eye.'

Crane stayed in Scottsdale for a month. On 28 June 1978, after signing autographs and chatting with people who had just seen his show at the Windmill Theatre, Crane went out for a double date with a friend and then returned to his rented apartment. The next morning he failed to show up for an interview. As he still hadn't emerged by two o'clock, his co-star, Victoria Berry, decided to knock on his door. There was no reply and the door was unlocked, so she walked in.

As she opened the door, she saw a body on the bed and thought that it was a woman. The body wasn't moving. She later recalled thinking to herself, 'Oh, Bob's got a girl here. Now where's Bob? Well, she's done something to herself. Bob has gone to get help.' Then she saw the blood.

The curtains were still drawn and in the half-light Berry saw Crane lying on the bed. He was curled up in a foetal position and wearing only his boxer shorts. 'The whole wall,' she later recalled, 'was covered from one end to the other with blood.'

The autopsy revealed that Crane had been dead since the early hours of that morning and had been bludgeoned to death while he had been asleep.

Crane, an avid home-movie maker, had a lot of film equipment in his room, but there was a heavy camera tripod missing, which police were convinced the killer had used to crack open his skull. Then, either as a sick joke or to make really sure that Crane would tell no tales, the murderer had wrapped a VCR cord tightly around his neck.

There were also traces of semen just below his shorts and as Crane was not known to be a homosexual police suspected that the killer could have masturbated over Crane's dead body. Further indication that the killer was male came in the form of the pattern of blood splatter. As there wasn't much blood on the ceiling, the pathologist speculated that the killer was probably male, or at the outside a strong female, as the attacker hadn't needed much swing as they had smashed in his skull – and so less blood had flown upwards on impact.

Apart from that, however, there were few other clues. There was no murder weapon, no signs of forced entry and guests in neighbouring apartments hadn't seen or heard a thing.

As police dug more deeply into Crane's past, however, they discovered something unexpected, something that might possibly provide a lead. Crane was into a very special kind of home movie. There was much more to Crane than the wholesome television image the American public had been swallowing since *Hogan's Heroes*.

It turned out that for years Crane had been addicted to sex, and had become a formidable sack artist in the process. Using 'auto focus', a remote-control device that allows a cameraman to film himself, Crane had recorded himself having sex for hours on end and then meticulously edited his footage in the basement of his own home – amassing in the process literally thousands of hours of pornographic footage and photos.

The further the police delved into Crane's past, the longer the list of possible suspects grew. It could have been any one of hundreds of angry one-night stands, or any one of their devastated husbands or boyfriends.

The murder made headlines all over the country, and rumours and allegations about Crane's sexual exploits were public knowledge soon afterwards. He had kept a photo album featuring nude photographs of women he had had sex with. He had spent thousands of dollars building a string of S&M-equipped dungeons and had employed the services of a vicious dominatrix called 'Tiffany Moonlight'. Indeed, so seriously was he into dominance and submission that he had been sighted at a notorious S&M club called The Castle. He had put out ads in swinger magazines, took part in orgies whenever he got the chance and was even said to have had metal penile implants in order to enhance the size of his penis.

Allegations of Crane's spectacular sexual exploits became legion, but the most damaging of all was that he also illegally filmed women without their consent or knowledge. Added together, it painted an extraordinarily dark tale of a washed-up TV has-been on a self-destructive quest for endless sexual encounters.

Somehow, it was all TV's fault: the story went that Bob Crane had been a churchgoing family man who suddenly turned into some kind of sex maniac the moment TV came calling. Until now, most reports have laid the blame for his rise to fame on *Hogan's Heroes*, but, as I found out when I talked to his son Scotty, Bob Crane was busy taking 'intimate' pictures 20 years before *Hogan's Heroes* even began. Scotty has photos dating as far back as the 1940s and films dating back to 1956. Crane certainly wasn't the good Catholic boy suddenly turned bad by TV stardom.

'My father did attend church – when people died. He wasn't religious and he didn't raise me to be religious,' Scotty said. 'The whole mythology about him being this churchgoing saint that was brought down and corrupted by the evils of Hollywood is really just a dramatic way to dress up a story. But it's totally untrue. He was an overly sexual person from an early age. In the 12 years that my mum knew him, he went to church three times: my baptism, his father's funeral and his own funeral.'

Twenty years after his death, the story of Robert Crane's life is still being told as if it were some kind of morality tale about the dangers of fame and too much sex. Reading through the books and articles and watching the recent Hollywood film about his life, *Auto Focus*, it is almost as if Crane somehow deserved to get his head caved in. Perhaps his biggest sin in the eyes of the American public was the fact that he had fame and somehow managed to lose it, becoming in the process that most hated of TV personalities – the ex-celebrity.

'A lot of these rumours paint a really ugly, dark portrait of my dad,' Scotty told me. 'Bob Crane was not a dark person at all; he was extremely funny, charismatic, quick-witted, silly and a very driven, hard-working guy! A workaholic, in fact. At one point in his life he did a radio show, a television show, sat in as a drummer with various big band jazz groups and had an active sex life! I barely have time to take a shower! My dad was an amazing guy and I continue to be motivated by him. He achieved an amazing amount of success at a very young age.'

Although there were an awful lot of angry boyfriends who would have happily seen Crane dead, the police quickly focused their investigation on his best friend, Sony video technician John Carpenter (no relation to the famous director). Crane had been introduced to Carpenter on the set of *Hogan's Heroes* by fellow cast member Richard Dawson. To begin with, he just used Carpenter for cheap video parts, but in 1975 they started to hang out together, cruising for sex.

They made an odd couple. Aside from Crane's obvious charms and good looks, many women jumped at the chance of sleeping with a celebrity – *any* celebrity – especially one who was synonymous in their minds with the dashing Colonel Hogan. Carpenter, on the other hand, came across as desperate and slightly sleazy; he picked up what was left. The two of them frequently took part in foursomes and recorded their exploits on film for prosperity.

Why did Carpenter become the prime suspect? Firstly, he had flown down from Los Angeles a couple of days before to hang out with Crane in Scottsdale and had spent much of the previous night with Crane, having arranged a double date. The date had been a blow-out, though, and Carpenter told police that he had driven to the airport to catch a flight back to Los Angeles. He did have a motive, however. According to Scotty, his father had seriously started to reassess his relationship with Carpenter. 'Carpenter had made a life out of being Bob Crane's associate, posing as his manager and getting nothing more than his sexual cast-offs. My dad treated John like a second-class citizen and, when John found out that their friendship had come to an end because my dad had made plans to move home and resume a life with my mother and I, he was mad... According to the police, this angered John so much that he murdered him. My father had a very rare blood type, and blood that matched his was found in John Carpenter's car.'

There was no DNA testing in those days, though, nor any other concrete physical evidence that could tie Carpenter to the murder scene, so the case was closed unsolved. It looked like it would stay that way, but in 1994 John Carpenter was suddenly arrested and tried for murder. Police claimed that they had discovered a photo of Carpenter's rental car that showed a small speck of 'brain matter' on the inside passenger door. From the start, however, their case looked unlikely to succeed, as it was based mainly on just one new photograph, and indeed it rapidly fell apart. Carpenter walked. He didn't have much longer left, though. In 1998, by which time he was a convicted child molester, Carpenter died of a heart attack, aged 70.

Bob Crane's death will in all likelihood remain a mystery. There were many other suspects but Scotty Crane for one believes Carpenter got away with murder. 'John Carpenter was accused of murdering my father in a Scottsdale hotel room, in June of 1978. The police told us that, in the middle of the night, John crept into my father's room, picked up one of my father's own camera tripods and bludgeoned my father to death. The police said that my father was asleep when he died, and that the impact was so forceful that he died instantly.

'I have always gone back and forth about who murdered my father. There are plenty of suspects, as my dad didn't practise discrimination when it came to married women or girlfriends of cops and mob bosses. In the 1970s Scottsdale was overrun with mobsters in the witness-relocation programme. The cops there will tell you that. The hard fact is that all of the roads with hard, tangible evidence lead to John Carpenter.

'I did not attend John Carpenter's trial for the murder of my father in which he was acquitted. That trial was more about John Carpenter than my father, who was already gone. Most people act as if knowing who killed my father will bring some kind of closure to me. The thing is, it won't. It won't bring my father back. It won't change the history of my life and I don't care to relive the murder through another trial. My dad is gone and nothing will change that. I prefer to think of the happier times and leave it at that.'

Meanwhile, Crane's legacy lives on in the strangest of places. *Hogan's Heroes* is still extremely popular today – even in Germany, where it is dubbed in German. Originally called *Stacheldraht und Fersengeld* ('Barbed Wire and Turning Tail'), it has since been retitled *Ein Käfig voller Helden* ('A Cage of Heroes'). There are numerous websites dedicated to the show and legions of loyal fans and avid collectors of *Hogan's Heroes* memorabilia. David Smith, who started one of the first *Hogan's Heroes* websites, told me that he had even considered buying the apartment where Crane was murdered when it went up for auction on eBay; he says that his most valued possession is dirt taken from Crane's grave. Perhaps unsurprisingly, what David Smith finds most compelling about the show today is the strange death and double life of its star, Bob Crane.

Crane was certainly no saint, but Scotty argues that many of the rumours of his father's sexual exploits are untrue. He is especially angry about allegations that his father filmed women without their consent. In an effort to set the record straight, Scotty started his own website, where for a time you could actually view the movies his father made, in order to show that the women knew that they were being recorded. The site has since received more than three million hits.

'My father was a performer in every aspect of his life; his sex life included. During the trial for his murder, CNN broadcast a segment of the trial that included videotape of my father having sex. My mom just looked at me and said, "If your father could see that so many years later, people are still talking about him and that his sex life is worldwide news, he would be thrilled. I think that, if he were alive today, he'd probably be running the website himself."'

## CHAPTER TEN

# 'BAD BOB' HANSEN AND THE HUNTERS OF HUMAN PREY

In his free time, crack shot Robert Hansen flew out in his private plane to his hunting lodge and killed game with his high-powered .223-calibre rifle. But animals weren't the only thing that 'Bad Bob' was hunting out there in the Alaskan wilderness.

Compared to the crimes carried out by many serial killers, in some ways there is nothing particularly shocking about Robert Hansen. He wasn't a cannibal, he wasn't a necrophiliac and he didn't dismember his victims or torture them to death. Yet there is one thing that puts Hansen in a league of his own and that is the sick game of cat and mouse that he devised in the Alaskan wilderness. It sounds like a somewhat unlikely premise for a film, but Hansen hunted human *literally*. While his victims fought for their lives in sub-zero temperatures, he would track them down and dispose of them like wild animals – for sport.

Hansen's hunting ground was the wilds of Alaska and his stalking ground was the then red-light district of Anchorage. At the time, Alaska was going through a huge transformation after the discovery of oil – and with the oil boom had come vice. Bars and strip clubs opened at breakneck speed; prostitution, violence and drug-related crime swiftly rose and went virtually unchecked amid three-hour happy hours, bar fights and the occasional murder. For Hansen, the conditions were perfect.

He lived in an affluent part of town on Old Harbour Road, ran his own bakery, was married with two children and owned his own plane, which he used to go out hunting. Hansen had built himself a good, solid business out of his bakery and enjoyed a reputation as an upstanding member of his community. In fact, while the vast majority of serial killers are friendless and often socially inept, Hansen seemed to make friends easily and on one occasion was even able to convince pals to provide him with a false alibi.

The fact that he was also an excellent shot and hunter only served to ingratiate him further in his community and for a man born and raised in Iowa he had adapted well to the rigorous life of the weekend outdoorsman. Over the years, Hansen had become something of an authority on the complex behavioural patterns and seasonal movements of big game specific to Alaska, such as Dall sheep, moose and bears, and had mastered the techniques necessary to survive in the hostile Alaskan wilderness. In fact, by the time he was finally arrested, his walls were lined with mounted trophies celebrating his most spectacular kills. But, as police were to learn, animals hadn't been enough.

When prostitutes suddenly began to vanish amid the nightly pandemonium on the strip, the police didn't pay much attention. Prostitutes have a tendency to pull up sticks at short notice anyway and this was especially true of Alaska, where girls had come to make a quick buck. All the same, for years there had been rumours of ladies of the night simply disappearing and for no apparent reason.

Then, three bodies were discovered; the victims – all prostitutes – had been shot and buried in shallow graves in remote corners of the Alaskan woods. For the girls working the strip, it was confirmation that someone had been stalking them for some time. And, when another of the girls suddenly vanished, her friends had a terrible feeling that she wouldn't be coming back.

Alaskan filmmaker Mary Katzke interviewed many of the prostitutes working in the area during the period of the Hansen killings and shortly after his arrest. One of the girls she talked to, Jazz, told her that one of her friends, Tiffany, had gone missing and had been found murdered and buried in the woods. 'Later I knew something was wrong because it was payday and she didn't get her tips envelope,' Jazz recalled. 'We might be late for work, or even miss it now and then, but we sure as hell don't miss out on getting our cash. And I knew it wasn't right she was gone on account of another reason – it was her son's birthday. She was wearing sandals. Sandals and it was below zero. All I could think about was how she would freeze – from the feet up, since her coat only went to her knees.'

The police remained more or less indifferent, although they did warn the local prostitutes to be on the lookout for a man offering them money to take their photograph. Meanwhile, the girls collected money between them and hired a detective to find out what had happened to their missing colleagues. The atmosphere on the strip quickly turned to one of edgy mutual distrust: 'I suspected everyone – my friends, clients, even my boss's friends. I had dreams I was by a river being shot,' Jazz reflected. Then they came out with a description of a suspect – saying he might want to take your picture or something. I tripped out, told the bar manager about the guy who had done that. We called the police – but the guy never showed. Every time I saw him my adrenaline would start.'

Hansen was not a suspect, even though he had a criminal record in Alaska dating back 13 years for crimes and attacks against women. As well as having two convictions for assault and abduction, there had been numerous other complaints made against him from prostitutes working in the area. But, because of his ostensibly respectable standing in the community, he remained in the clear. He might well have continued killing for several more years had it not been for the bravery and quick thinking of one prostitute.

On the morning of 13 June 1983, Hansen approached her in his car – a green Buick. To the woman, he looked harmless enough. He was in his mid-forties, had a stutter, wore glasses and was lightly built. In fact, he seemed a bit nerdy. She was well aware that there might be a killer of prostitutes on the loose, but she accepted his offer and got in his car.

Hansen immediately knocked her unconscious, shoved her to the floor and put an army blanket over her body. He then drove her back to his home, where he led her downstairs to the basement. On the way down, she tripped on some children's toys, and would later remember that the basement walls were covered with hunting trophies. Hansen handcuffed her to a pole, raped her and then promptly fell asleep on the couch. While he was asleep she wet herself and, afraid that he would be angry if he saw what she had done, she used her foot to drag the blanket into the puddle to soak it up.

When Hansen woke, he bundled her into his car and drove

her to nearby Merrill airfield, where he shoved her inside his plane, warning her not to move: 'I'd hate to have to shoot holes in the side of my plane,' he told her. As she lay bundled in the back, she could hear him chatting affably to the airfield personnel and learned, to her horror, that he was off to his cabin in the woods.

By the time he assaulted the young prostitute, Hansen had developed a method that enabled him to draw out and savour the deaths of the terrorised women whom he had abducted. He would fly his victims in his Super Cub plane to his hunting shack, in an area near the Knik River. It was a popular spot with fellow moose hunters, but it was also Hansen's killing ground. Inside his shack was an iron rail suspended along the ceiling. This was where Hansen hung dead moose, and also where he tied his victims before repeatedly raping them.

It's unknown exactly how many times he did this, but afterwards Hansen would release his victims and give them a head start so that they could run for their lives. He would then pick up his rifle and knife and then calmly hunt them down. It was like 'going after a trophy Dall sheep or a grizzly bear', he said later, and referred to it as his 'summertime project'.

This victim, of course, had no way of knowing this, but she did know that she faced certain death if the plane ever took off, so she took the only chance she had. The plane didn't start immediately, so Hansen had to jump out and start the propeller by hand. She rolled out, saw the highway and ran towards it, managing to stop a truck. Hansen ran after her but when he saw the truck stopping he backed off.

Because the victim was a prostitute, however, police didn't believe her at first – even though she was able to identify the plane and later its owner; plus, one of Hansen's friends provided an alibi for him. Then, less than three months later, another body was found, buried like the others in a shallow grave in a remote corner of the Alaskan wilderness. Hansen's friend was interrogated a second time and eventually confessed that he had been covering for his pal.

This time the police sought the assistance of profiler John Douglas at the FBI's Behavioral Science Unit. Detectives had told Douglas that Hansen was a well-known hunter and that his family had been away when the woman had been abducted. Douglas later wrote about the case in an article: 'It gave me a cold, sick feeling in my stomach. It seemed clear to me that he was definitely the killer, but he wasn't simply killing these women. I believed he was releasing them into the woods and then hunting them down like animals – and this proved to be the case.'

Hansen's home was searched, initially to no avail. Just as investigators were about to give up, though, they found a stash of 'souvenirs' including items of jewellery and ID cards belonging to women known to have suddenly disappeared. They also found a .223-calibre Mini-14 rifle that matched the type that had been used to kill the girls. When brought in for questioning, Hansen quickly cracked and during his two-day confession would reveal to police the extent and method of his murder binge. He had apparently got tired of the complaints made against him by prostitutes after he had brutalised and raped them and so had started to kill them instead. He had also developed a tried-and-tested method to make the prostitutes co-operate.

'I scare them right off the bat,' he told detectives. 'I just say, "Hey, it's your word against mine. I'm a businessman, a family man, and you're a prostitute"... As long as they didn't panic on me, as long as things went the way I wanted them to, it was go home and that was it.'

Hansen really didn't like it when prostitutes asked him for more money. In fact, that made him mad. 'And when I get mad,' Hansen said, 'what happens is – I just don't put up with it… I'd just say, "Hey, you're a professional, you know there's some risk to what you're doing and if you do exactly what I say you won't get hurt. You're going to count this off as a bad experience and be a little bit more careful next time."… Now don't get me wrong. Any girl I was ever with is one who agreed to meet me for money for sex. I didn't do nothing to decent girls. They had to approach me. She had to come out and say it – you know – that it was going to cost money.'

Police had also found an air chart of the surrounding area in Hansen's house. On the map were three dots, which marked the shallow graves where the bodies of three prostitutes had already been discovered. But there were 17 other dots on the map. So did the police need to go looking for 17 more bodies?

The answer, unfortunately, was yes. Hansen had buried almost all of his victims in shallow graves by the banks of the 25-mile-long Knik River in the Matanuska-Susitna Valley. To their horror, the detectives now realised that Hansen had been murdering and hunting prostitutes for ten long years.

In all, Hansen admitted to committing 17 murders and raping 30 women; in 1984, he was sentenced to 461 years in prison. Six years later, it was revealed that Hansen had formulated a fairly elaborate plan to escape from the Lemon Creek jail where he was then being held. He had hidden air charts and other documents, which were found stashed in an air duct, and had planned to steal a plane from the nearby airfield, but the plan was foiled at the last minute after he was ratted out by a fellow inmate. As a result, Hansen was promptly transferred to the new maximum-security prison in Seward, Alaska.

Not all of Hansen's victims were discovered, even though he pointed out where he had buried them. And, even when they were recovered, the ground was often too hard to bury them right away.

When it was all over, Jazz remembered visiting Tiffany's grave. She had been one of Hansen's last victims. 'On Memorial Day, we went to Potter's Field to put some white roses on her grave,' she recalled. 'They said once the ground thawed they'd bury her. The dirt was muddy and there wasn't any grass there yet. I can still feel the way my heels sunk in the wet ground while we were walking around, trying to find where they put her. All there was, and it took a while to find, was a wooden stake with a strip of orange tape to mark her grave.'

## THE ZODIAC

Hansen was not alone in his love of hunting humans for sport. In fact, his passion for human hunting is shared by one of the most infamous serial killers of all time: the Zodiac. Unfortunately, the identity of this infamous killer and the number of people he murdered will almost certainly remain a mystery. In one of the many letters he sent to the local press in California, he boasted that he had murdered 37 people (although he has an officially confirmed five kills). These letters first began on 1 August 1968, with three letters sent to three different newspapers, all of which contained a page of code. When the three parts of the code were combined and deciphered, it was evident that the self-named Zodiac was making a reference to hunting humans.

'I like killing people because it is so much fun,' the Zodiac wrote. 'It is more fun than killing wild game in the forest because man is the most dangerous animal. To kill something gives me the most thrilling experience. It is even better than getting your rocks off with a girl. The best part is that, when I die, I will be reborn in paradise and all that I have killed will become my slaves.'

The 'most dangerous animal' is widely believed by Zodiac experts to refer to a famous short story published in 1924 by Richard Connell called 'The Most Dangerous Game'. In the story, a big-game hunter must fight for his life as he is hunted down for sport by a deranged Russian aristocrat, Count Zaroff. But Zaroff meets his match, learning too late that man is indeed the 'Most Dangerous Game' of all. Connell's short story was made into a film in 1932, though the film reels had been lost at the time of the Zodiac killings and were not recovered until the 1970s.

The prime suspect in the Zodiac murder case was Arthur Leigh Allen, who once told police that he had read the story in high school and had been fascinated by it. But Connell's piece, a classic of the genre, was widely read in school at the time as required reading and there is absolutely no physical proof linking Allen with the killings. In truth, Allen is just one in a very long list of possible suspects.

## IVAN MILAT

Another killer who hunted down humans for fun was Ivan Milat, Australia's worst serial killer, who shot and stabbed his victims and then buried them in shallow graves in the Belanglo Forest south-west of Sydney.

A keen hunter and gun nut, Milat (or 'Tex', as he liked to call himself) is believed to have given his victims a head-start before tracking them down and killing them in the Australian outback. Suspected of being involved in at least three other murders besides the seven he was actually convicted of, it is also thought that Milat beheaded German student Anja Habschied with a cavalry sword that he later stashed in his mother's apartment and used an English backpacker's head for target practice with a .22-calibre rifle.

Milat was finally convicted thanks to the sworn testimony of Paul Onions, a British backpacker who managed to escape from an attack in 1990. Onions was a British ex-navy sailor and had been hitchhiking on the Hugh Highway when Milat stopped his truck and offered him a ride outside a petrol station. Milat introduced himself as Bill.

To begin with, Milat seemed pleasant and chatted affably enough, but he soon turned nasty and pulled over to the side of the road, where he produced a gun. Onions fled for his life as Milat attempted to shoot him down. Luckily, Onions managed to pull over another car for help and later reported the incident at the local Bowral police station. Shortly afterwards, Onions returned home and soon discovered that several bodies had been discovered just five miles away from where he had been attacked. He immediately phoned the police in New South Wales; he was flown back to Australia and made a positive ID. When police raided Milat's home, they found possessions belonging to his victims, such as a sleeping bag and items of clothing. In 1996, he was found guilty of murder and handed down multiple life sentences, to be served consecutively, for the slayings of seven backpackers. In June 2006, he threatened suicide when his TV and toasted-sandwich maker were taken away from him and when he's not on hunger strike he spends his time whinging about his lack of rights in the high-security wing of the Gouldburn jail in New South Wales.

## CHAPTER ELEVEN

# 'BUTCHER BROWN' AND THE DEADLY DOCTORS

In May 1998, stump lover Philip Bondy paid ten thousand dollars to get his perfectly healthy leg amputated in Tijuana. Because no one else would do it he chose renegade surgeon Dr John 'Butcher Brown'.

For his entire adult life, Philip Bondy had been looking for a doctor to amputate his leg. Bondy suffered from a rare mental disorder called apotemnophilia; bizarrely, he had despised his leg throughout his life and, for reasons that he had never been able to adequately explain, he had wanted to be an amputee for as long as he could remember. He also felt a strong sexual attraction to amputees. He was 79 years old now, though, and because his leg was perfectly healthy no qualified surgeon in the country would ever agree to remove it.

Like many apotemnophiliacs, Bondy was prepared to go to extreme lengths in order to rid himself of his hated limb. Unlike many fellow sufferers, however, he was not prepared simply to maim himself and hope that his leg would later be amputated in hospital. He wanted a qualified surgeon who would do a clean, painless job and then make sure that he recovered in comfort and in safety.

He had heard about someone who might do it, too. That person was Dr Brown, whom he had been told about by a close friend and fellow apotemnophiliac, Gregg Furth; Furth had travelled to Mexico only three weeks previously for a similar operation, though he had backed out at the very last minute when he saw one of Brown's assistants wielding a butcher's knife. So Furth had proposed a swap and phoned his friend Bondy. The latter had jumped at the chance to get his long-awaited amputation and almost immediately booked a flight from New York to San Diego.

There were risks, though. He was retired, a septuagenarian and not exactly in great shape. Actually he was in much worse shape than he knew. He was emaciated, had a very weak heart and was suffering from pneumonia when he finally decided to go through with the operation. To a qualified surgeon, any one of these factors would have instantly ruled Bondy out of undergoing a major operation. Not to Dr Brown, though, who instantly agreed to the swap, with no questions asked. All Bondy had to do was to come up with $10,000 and then get down to Tijuana, where Brown ran a clinic.

So why would someone like Bondy want to take the risk? Why, for that matter, would anyone want their own perfectly healthy limb removed? According to amputee and apotemnophilia expert Alex Mensaert, for people like Philip Bondy it is an unavoidable need, a need that they have had since birth. 'They are born with this feeling,' Alex told me. 'The day they find out that there are amputees in this world they know that they want to become an amputee too. Most discover that they have this desire very young – at the age of five to seven. The people I know who are now amputees are completely happy – much more happy than before, when they still had all their limbs.

'Some of them start with a toe or a finger and end up amputating a whole leg. The majority of them want to have a leg removed, but I know some people who even want to have two arms and two legs removed. There is even a 19-year-old girl I heard about from the Netherlands who wants to have all of her limbs removed!'

Needless to say, there are risks attached: 'There are always a few deaths – certainly when you see how far some people are prepared to go sometimes. The only problem is that the medical world doesn't want to help them. Some of them cut off their own toes or fingers. They do it mostly with the use of xylocaine, a local anaesthetic. I know a woman who is legless after she froze her legs with dry ice. I also know a doctor who is now a left below-the-knee amputee. He injected his leg with xylocaine and hooked his foot off with a hammer. He then told the hospital that he had had a motorcycle accident. I also know a woman who cut off her own arm with a circular saw.'

Amputations were a new field for Dr Brown, but already seemed like a potentially lucrative sideline. Almost all his work until then had revolved around sex changes and plastic surgery. Back in 1973, Brown had first begun to make a name for himself as a sex-change specialist in Los Angeles. In order to obtain gender-reassignment surgery, transsexuals usually have to undergo three months of strict psychotherapy at the very least, but Brown cut through all the red tape and offered sex changes for as little as $2,500 dollars on a walk-in basis.

To begin with, his rock-bottom sex-change business got rave reviews from his transsexual patients and his office soon became known as 'the House of Dreams'. But Brown only spent five years practising in LA, because in 1977 he lost his licence owing to gross negligence. So he moved – and subsequently managed to get himself banned from ever practising medicine again in Alaska, Hawaii and St Lucia.

During his career, Brown carried out an estimated 600 sex-reassignment surgeries. The fact that he was not a qualified surgeon (he had failed the general surgeon's exam twice and the plastic surgeon's exam three times) hadn't deterred him for a moment. Despite his lack of qualifications, Brown had created a revolutionary new process that he called 'miniaturisation', which involved reducing the penis and turning it into a pleasure-sensitive clitoris. He also regularly carried out vaginoplastys – an extremely delicate operation that involves splitting the penis open and turning it into a vagina.

Brown also dabbled in facial reconstructive surgery, breast augmentation and penis enlargement. Unable to work out of a proper surgery, he carried out the majority of his operations in garages and hotel rooms. According to one report, he once carried out a sex change on a kitchen table, which promptly collapsed halfway through the operation. His absent-minded manner and scruffy appearance went hand in hand with his often primitive surgical techniques.

Along with tales of horribly botched breast jobs and gaping surgical wounds super-glued shut, there were also disturbing reports of patients regaining consciousness midway through his operations. Brown, it appeared, was causing absolute havoc in the surgery room. In fact, the catalogue of blunders had become so bad so quickly that Brown's popularity in Los Angeles didn't last long. Among LA's transsexual community, he had swiftly become known as 'Butcher Brown'.

It seemed that nothing, however, could stop Brown from putting his scalpel to bad use. Even after he was finally arrested in 1996 and spent 19 months in jail for a botched sex-change operation, he carried on regardless; he simply moved to San Diego and opened up a surgery across the border in Mexico, where he offered cut-rate plastic and sex-change surgery at even lower prices. The medical mayhem continued.

According to court records, in 1995 a patient who had undergone transsexual surgery in Europe contacted Brown concerning reconstructive surgery on her labia. Brown performed the surgery in Tijuana but failed to examine the medical reports on her operation in Europe, nor did he take a medical history. He also failed to give her any pain medication, antibiotics or post-operative instructions. In fact, the reconstruction was a total failure and like many of his patients the woman was sent on her way to fend for herself. Brown messed up again two years later on another genetic female undergoing transsexual surgery. On returning home, she developed complications and required urgent surgery to correct serious problems caused by Brown's surgical errors. This time, his patient very nearly died.

Seemingly indifferent to the mounting complaints against him, Brown continued to advertise a full list of procedures. His self-proclaimed revolutionary penis-enlargement technique seemed particularly popular and had men from all over the United States hopping across the border into Mexico; but, as he continued his work, the list of complaints grew, including some truly harrowing accounts of plastic surgery gone hideously wrong.

According to a report in *LA Weekly*, when Brown inserted breast implants into one of his patients, the breasts rotted, went black and began to smell of 'cat piss'. When he castrated a transsexual, the patient got a wound 'the size of a softball'.

Brown also made one transsexual's vaginal walls so thin that they tore wide open during intercourse and made another transsexual's vaginal entrance too small.

Once, when he removed a rib in order to narrow a transsexual's waist she developed a huge abscess 'the size of a baseball' that nearly killed her. In another instance, after a botched vaginoplasty, he created a recto-vaginal fistula, which caused faeces to pour out of his patient's vagina. The unfortunate individual was found six days later covered in her own faeces and she very nearly died too. (The grisly details were revealed in Paul Ciotti's *LA Weekly* article 'Why Did He Cut Off That Man's Leg?')

So, by the time Philip Bondy travelled to California for his surgery, Dr Brown had very nearly killed four people at the very least. He didn't seem to have learned from his mistakes, though. He knew full well that his new patient had a heart condition, but as usual he didn't bother to carry out a medical assessment when Bondy arrived in San Diego. Instead, the pair went to a medical-supply store in Chula Vista, where Brown helped the would-be amputee pick out a pair of brand-new crutches. The next day, they travelled across the border into Mexico.

The idea was that Brown would perform the operation in his private clinic in Tijuana and then drive Bondy back across to a hotel in the suburbs of San Diego, where he could recover. It was less risky to perform the operation in Mexico because Brown didn't have a licence to practise in the States, and if complications did set in Brown could always claim that the act had been committed outside America's borders.

The operation went according to plan: Brown sawed through Bondy's leg just below the knee. Then, before driving his patient to the National City Holiday Inn in San Diego, he drove into the desert and buried the leg. According to court records on the day's events, after the surgery, Bondy called Furth from his hotel. He was apparently 'delighted' that his leg had been amputated, but said that he was having difficulty using the crutches and had fallen several times. Furth also noticed that his friend did not sound well, and so he decided to fly to San Diego and check up on him.

In the early morning of the next day, hotel security was called to Bondy's room; he was naked, on the floor, leaning against the bed. As he helped Bondy on to the bed, the guard noticed that one of the man's legs was missing and the stump was bloody. Later the same day, Bondy phoned Brown and complained of pain and bleeding. According to court transcripts, Brown 'examined the wound, noted it was bleeding but not profusely' and saw 'a blue tint, which he associated with gangrene'. Brown told Bondy to increase the amount of medication he was taking. It seemed to work. When Furth arrived at the hotel, Bondy seemed to be doing much better.

The next morning, however, when Furth went to check up on Bondy again, he found his friend dead. The phone had been tipped over, Bondy was lying half on the bed and blood was dripping from the stump. The room was in chaos.

When Brown found out, he sounded as if he had been half-expecting it. After all, he told Furth over the phone, Bondy was 'brittle'. He didn't seem to think that he would ever be prosecuted, though, as he had carried out the operation in Mexico and had only been doing his sworn duty as a doctor. But the coroner ruled that Bondy had died of gas gangrene – a condition associated with dirty surgical conditions and improper wound care that is lethal unless treated within 24 hours.

Dr Brown's long career was finally at an end. Despite carrying out the operation in Mexico, he was convicted by a Californian court of second-degree murder and was handed down a sentence of 15 years to life. In a decision that was to be later upheld by the California Court of Appeals, the court ruled that Brown had known full well the risks he was taking. Brown had acted in a criminally negligent manner with conscious disregard for human life; as a result, his patient had, in all likelihood, died a slow and very painful death.

A year after his friend's death, Furth was still looking for a surgeon willing to amputate his right leg. He found one who had already carried out two voluntary amputations on patients. When the media got wind of them, the surgeon immediately found himself in the spotlight.

According to an interview he gave in January 2000, both of his patients had been convinced that surgery had been 'the only possible redress for this quite seriously disabling condition'. He also said that those with the disorder faced great risk of injuring or even killing themselves in attempts to rid themselves of their hated limbs. 'The one concern is that many of these individuals will, in fact, injure themselves,' he said. 'There are quite a lot of anecdotal reports, largely from the States, of people taking the law into their own hands, lying on a railway line or shooting their legs off with a shotgun.'

However, the hospital ordered that no more voluntary amputations be carried out and Furth did not get his amputation.

## EVEN WORSE THAN BROWN? REINALDO SILVESTRE

Although Cuban Reinaldo Silvestre had absolutely no training as a plastic surgeon, or even a licence to practise medicine in the United States, it didn't stop him from offering cut-price nose and breast jobs on South Beach, Florida. Often using the animal tranquilliser ketamine instead of a general anaesthetic, he sliced into the flesh of his unsuspecting patients in a hit-and-miss 'learn on the job' approach to plastic surgery.

When Silvestre was finally investigated, even hardened detectives were shocked at the mess the smooth-talking con man had left behind him. As part of the investigation, one of the investigators in the case had to watch a videotape of Sylvester operating, which made for painful viewing: 'It was a butcher job you wouldn't want to have happen to your dog,' he told the New York Times.

Operations scheduled to last for a relatively short time would drag on for up to eight hours as the hapless doctor struggled to figure out the best way to insert breast implants. As he did so, he blithely severed muscle tissue as he went along, before crudely stitching up the mess and hoping vainly that the wounds wouldn't become infected.

One female patient, while tripping out on the ketamine anaesthetic, remembered Silvestre literally putting his hand inside her breast to try to correct an already horribly botched breast job before stapling it shut. In another case, a Mexican bodybuilder, who had come in for a simple pectoral enhancement, ended up with a woman's implants, becoming overnight the not-so-proud owner of two female breasts. As Spencer Aronfeld, a lawyer for the alleged victims of Silvestre, told the press, 'So this big bodybuilder from Mexico wakes up from this surgery expecting to look like Tarzan and instead he looks like Pamela Anderson Lee and Dolly Parton.'

When the complaints against him started mounting, the Cuban doctor simply upped sticks and disappeared, leaving a trail of misery and permanently scarred people behind him. He was finally spotted in Belize in October 2004 thanks to someone who had recognised him from the TV show *America's Most Wanted*; at the time he was teaching classes to medical students at a private university. Silvestre was extradited to the States, where he was charged with aggravated battery and practising medicine without a licence. He was found guilty and sent to jail for seven years.

## SURGICAL SLAUGHTER: AMADO CARRILLO FUENTES

People recovering from the effects of surgery are vulnerable and the surgeon's recovery room has been the scene of more than one murder – including that of one of the most dangerous people on the planet.

Multi-billionaire drug baron Amado Carrillo Fuentes died hours after going under the plastic surgeon's knife. The founder of the Juárez cartel – the most powerful Mexican drug cartel in the 1990s – Fuentes smuggled thousands of tonnes of cocaine into the States with his own private fleet of jet planes while enjoying the protection of corrupt, high-ranking members of the Mexican police and military.

When a warrant was issued for his arrest in 1997, Fuentes opted for plastic surgery before a planned emigration to Cuba. After an eight-hour-long operation designed to utterly transform his face and body, he was given a deadly mixture of anaesthetics and the sleeping potion Dormicum by his doctors and died in a recovery room in a Santa Monica hospital on 4 July 1997.

According to some newspaper reports at the time, Fuentes had recently struck a deal with drug-enforcement officials to rat out his associates and the surgeons had been paid to make sure that Fuentes told no tales. But had the death been simply a mistake, or was it a carefully planned hit? Authorities believed it was the latter and immediately charged the three surgeons who had operated on Fuentes with murder one.

Predictably, police never got the chance to question them. On 2 November, three bodies were found stuffed into oil barrels and dumped beside the side of a Mexican highway. All three of the surgeons had been bound, gagged and tortured for the 'longest time possible.' Two of them had been strangled and the third had been shot.

Since then, other rumours about the case have surfaced, though. Today, many journalists in Mexico are still convinced that Fuentes faked his own death and that it's not his body buried there in the family mausoleum in his hometown of Guamuchilito. According to some reports, Fuentes himself had the surgeons killed – as they were the only people who knew what he now looked like – and continues to pull the strings of his $25 billion-a-year drug-smuggling business.

# CHAPTER TWELVE

# CONSTANTINO MACHUCA AND THE KILLER COOKS: MEAT IS MURDER

Wholly tamale? Snack lovers in the small
town of Morelia in Mexico got a nasty surprise
when they discovered that there may well have
been an extra ingredient in their beloved
tamale meat pasties.

Fifty-six-year-old Carlos Constantino Machuca had been cooking and selling his tamales in the Mexican city of Morelia for over five years. The tamale has a long and illustrious history in Morelia, and Machuca with his hot-food cart was a familiar figure in the city, with a steady trade and a wide beat. He prepared the dough himself, filled the tasty pastries at home and then sold them out of two food carts at various points throughout the city, such as parks and outside the city's main hospital as well as on the children's ward there. They were always well received.

But in April 2004, residents on the road where Machuca lived – Fernández Street – who were accustomed to the smell of frying meat and dough, noticed another far less pleasant smell emanating from their neighbour's house. Not only that, but stray dogs were now crowding outside his back door in unusual numbers trying to get in and the owner's two dogs were in a frenzy.

The police were called in and arrived at the premises to find the house empty. But there was something cooking out on the back patio and it was clear that the chef had only just stepped out. Rather than waiting for Machuca to return, the police broke down the door. Machuca's two dogs – loyal to their master, who had fed them all kinds of unexpected treats lately – wouldn't let them in, so they shot them.

Inside the living room the police found a dismembered corpse shoved beneath a table. The legs and arms had been hacked off and all that remained was the torso, the head and the spinal column. Although the smell inside was truly awful, beneath it was a second, sweeter aroma that actually made everything much worse: the smell of herbs.

The police made their way through the hall and into the kitchen. On the table were 80 filled tamales, several kilos of corn gruel, 10kg of fresh dough and several cans of salsa. In short, all the ingredients to make another large batch of tamales – minus one. The only thing that Machuca didn't have in his kitchen was any trace of meat. No chicken, no pork and no beef. So what was out on the patio, gently simmering in those two pans?

It didn't need a forensic scientist to figure it out. Machuca had carefully removed the limbs of his victim piece by piece. He had then stacked them by the side of the industrial-sized pots while the other parts slowly boiled just metres away from the fresh dough.

But Machuca was no master criminal. While the police were busy securing the scene, he joined the other gawpers outside, until one of the neighbours recognised him and started screaming, 'Here's the murderer!' After trying to escape on his bicycle, Machuca was promptly arrested, taken to a holding cell and interrogated for six straight hours; eventually, he broke down and confessed.

Carlos Machuca had met his old friend, 61-year-old Rigoberto Zavala, on the previous Monday at 2 p.m. Machuca had a whopping hangover and his friend bought him a sherry to kill it off. They started drinking in the street until 5 p.m., when Machuca invited Zavala home. They bought a bottle of brandy on the way and carried on drinking until 8 p.m., when Zavala crashed out on the sofa.

'He was driving me crazy,' Machuca told reporters after the interrogation. 'He always thought he was such a big shot and stronger than me, even though he was older.' Machuca claimed that Zavala had been mocking him non-stop all day and had even given him a couple of playful slaps. Machuca hadn't liked that one bit and besides, in his words, his friend 'was a big chap.'

Machuca had had plenty of practice with a blade, having worked as a butcher for several years in Mexico City. After grabbing a knife out of the kitchen, he slowly approached Zavala and then stabbed him right in the heart while he was asleep. A few hours later, Machuca's family showed up at the door, but when they saw what their relative had done they fled.

Aware that his family might at any moment denounce him, he panicked. How to get rid of the body? While polishing off what was left of the brandy, he figured out what to do. A quick look around his immediate surroundings and he formulated his first plan. Rats thrived in the sewer labyrinth. He'd use the pots to soften up the meat, dump it down the drain and let the dogs feast on the rest.

At around 3 a.m., he started on the body, which he took apart on the living-room floor with the same knife he used to prepare his tamales. He even tried to feed some of the organs to the dogs, but they didn't think too much of the menu and threw up. Machuca had already boiled three batches and dumped them down the sewer by the time he was arrested.

The interrogators had other suspicions, though. A carved-up body beneath a table, two simmering pans on the patio, the dough and a cart waiting outside the front door to take them out. It looked pretty clear to police just where this was going. Had Machuca already taken his cart out and sold tamales filled with human flesh to the general public?

While there have been many cases of cannibalism, cases of actually selling human flesh are rarer (see below). People do, after a while, have a tendency to notice something odd about the taste of the meat. Yet the tamale has something in its favour in this regard, for it shares, like most Mexican food, one whopping and heart-stopping dose of chilli.

Tabloid headlines screamed 'Tamales of Death!' and the citizens of Morelia quickly checked their culinary memory. Had they ever bought their favourite snack from a vendor with a guilty look in his eye? Fortunately for them, the meat in the pre-prepared tamales was quickly determined to be chicken, and Machuca's food carts were declared free of traces of human remains.

Pieces of human flesh were discovered near the fresh dough, though, and this, combined with the herbs and the boiling water, pointed to dark intentions. Police suspect that Machuca had been on the brink of trying out a new way of disposing of the body. Thanks to that anonymous tip-off, he simply hadn't had the time.

Machuca was formally charged with the 'murder calificado' of Rigoberto Zavala on 22 April 2004, which meant that he also received a further sentence for the fact that he'd tried to cover up his crimes. Prosecutors pushed for the maximum penalty the law allows: 40 years' imprisonment. With a confession and the overwhelming forensic evidence staked against him, he was sentenced to 30 years in jail in August 2006 and will therefore almost certainly die there.

Before Machuca's trial in Morelia, he was questioned in his holding cell by reporters. But while he was open about some of the details of the murder, he remained distinctly cagey about others. Did he now regret what he'd done? Yes he regretted it: it had been a stupid thing to do. He had been afraid and if he hadn't have been so scared he would have turned himself in. But why the boiling water and the dough? Did it ever cross his mind to put the meat in the tamales? Not even for a single moment, he explained. What about the herbs, then? He didn't know. Maybe to make the smell better. But why bother softening up the meat? He wasn't sure about that either.

Kneading so much dough comes closer to manual labour than cooking and it's hard work on the arms; although he had no previous criminal record, Machuca is a pretty tough customer all the same. He is being held in the maximum-security wing in the State of Morelia and, according to a recent report in *Mural*, his neighbours complained that he was often aggressive and had recently attacked one of them.

Yet Machuca still refers to his victim by his nickname, 'Rigo', and at times seems like a kid facing a detention rather than a murderer facing a life sentence. Recent photos show him with his hand in his lap looking stunned and bewildered – and guilty – although according to a preliminary psychological study he shows no signs of mental illness. In fact, when conversation comes round to the issue of the tamales, he becomes somewhat indignant. Looking a little bit sheepish, he declares, 'I know there's no such a thing as a perfect crime, but something had to be done with Rigo's body. That's why I cut him in pieces, to throw in the sewer. Not to make tamales! No way, man, am I crazy enough to do that!'

But the fact remains that, while Machuca claims he acted out of panic and fear, he was quite capable of carving up a human being and was in the midst of eliminating every single trace of his crime when discovered by the police. While Machuca remains adamant that he had no intention of filling his tamales with his friend, Rigoberto's wife is now demanding justice. 'My husband might have been a drunk but he was never a brawler,' she has stated.

Most of the dismay, however, has been directed at the harm this story will do to the reputation of a much-beloved snack. According to a report in the Associated Press, one police spokesman for the district said, 'People are very upset because the tradition of the tamale is very important here.'

The harm to the tamale notwithstanding, the local population can be thankful: stabbing, chopping up your friend, boiling him and feeding him to the rats is bad enough, but if the police hadn't arrived when they did it could have been an awful lot worse. Only time will tell whether the people of Morelia will ever be able to sink their teeth into their favourite meaty treat in the same way again, though.

## A MEAL TO DIE FOR

In Roald Dahl's famous short story 'Lamb to Slaughter', a pregnant housewife learns that her husband, a policeman, is about to leave her for another woman. In a rage she bludgeons him to death with a frozen leg of lamb. Then, in order to dispose of the murder weapon, she defrosts the joint and feeds it to her husband's policemen friends who are investigating the murder case. Thomas Harris, writer of the Hannibal Lecter novels, took this idea much further. Lecter, of course, feeds carefully selected parts of his victims to his guests during lavish dinner parties.

Cases of real-life killers feeding their victims to other people are extremely rare. But that's not to say that they are completely unheard of. There was Fritz Haarman, the 'Hanover Vampire', who confessed to having killed over 30 boys and selling parts of them in his butcher's shop in the 1920s and more recently Russian serial killer Nikolai Dzhurmongaliev. Also known as 'metal fang', because of his false metal teeth, Dzhurmongaliev is said to have served up an estimated 70 prostitutes in stews to his neighbours. Dzhurmongaliev was declared insane and not responsible for his acts and was released ten years ago from an institute for the criminally insane. He is said to now reside somewhere in Uzbekistan.

## A BAD KNIGHT: HANI LECTER

Not so long ago, a related case arose in Australia, centring on slaughterhouse worker Katherine Knight, who was frequently referred to in the local press as 'Hani Lecter'. Despite her nickname, however, it is highly unlikely that Knight's intention was for anyone to actually eat the remains of her victim. Instead, it seems to have been part of a very sick joke that she played on her lover's two children.

In 2001, Knight stabbed her lover to death after they had had sex. She then skinned him with such expertise that his skin, including that of his head, face, nose, ears, neck, torso, genital organs and legs, was removed to form one pelt. According to court transcripts of her trial, the ex-mental patient, who had spent her entire working life in slaughterhouses all over Australia, carried out the sickening desecration of the body with a very steady hand: 'So expertly was it done that, after the post-mortem examination, the skin was able to be re-sewn on to Mr Price's body in a way that indicated a clear and appropriate, albeit grisly, methodology... The excised parts of Mr Price were then taken to the kitchen and at some stage, after she peeled and prepared various vegetables, she cooked Mr Price's head in a large pot with a number of vegetables she had prepared so as to produce a sickening stew. The removal was clean and left an incised type wound. To remove Mr Price's head in such a way required skill, which was consistent with the skills acquired by the prisoner in the course of her work as a meat slicer.'

Knight then moved the skinned and decapitated body into the lounge, where she placed it on a sofa, crossed its legs and put the left arm in such a position so that it looked as if he was holding an empty bottle of pop. When that was done, Knight hung the pelt to dry on a meat hook in the lounge and put two buttock steaks in the fridge for her husband's two children to eat. She then left the stew to boil on the hob.

Police were called to the scene at eleven o'clock the next morning; they found that the stew was still warm and Knight, who had crashed out on the bed after her long night's work, was fast asleep. During the subsequent trial, it was revealed that

Knight had once cut the throat of a boyfriend's eight-week-old puppy, slashed a woman across the face with a knife and even threatened a child at knifepoint.

## COOKING UP A MURDER: EMILIA BASIL

One professional cook did actually kill someone and then feed the remains of her victim to customers in her restaurant: Emilia Basil, in Argentina. In the early hours of 23 March 1973, Basil strangled her 65-year-old lover, Jose Petriella, to death with a nylon cord. Petriella was a tenant who lived in one of the rooms at the back of the restaurant and the two had been having an affair for almost five years.

But, while Basil's ardour for Petriella had recently begun to wane, Petriella's love had only grown; he often told a completely unimpressed Basil that he was head over heels in love with her. In fact, he had recently announced his intention to tell her husband that the two had been having an affair behind his back and right under his own roof.

The affair had provided Basil with a bit of excitement in the past as well as cash (Petriella regularly paid her for sex), but Basil had three children and did not want to lose her home, her husband or her restaurant. When Petriella started throwing stones at her windowpane at five in the morning, begging her to come downstairs and have sex with him, it proved the final straw.

Basil put on her dressing gown and slippers and went to his room in the back of the house, but, when Petriella went to embrace her, she strangled him. Basil hid the body under the bed and then came back for it the next day, when she had the kitchen and the whole house to herself. Basil had had plenty of practice slicing meat for the Lebanese stews and meat pasties that she was famous for in the area and immediately went to work.

She stripped the body and removed the arms and legs at the joints. She then sliced the meat off the arms and legs and cut it into small, bite-size pieces. She mixed the chunks of tender flesh with boiled eggs and spices then put the meat into Arabian-style meat pasties. Meanwhile, she salted and seasoned the larger, tougher pieces of flesh, added vegetables and stock and boiled them in a stew. Basil slowly fed the remains of the body to her customers, none of whom seemed to notice anything odd about the food they were eating.

Some parts proved easier to get rid of than others, though. She was able to dump his shoulder blades and genitals down the drain outside her house. As for the head, she carried that by the hair to her largest saucepan in her kitchen and boiled it until the flesh and hair had all fallen off. That hideous liquid went down the drain as well. She then wrapped the fleshless head in brown paper and left it at the bottom of a cupboard while she figured out what to do with it.

Her undoing was the torso. Unwisely, she decided to put it in a box, cover it with vegetable waste from her kitchen and put it in the front of the shop for the refuse men to take away. Because the box was so heavy, the refuse collectors (in classic Latin American fashion) shrugged their shoulders and refused to move it; before long, the neighbours noticed a terrible smell coming from the box and called the police.

When the police arrived and brushed aside the rotting vegetables, they discovered the old man's rotting torso. They knew that a man living on the same block had been reported missing by his brother two days before. Basil's house was searched and police found Jose Petriella's head at the bottom of the wardrobe (Basil still hadn't made up her mind what to do with it). Of the stew and the pasties there was no sign. The customers had seen to that. Basil was promptly arrested and spent the next 14 years of her life in jail.

# CHAPTER THIRTEEN

# MURDEROUS REAL-LIFE WITCHES

Meet the real-life killer witches who make the fairy-tale hags of old look like the fairy godmother herself.

In 1612, 13 individuals stood trial for the witchcraft-inspired murder of 17 people in and around the Forest of Pendle in Lancaster. At the trial, alleged witch Alizon Device told the magistrate that her grandmother, Demdike, had persuaded her to let a 'familiar' spirit suck her blood in return for great murderous powers. Alizon then went on to accuse her grandmother of murdering three other victims, and another witch of murdering a further five. Three men and seven women were hanged for the crimes.

Historians estimate that there may have been as many as 50,000 'witches' killed in Europe alone since the first witch hunt in 1427. For centuries, witches were drowned, burned at the stake, strangled, tortured, forced to commit suicide, had their tongues cut out and were even buried alive. And it's pretty safe to say that none of them ever 'blasted' a crop, had the ability to shape-change into an animal or had personally met the devil himself at a crossroads.

Even as late as 1945, however, there was a murder thought to be related to witchcraft in the UK and there have been real-life witches whose exploits make fairy-tale hags look like fairy godmothers.

## THE CHILD KILLER: ENRIQUETA MARTÍ RIPOLLÉS

In 1910, tales began to circulate of children vanishing from the streets of Barcelona; by 1912, they had become so commonplace that the Governor of Barcelona, in the face of widespread mounting panic, had to claim publicly that they were unfounded. Yet the stories persisted. At the time, Barcelona was infected with a fast-spreading tuberculosis epidemic and it was believed, especially in the poorer areas of the city, that someone was killing children and drinking their blood, as this was rumoured to provided a cure for the disease. The most common story of the time told of a dark rider who took children from the streets of Barcelona at night, killed them, bottled up the blood and then sold it to the highest bidder. Horrified witnesses came forward and claimed to have seen him driving a sinister carriage pulled by two jet-black stallions. Another rumour told of a deranged maniac, stricken with tuberculosis, who walked the streets at night and left a trail of bloodless child corpses in his wake.

Despite the Governor's constant reassurances, children were indeed disappearing and dying – not at the hands of a vampire or a sinister horsemen, but of someone all too real and far, far worse. Her name was Enriqueta Ripollés and she was not only a child snatcher and peddler of children to adults for sex but also a real-life witch, who, once finished with her helpless victims, literally boiled their bones in a cauldron and made potions out of their blood and fat.

Enriqueta Ripollés had tried her hand at various professions over the years. She was a domestic servant girl at 15, had become a prostitute by the time she was 20 and was madam of a child brothel when she was 32. When the brothel was raided in 1909, she was arrested and sent to jail for four years, after which she went straight for a while, opening an antique shop in 1914, and living above the premises with her partner, a failed artist. But the enterprise soon collapsed and she broke up with her lover shortly afterwards. So, instead of opening another child brothel and risking another police raid, she hit upon another idea. This time she decided that she would provide a door-to-door service to the sick and depraved clientele she had acquired through her many years working in the child sex trade.

In the mornings, she would dress up as a beggar, disguise the children she had kidnapped in rags and take them into the city centre to help her beg for money. In the afternoons, she would bring the children to the more affluent parts of town and sell them for sex to her old and trusted customers. She soon had a lucrative and exclusive list of clients and had also hit upon another profitable sideline: mysterious potions, which she claimed could cure impotence and old age.

To acquire the ingredients for her concoctions, Ripollés dismembered her victims, drained them of their blood, boiled away their flesh and even crushed their bones. Her rich clients, knowing full well what was in them, snapped them up.

Police finally became suspicious of Ripollés when a neighbour noticed a child peering forlornly from the window of an apartment across the road and contacted the local police station. For three weeks, police had been on the lookout for five-year-old Teresa Guitart, who had vanished from the street outside her house in February 1912, and the disappearance had made headlines the city over. When police knocked on her door, a little girl answered and told them that her 'mother' was not in. The girl's head had been shaved and she said that her name was Felicidad (Happiness) but when gently questioned by police it was clear to the authorities that this was indeed the missing girl and that she had been instructed to call the owner of the apartment 'mother'. There was another little girl in the house too. She was called Angelina, a variant of her real name – Angela.

When police went to interview the neighbours, they told them that they had often seen a little boy called Pepito with Ripollés only recently, but now he was nowhere to be seen. As police soon learned when they talked to the girls, Pepito was in fact dead and Felicidad and Angelina were both extremely lucky to be alive. Their account of their ordeal at the hands of Ripollés, especially that of five-year-old Angela, sounded like a sick version of Hansel and Gretel. Unfortunately, as police soon discovered, it was all too true.

Before Teresa had arrived, Angela had had another playmate: a six-year-old called Pepito. One day, Angela told police, Ripollés had picked him up, put him on a table and calmly stabbed him to death. She had then forced Angela to eat some of his cooked remains. On searching the witch's lair, police found a bag of laundry at the bottom of which was a pile of charred children's bones. In the kitchen they found another sack containing a large knife and a bloody pile of boy's clothes, confirming Angela's story. And the more police searched, the worse it got.

In a locked room, they found more than fifty vials containing blood and the fat from children's bodies, along with ancient books containing mysterious recipes. Evidence that Ripollés had indeed been doing a brisk business came in the form of a luxurious room completely out of keeping with the rest of the house. It was decorated with rich fabrics and furniture and contained cupboards full of expensive women's clothing and jewellery. They found several sets of silken children's clothes too and also, legend has it, a cage with two dead children locked inside it.

The method Ripollés employed to kill children was revealed during her sensational murder trial, which saw headlines all over Spain baying for her prompt execution. One witness came forward and positively identified Ripollés as the woman who had stolen her child back in 1905. According to her testimony, she had originally come from the nearby village of Alcañiz to look for employment. One day she was standing in a cold doorway in Barcelona with her baby in her arms when Ripollés approached her, asked her if her baby needed milk and then offered to buy some. The woman gratefully accompanied her to a shop, where Ripollés bought her milk. Having gained the woman's trust, Ripollés then offered to buy the baby bread and took the infant in her arms, saying she was going with her to the local bakery and would return shortly. The woman never saw her baby again.

Police were ordered to search all of Ripollés's previous lodgings and there they found children's bones under floorboards, as well as a bundle of tiny hands and wigs made of children's hair. When their stomach-turning investigation was complete, horrified police estimated that Ripollés had murdered and made potions out of at least ten children over a ten-year period.

While in prison and awaiting trial, Ripollés tried unsuccessfully to kill herself by cutting her wrists. In the end, her fellow inmates did the job for her. Before she could be sentenced, she was beaten to death while she was exercising in the prison courtyard.

## THE VIRGIN AND THE MADWOMAN: LEONARDA CIANCIULLI

A gypsy fortune teller once told witch Leonarda Cianciulli that all of her three sons would die young and that she herself would end up dead and deranged in a madhouse. World War II was fast approaching and as the conflict drew closer Cianciulli became increasingly convinced that the fortune teller was right and that her sons would all meet violent deaths on the battlefield.

At a young age, she had married an impoverished government clerk called Raffaele Pansardi. From the outset, their marriage had been marred by misfortune and tragedy. Cianciulli had given birth to 14 children, but only four of them had survived: three boys and one girl. In 1930, their home and all of their meagre possessions had been destroyed in a single afternoon by an earthquake. The couple had been forced to move and had been living in the impoverished village of Correggio in the Po valley ever since. There, in order to help supplement her husband's small pay, Cianciulli made soap and candles and read tarot cards to the locals. She soon earned a reputation as a matchmaker and an expert in the affairs of the heart.

When, in the summer of 1940, Cianciulli got the news that her favourite son, Giuseppe, had been drafted into the army, she became convinced that the gypsy's prophecy was about to come true. One night, shortly before Giuseppe was scheduled to present himself at the nearby army barracks for training,

Cianciulli had a vivid dream in which the Virgin Mary came to her and told her that she would spare the lives of her sons but required three human sacrifices in return. The next day, without any hesitation at all, Cianciulli went to work.

She told three of the older women in the village that she had found a suitable husband for each one of them. Even better still, each husband lived far away from the confines of Correggio and all were in a position to offer the women happy, comfortable lives. The women would, of course, have to pay for the service rendered by the matchmaker and it would be better also, so as not to cause any fuss, to keep it all a secret until they had left the village and had established themselves in their new lives. So that their relatives would not worry about them in the meantime, Cianciulli persuaded all three women to write letters to their families, telling them that they had found happiness elsewhere. She promised that she would pass the letters on later.

When everything had been arranged and the women came to her house to pay her, Cianciulli drugged them and murdered them with an axe before turning their bodies into soap and cakes. Both products were big hits with the neighbours.

Fifty-year-old Faustina Setti was the first to end up in one of Correggio's pots, having just handed her 30,000 lire for the privilege. Correggio drugged her wine and then cut her up into nine pieces with an axe. She then dropped the victim's flesh and bones into the large cauldrons she used for making soap and boiled the mixture for 24 hours straight.

'I threw the pieces into a pot,' Cianciulli later testified at her trial, 'added seven kilos of caustic soda, which I had bought to make soap, and stirred the whole mixture until the pieces dissolved in a thick, dark mush that I poured into several buckets and emptied in a nearby septic tank. As for the blood in the basin, I waited until it had coagulated, dried it in the oven, ground it and mixed it with flour, sugar, chocolate, milk and eggs, as well as a bit of margarine, kneading all the ingredients together. I made lots of crunchy tea cakes and served them to the ladies who came to visit, though Giuseppe and I also ate them.'

Her second victim was 53-year-old Francesca Soavi; her third and last victim was a 60-year-old widow called Virginia Cacioppo: 'She ended up in the pot, like the other two,' Cianciulli later remembered, happily. 'Her flesh was fat and white; when it had melted, I added a bottle of cologne, and after a long time on the boil I was able to make some most acceptable creamy soap. I gave bars to neighbours and acquaintances. The cakes, too, were better: that woman was really sweet.'

But Virginia Cacioppo's sister became suspicious when Virginia disappeared after her visit to Cianciulli and contacted the police. Now that her work was over, Cianciulli immediately confessed to the three murders. She was sent to the madhouse in Pozzuoli, where she died 30 years later – fulfilling part of the prophecy made to her by the fortune teller.

## A COTSWOLD KILLING: CHARLES WALTON

On Valentine's Day 1945, the body of 74-year-old farm labourer Charles Walton was found lying face up under a willow tree on the lower slopes of Meon Hill in the Cotswolds. A pitchfork had been driven through his body with such force that it took two policemen to pull it out. His throat had been slashed with his own trouncing fork and a cross had been slashed on his chest.

The oddest murder in recent history. 41-year-old cannibal Armin Meiwes found somebody who wanted to be eaten. The message Meiwes had posted online was: 'Seeking young, well-built 18-to-30-year-old for slaughter.'

© Rex Features

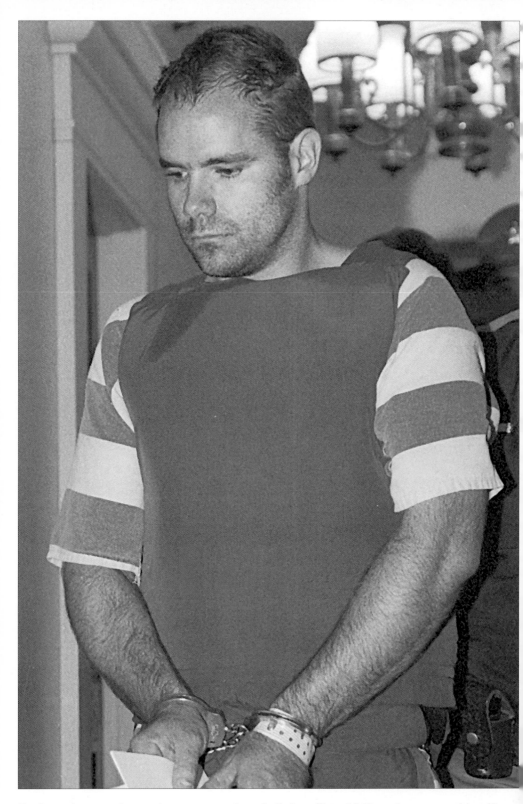

Perhaps the most harrowing revenge plot of all time. Ronald Shanabarger got his wife pregnant so that he would one day be able to kill their baby. The reason? She hadn't been there for him when his dad died...

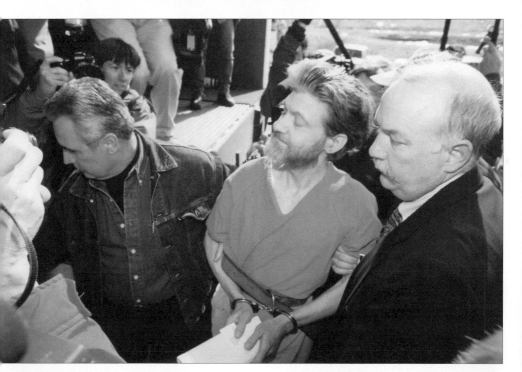

*Above*: A genius who was fast-tracked to Harvard aged 16, Theodore Kaczynski became a bomb-building hermit determined to murder and maim scientists and researchers involved in modern technology, which Kaczynski saw as evil.

© *Rex Features*

*Below*: One of the most notorious killers in history, farmer Robert Pickton fed his victims' bodies to his pigs. Convicted for six murders, he is suspected of up to 40 more.

© *Corbis*

Jerome Brudos (top left) brutally murdered four women before performing fetish rituals on them in the garage behind his house (below). He lived a double life and his wife (top right) had no idea there was anything wrong until the police came knocking.

© Above left: Topfoto; Above right: Corbis; Below: PA Photos

Best friends Pauline Parker and Juliet Hulme murdered Juliet's mother using a brick. It took forty blows to kill her. The girls served five years in prison, and were released on the condition that they never met each other again.                                    © *Corbis*

*Above*: Japanese cannibal Issei Sagawa told the authorities that he had been waiting for his chance to eat another human being; and when it finally came, he ate her raw within 24 hours.

*Below*: Serial killer Randy Kraft picked up hitchhikers and men in gay bars, drugged them, raped them, strangled them with their own shoelaces or belts and then mutilated their dead bodies. His co-workers described him as 'pleasant, reserved and friendly.'

© *Corbis*

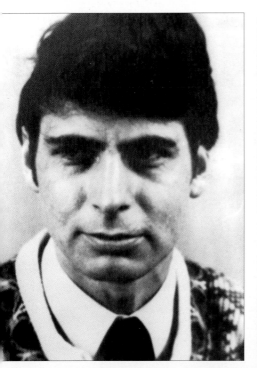

*Above left*: Living with the dead. Dennis Nilsen disposed of his victims in his north London flat, and stored them there. He would fetch them from beneath the floorboards, bath them, and prop them up on his living-room sofa.

*Above right*: The murder of sitcom star Bob Crane was shrouded in mystery. It was only after his death that the dark side of the 'family man' came to light.

*Below*: Hollywood actress Susan Cabot was found bludgeoned to death in her Los Angeles home. But had the murderer really been a Latin American ninja, as her son claimed?

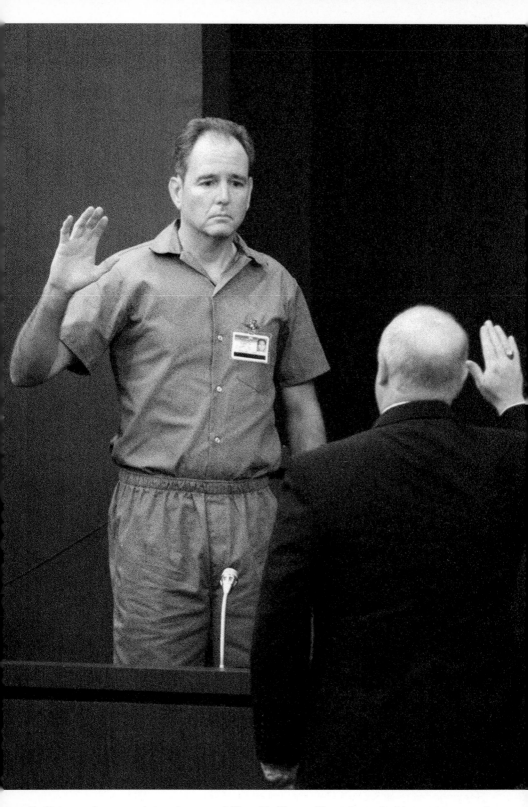

Sadist, murderer, rapist and necrophiliac, Rolling will go down in history as one of America's most savage and unrepentant killers of all time – which is exactly what he wanted…

© *PA Photos*

In one of the largest investigations in police history, every inch of the field was searched and every one of the inhabitants of the nearby village of Lower Quinton was interviewed – to no avail. In fact, the local population seemed peculiarly reluctant to talk. All police could uncover were strange coincidences and whispered rumours of witchery.

Since well before Tudor times, the local Rollright Stones have been a meeting spot for witches; Walton himself was rumoured to be a high-ranking member of one of the many witches' covens said to be operating in the area. Locals believed that he had the power to control animals, that he was clairvoyant and that he could also call and direct small animals at will. Police also learned that Walton had a rather sinister hobby: raising natterjack toads, which he was said to have harnessed at night to blight the crops.

Walton's rumoured clairvoyance stemmed from a very old story about a black dog that had been recorded 80 years earlier by a local priest and amateur local historian. In the tale, an eight-year-old apprentice called Charles Walton had seen something called a 'shuck' on eight successive nights; according to local rumour, a 'shuck' comes in the form of a large black dog and its presence signifies impending tragedy. On the eighth night, the boy had heard the rustling of a silken dress and when he turned around he had seen a headless woman. He was later informed that his eight-year-old sister had been tragically killed.

The silence around the death of Charles Walton only deepened when one of the detectives in the case said he had seen a black dog on Meon Hill. Later that same day, a black dog was found dead, hung from a tree in close proximity to where Walton's body had been found.

Police also discovered that Walton was not the first supposed witch to die in such a gruesome manner. Almost exactly a hundred years before his death, a mentally backwards stable boy had murdered a so-called witch in almost exactly the same way. When the boy was asked why he had killed her, he replied that he had done so to lift a curse that she had cast upon that year's crop.

The area had seen other, related incidents over the years. In 1912, a farm hand in neighbouring Shipston on Stour had killed an 80-year-old woman with a pitchfork, claiming at his trial that she had bewitched him. There was even a name for the manner in which Walton had been killed: 'sticking', a way to kill a witch while preventing them from rising from the grave and seeking vengeance. So had Walton been murdered in this way as self-defence against a curse or as retaliation for a supposed hex upon the land?

The idea of witchcraft led to yet another bizarre theory. According to the old Julian calendar, in use until the Middle Ages, today's 14 February had fallen on 2 February, which, according to local superstition, was traditionally the best day for a blood sacrifice. Walton had been thrown to the ground and the fork had then been driven in at an angle – possibly to allow his blood to flow into the earth.

The absence of Walton's pocket watch, which he was said to carry with him wherever he went, made for another possible clue. Believing it might provide a link to the killer, police searched widely for it, without any luck. Inside the watch, Walton was said to keep a witch's glass – an instrument that would protect him from spells and enchantments. Although it remained undiscovered at the time, the watch was unearthed 20 years later by a builder when he was remodelling

Walton's old cottage. The piece of glass that Walton kept inside it was missing.

The case remains unsolved to this day and the locals are still extremely reluctant to talk about it. While looking for Charles Walton's grave, I asked one of the locals if there was any talk in the village today about who actually killed him. I was warned politely but firmly to mind my own damn business.

## CASTLE OF BLOOD: ELIZABETH BATHORY

When Elizabeth Bathory was seven, she sneaked away from her nanny to witness the execution of a gypsy who, in one of the most appalling deaths known to man, was sewn up alive inside a dead horse. Such demented conduct was not uncommon in the 16th century, when the Hungarian nobility murdered and tortured the peasant population almost at will. That said, being a servant girl in the household the adult Bathory later controlled would turn out to be just about the worst job you could get.

Bathory had pale, almost translucent skin, and was of noble birth, hailing from one of the richest and most powerful families of Eastern Europe. Well educated and fluent in three languages, she was also (probably due to hundreds of years of intermarriage) hideously psychotic. At the age of 15, she was married off to a nobleman named Ferenc Nadasdy and moved to Cachtice Castle. Three years after her marriage, her husband was appointed Chief Commander of the Hungarian army and was from then on almost permanently absent warring and whoring, making a great name for himself against the Turks. Left to her own devices, Bathory soon started torturing servant girls, dabbling in witchcraft and, witnesses at her trial insisted, having regular sex with the devil.

The first official complaint against her reached the royal court in Vienna in 1602, when Lutheran parish priest Istvan Magyari raised concerns about the atrocities Bathory was allegedly carrying out on the local population. The authorities were slow to react, though – these were just peasants, after all – and it wasn't until another eight years had passed that they actually sent an official team down to investigate further. In the meantime, Bathory's husband died after being stabbed by a prostitute in Bucharest when he refused to pay her.

Under the guidance of witch Ilona Joo, witches, wizards, sorcerers, alchemists and devil worshippers found a warm welcome in Bathory's castle and she soon started paying regular visits to her aunt, another witch and also rumoured to be a lesbian. She received further instruction from an old maid and sadist named called Dorka, a 'forest witch' well versed in the ways of witchcraft and black magic.

Bathory whiled away the lonely hours in the castle by shoving needles into the nails of young girls and then cutting off their fingers with red-hot shears. If the maids were caught gossiping she would sew their mouths firmly shut and if the ironing wasn't quite up to scratch she was known to shove a red-hot iron down the offender's throat. When feeling a bit down and too tired to get out of bed, she was known to call upon a servant, grab them and bite them in the face. According to some accounts, one winter she poured water over a domestic helper and then let the victim freeze to death outside. But most of her victims (and they may number six hundred) were beaten to death.

During one characteristic attack on a servant girl, Bathory discovered a novel new skin product: human blood. She was almost 40 at the time and was becoming concerned that she was losing her looks; it seemed to her that when blood splashed on her skin it appeared to make it look younger. Soon she was wallowing in human blood and drinking it by the gallon. To acquire it, she often employed a cage suspended from the ceiling by a rope, with spikes on the inside. According to rumour, when one 12-year-old girl tried to escape from the castle, she was put in the cage and one of Bathory's male helpers, a dwarf called Ficzko, poked a red-hot poker through the bars. Trying to avoid the poker, the girl slowly bled to death – and Bathory wallowed in the rain of blood below.

However, after a while, it seemed to her that the blood was losing its beneficial effects. Was it perhaps because the blood was from peasants? On the advice of a fellow witch, in 1609, Bathory began to invite daughters of the nobility to come to her castle and learn upper-class etiquette. They were, of course, promptly murdered.

Whether Bathory actually did bathe in and drink human blood is unconfirmed. But, when word finally reached the Hungarian king that girls of noble birth were disappearing in the area, a party was sent to investigate; they found cages in the castle full of women awaiting torture and execution. Legend has it that, at that moment, knowing that her murderous rampage was nearing an end, Bathory called on her cats for help. 'Protect me, Erzsébet, and grant me a long life. I am in peril, O cloud!' she is reported to have said. 'Send me 90 cats, for thou are the supreme Lord of cats. Give them thy orders and tell them, wherever they may be, to assemble together, to come from the mountains, from the waters, from the rivers, from the rainwater on the roofs and from the oceans. Tell them to come to me.'

Legend has it also that the cats appeared and attacked the priest who was leading the expedition, but when the soldiers gave chase the cats simply vanished into thin air. As the expedition continued their search of the castle, they came across countless bodies of young women outside the surrounding walls; they had been simply tossed over the ramparts. Many of the bodies had no arms or legs. 'We watched in horror as the dogs ran about with parts of the girls in their mouths,' one shaken observer wrote.

Those who had helped Bathory in her crimes all suffered a horrible death. Their fingers were plucked out with red-hot shears and they were then thrown on to a fire and burned alive. Bathory's dwarf helper Ficzko got off reasonably lightly with a relatively quick death: he was beheaded.

As punishment for her terrible crimes, Elizabeth Bathory was walled up inside her own castle, with only a small slit through which food was passed to her. She died four years later.

## ONLY TRYING TO HELP: MIGUEL ANGEL RODRIGUEZ

According to Marisa Grinstein in her excellent book *Mujeres Asesinas* ('Killer Women'), Buenos Aires had its very own killer witch: an effeminate, overweight homosexual who persuaded three women to kill their husbands in 1966. Arturo Miguel Angel Rodriguez was an ex-priest and tailor who read cards and offered advice and occult remedies for everyday problems to lonely – not to mention extremely gullible – women. Rodriguez (who also answered to the name of Monica) claimed that he had command over the spirit world, having learned his art in a long-lost Brazilian village, and hinted that his speciality was the creation of murder potions.

The first woman to kill her husband with Rodriguez's help

needed little persuasion. Juana Pugnetti was sick of her husband breathing down her neck and nagging her and wanted freedom to indulge in affairs. Her daughter, who was only 17 at the time (half her mother's age), pretty much wanted the same thing. The two of them agreed that it would be better for them both if he dropped down dead. And the quicker the better.

Rodriguez initially refused to help, though. Seeing a useful way to draw the business out, and earn a fistful of pesos in the process, he told Pugnetti that the spirits wanted to give her husband a second chance. He told her to cut up a living toad, remove its entrails, put her husband's name inside and then bury it. This, he claimed, would put her husband into a trance-like state for months, allowing her to come and go as she pleased. A furious Pugnetti came back a few weeks later: it hadn't worked, she told him. In fact, her husband was even worse than before. So, after much consultation with the spirit world, Rodriguez told her that he had been given permission to create a murder potion. He asked her to meet him outside a nearby cemetery at eleven o'clock.

When they met that night, Rodriguez disappeared for an hour to find the ingredients and came back with what he claimed were the crushed bones from an arm and a human eyeball. This, he told Pugnetti grandly, was 'the liquor of the gods' and would kill her husband without arousing any suspicion. Pugnetti obediently slipped the potion into her husband's food and hey presto – nothing at all. Once more, Pugnetti approached the witch. But Rodriguez, knowing that he couldn't spin things out any longer, now offered a far more worldly solution: arsenic. And – for a fee, of course – he would commune with the spirit world to make sure that the manner of her husband's death would remain undetected.

Rodriguez did almost exactly the same thing with two other unhappily married women. Nina Ponorilox's justification for wanting her husband dead was that he regularly beat her. As well as going through the entire toad routine (which actually seemed to work!), she was told to light seven black candles over seven days and then flush the remaining wax in the toilet so that it would enter the river. She put arsenic in a cup of coffee and a lemon tea for her husband, who died that very same day.

The third unhappy wife, Margarita Tiadini, needed more persuasion, though. Tiadini was reluctant and squeamish. She had vomited when she had cut up the toad and subsequently had nightmares about it for weeks. Rodriguez, however, introduced her to his other two satisfied clients and they eagerly persuaded her to go ahead with her plan.

This time, though, it wasn't so easy. Tiadini put arsenic in her husband's soup, but the quantity wasn't enough and he simply asked to see a doctor. Tiadini ran out of the house, saying she was on her way to fetch help, and came back instead with Rodriguez dressed up in a white coat. In the end the pair decided to inject the husband with the arsenic directly, but still her husband held on grimly to life for another two days. Indeed, he nearly managed to escape out of a back door at one point, but Rodriguez dragged him back in.

Meanwhile, Rodriguez's first murderous client was now enjoying her newfound freedom and was running a brothel along with her daughter in their own home. Police had become suspicious about her husband's sudden demise, however, and obtained a court order for an exhumation of the body; on discovering traces of arsenic, they came calling. It was the daughter who broke down and confessed first. When her

MURDEROUS REAL-LIFE WITCHES

mother learned that her daughter had blabbed, she led police to the other two murderesses too, and to Rodriguez. All were sentenced to 15 years in prison.

According to Marisa Grinstein, none of the widows showed any remorse for their crimes whatsoever, expressing instead profound relief that their husbands would bother them no longer. It was Rodriguez who felt the most hard done by. He told cellmates that he had only been trying to help and declared that it was because of those three women that he was now in prison. True to character, he cast a terrible spell to ensure that they would each endure a long and terrible death.

# CHAPTER FOURTEEN
# TEENAGE KILLERS

Sometimes the bloody consequences of teen
tantrums can be a truly terrible sight
to behold.

Every year in the Unites States there are around 300 cases of teenagers who kill their own parents. While the vast majority of these cases involve teenagers who are lashing out against physical or sexual abuse, there are always a handful of cases of teens who kill for such mundane reasons as more pocket money, or simply because they want more time to hang out with their friends at the local mall. Cases like these invariably make headlines the world over; these are teenagers from loving families who kill their own parents for absolutely no real reason at all.

Take, for example, the murder of Peter and Patty Niedere by their son and his best friend in October 2005. Among other things, Matthew Niedere was sick of his parents nagging at him to go to church. So, one day, during physics class, he persuaded his best friend, Clayton Keister, to help him kill them both. After the pair had cold-bloodedly gunned down Niedere's parents, they went shopping, mowed the lawn and got ready for a school dance, where they were later arrested. Both teenagers were convicted of first-degree murder.

While mean teens can kill because they want more cash or freedom, they can also kill out of love. In fact, the most disturbing and bizarre teenage parricides are often the result of warped teenage infatuation and obsessed teenagers are known to have killed their parents and slaughtered romantic rivals without the slightest hesitation; adding insult to injury, these adolescent murderers often cast themselves afterwards as the heroic star-crossed lovers of the piece. But, as the following cases of teenage love gone homicidal show, Romeo and Juliet these teenagers certainly are not.

## HEAVENLY CREATURES: PAULINE PARKER AND JULIET HULME

No list of murderous teenage crushes would be complete without at least a mention of the most famous teenage crush of them all: the romance that is alleged to have developed between Pauline Parker (16) and Juliet Hulme (15) in the summer of 1954. The murder of Pauline's mother, Honora Parker, was the most famous murder case of the day in New Zealand and the story made headlines around the world after it was alleged by prosecutors at their trial that the two 'dirty-minded little girls' had been involved in an intense lesbian relationship for several months.

When both sets of parents began to suspect that their daughters' friendship had turned 'unhealthy', they decided that the two would have to be separated and that Juliet Hulme should go to boarding school in South Africa. The pair, unaware that this was part of a plan to split them up, hoped that perhaps Pauline could accompany Juliet to South Africa, but Pauline's mother strongly opposed the idea.

Unable to face the fact that they would soon be separated, the girls promptly started plotting. If Pauline's mother was dead, then they just might be able to remain together and travel to South Africa with Pauline's father. As they plotted the murder, Pauline Parker kept a diary in which she detailed her own mother's impending death. 'We have worked it all out carefully and are both thrilled with the idea. Naturally we feel a trifle nervous but the anticipation is great,' she wrote. 'I'm trying to think of some way. I want it to appear a natural or an accidental death. We discussed the "moider" fully, so next time I write in the diary Mother will be dead. How odd, yet how pleasing.'

On 22 June, the girls and Pauline's mother went for a picnic in Victoria Park, Christchurch. When they reached a secluded spot, Juliet Hulme dropped a bright-pink stone on the path, which she had brought along with her for that purpose, and pointed it out to Honora Parker. When Honora bent down to look at it, her daughter beat her over the head with a brick wrapped in a stocking.

The girls had badly miscalculated, however, believing in their teenage rose-tinted fantasy world that Honora would somehow instantly drop dead with a minimum of fuss. Instead, it took over 40 blows to kill her. They had hoped to attribute the head injuries to a fall but the repeated blows, of course, made that impossible. Even so, they went ahead with their plan and rushed into a nearby tearoom, where they asked for help. They were immediately suspects in the case and when Pauline's diaries were found the next day they were both arrested. Promptly convicted of murder, the pair served five years in separate jails and were famously released on the condition that they never meet again.

Nothing was heard about them for many years, until it emerged that Hulme, who now lives in Scotland, is a successful writer specialising in Victorian mysteries; under the pen name Anne Perry, she has sold over three million copies of her books. Pauline Parker, meanwhile, also moved to the UK, where for many years she taught mentally handicapped children in a special-needs school.

## MATRICIDAL MANIAC: VALESSA ROBINSON

The story of Valessa Robinson, now serving a 20-year sentence for murder, makes Parker and Hulme's murder look positively quaint by comparison.

Back in 1998, Valessa Robinson was a teenager and she was in love. 'My true one and only love is Adam William Davis,' she wrote in her diary in May 1998, 'and pretty soon I'll be Valessa Lyn Davis. We're trying to get me pregnant because I want a baby so bad. Just imagine a little version of me running around, scary, isn't it!'

Valessa's boyfriend was 19-year-old Adam Davis – the archetypal bad boy from the other side of the tracks and any parent's worst nightmare. Davis, who went by the name 'Rattlesnake', was a drifter with a long criminal record. In fact, although Valessa and Davis had been 'going steady' for seven months, for much of that time Davis had been serving time in the local jail for robbery.

Valessa Robinson, on the other hand, was only 16 years old. She lived in a pleasant house in the quiet suburb of Carrollwood in Tampa, Florida, with her recently divorced mother. But mother and daughter had not been seeing eye to eye for quite a while. In her free time, Valessa was tripping out on LSD, getting drunk, smashing in post boxes, hanging out with the wrong crowd and not coming home at night. Her grades were slipping, she was smoking and she had also recently been arrested for shoplifting. Robinson's mother had watched all this with helpless horror, but the biggest point of conflict by far was Valessa's boyfriend.

Valessa's mother knew that her daughter was having sex, and had in fact caught the two at it under her own roof. She may also have known that the two planned to get married and there is evidence to suggest that she was reading her daughter's journal. What is known for sure is that Vicki Robinson was finding it harder and harder to cope with her teenage offspring. After months of yelling and increasingly acrimonious arguments, she had become so desperate that she planned to enrol her daughter into a Christian boot camp called Stepping Stone Farm for an entire year.

She never got the chance.

On the night of Friday, 26 June 1998, Valessa Robinson, Adam Davis and 19-year-old John Whispel, a mutual friend of theirs, bought some LSD. While tripping in a Denny's restaurant, Valessa suddenly announced to the two young men that she wanted her mother dead: 'Let's kill Mom.'

To begin with, it seemed like a joke – to Whispel, at least. But Davis and Robinson were serious and as they continued talking the two smitten teens soon became specific about the details. In the end, they hit upon a novel method. They would score some heroin and give Vicki Robinson an overdose.

But they couldn't score any. Instead, they bought a syringe and drove back to the house, where Davis filled it with kitchen bleach. When Mrs Robinson walked into the kitchen in her nightgown, Davis, still tripping, grabbed her from behind and stabbed her in the neck. The syringe and the bleach didn't work, though, so Davis stabbed her again – this time with a knife – killing her. Or at least that's what they thought.

As the trio sat around smoking cigarettes in Valessa's bedroom, they heard a low whimper coming from the kitchen. According to court testimony, it was at this point that Davis said, 'The bitch won't die.' He then grabbed the knife, returned to the kitchen and stabbed Vicki Robinson twice in the neck, finally killing her. According to Whispel, who later testified against the pair in court, Valessa Robinson had then declared, 'Well, now I'm free. I can do whatever I want.'

The three then stuffed Mrs Robinson's body in a plastic rubbish bin, took it to a deserted spot near Whispel's house and dumped it in some nearby bushes. Their initial idea was to encase the bin later in concrete and dump it in a nearby river. As it turned out, they never bothered. Instead, they used Vicki Robinson's cash machine (Valessa knew the pin number) to get tattoos, eat junk food and buy more drugs in the nearby town of Ybor City, where they stayed for three days. Apparently in no hurry to make a run for it, the three seemed quite content to stay in motel rooms and watch movies such as *Scream 2* on pay-for-view.

It wasn't until they saw a news report that Vicki Robinson had been reported missing that they finally decided to flee, getting as far as Texas in her minivan. When sheriffs identified the vehicle, however, the trio were arrested. To begin with, Valessa, probably in order to protect her boyfriend, claimed that she had stabbed her mother after an argument. Davis, meanwhile, in his initial confession told detectives that he had killed Valessa's mother because she had been trying to break the two up.

The love-struck couple tried to keep their romance going as far as it was possible even after they were arrested. While she was being led to a police car, Robinson told the assembled reporters, 'I love Adam!' And when the two were in the same court room during the pre-trial hearings, Robinson couldn't resist smiling at her dreamboat across the room and casting coy glances in his direction – much to the annoyance of Circuit Judge Cynthia Holloway, who ordered them both to cut it out.

Whispel had always been the odd man out and duly testified against Davis and Robinson in return for a second-degree murder charge, stating that Valessa had held her mother down while Davis had stabbed her with the syringe. Valessa was too young to face the death penalty but she did face spending the rest of her natural life in jail for the count of first-degree murder. In one of the biggest upsets in the history of the State of Florida, however, her lawyers were able to secure a conviction on the lesser charge of third-degree murder, persuading the jury that two adult men had manipulated her. The decision of the court means that in all likelihood Valessa will leave prison while still in her thirties. Whispel, as part of a plea-bargain agreement, got 25 years, while Valessa's ex-teenage love, Davis, now awaits execution on Death Row.

## GROUNDED FOR LIFE

Perhaps the meanest teen of all time is the 13-year-old girl in Canada who recently wiped out her entire family with the help of her boyfriend, just because her parents disapproved of the relationship and had grounded her. In one of the bloodiest murders in Canadian history, on 22 April 2006, the teenage duo stabbed the girl's parents to death, as well as her brother, who was just eight years old. According to court transcripts, he begged his sister to spare him his life but to no avail. His sister (who cannot be named here for legal reasons) stabbed him twice in the chest, then handed her brother over to her boyfriend who slit the boy's throat.

While it was the boyfriend who had actually carried out the killings, it was ruled that the girl had purposefully and intentionally encouraged and persuaded him to kill her family. This emerged after several witnesses had come forward to testify that they had heard her say that she hated her family and wanted them all dead, while others had overheard her asking her boyfriend to kill them.

Just two hours after the murder, the duo were seen kissing and laughing in a nearby restaurant. They also went to a cocaine dealer's apartment where they had sex and later attended a party where they boasted of the killings, the boyfriend telling appalled guests that he had gutted his girlfriend's family 'like fish'. The killers were arrested the next day. In jail, the two swapped gushing love letters and the boyfriend proposed. His still-smitten girlfriend accepted.

It took the jury just less than four hours to convict the minor of three counts of first-degree murder, making her the youngest person ever to be convicted of murder in Canada. She is now serving four years in custody in a mental institution, which will be followed by four-and-a-half years under close community supervision, where she will be given a new identity.

The case received an unexpected twist after it was revealed that the girl's boyfriend seems to have genuinely believed that he was a 300-year-old werewolf and was in the habit of drinking his own blood. He also called himself 'Lycan'. Both had posted their own profiles on ultra-gothic websites Nexopia and Vampirefreaks.com; in one of the many profiles that he posted online, he claimed that he believed in 'Blood, Destruction, Guts, and Gore & Greed'. He also posted some gruesome (in more sense than one) poetry online. In one poem he said that he was going to kill his girlfriend's parents and slit their throats because of their 'insulince' (sic). His girlfriend, meanwhile, who claimed online that she was 15, also posted a picture of herself holding a handgun.

In fact, as teenagers spend more and more time communicating with their peers via the internet, the web has become a rich new source of information for investigators in 'bad seed' murder cases. At the same time, teenage MySpace accounts and blogs often provide a chilling insight into the mind of an adolescent killer. This is especially true of blogs in which teenagers often post their most intimate thoughts to a worldwide audience of complete strangers.

This was perfectly exemplified recently by the story of a Japanese schoolgirl who admitted to trying to kill her own mother on her online blog. The teenager had apparently become obsessed with the famous English poisoner Graham Young. For those of you who might not be acquainted with the case, Young attempted to wipe out his whole family by giving them increasing doses of thallium (a potent rat poison) in their tea when he was just 14 years old. He succeeded in killing his stepmother before being caught and was sent to Broadmoor. After his release, he killed two of his co-workers. The Japanese schoolgirl followed Young's earlier exploits more or less to the letter and managed to put her mother in a coma by lacing her food with rat poison, all the while calmly noting down the results on her online blog.

## DEADLY CYBER CRUSHES

Strange as it may seem, due to the increasing popularity of social networking websites, nowadays a deadly teenage crush does not have to involve a real teenager at all. Take the recent case of Lori Drew, who posed online as a 16-year-old boy so that she could find out what a teenage girl was saying about her daughter.

Drew's daughter and Megan Meier had once been friends but had fallen out, as teenage girls have a tendency to do. Lori Drew created a fake profile of a boy she called Josh Evans and contacted Meier through MySpace. Josh, according to his online profile, had just moved to Michigan from Florida, was being home-schooled and played the drums and the guitar. Along with the profile, the middle-aged mother also posted a picture of a good-looking 16-year-old boy. Then, when Megan Meier had become sufficiently drawn in by the non-existent but apparently smitten 16-year-old, Josh suddenly turned nasty. He began to insult her and abruptly broke off their friendship. After an hour-long argument in which both continued to trade insults and abuse, the distraught 13-year-old, who was on anti-depressant drugs, went to her room and hanged herself with her own belt.

Drew was indicted by a Los Angeles Federal Grand Jury on one count of conspiracy and three counts of 'accessing protected computers without authorisation to obtain information to inflict emotional distress'. She is now awaiting trial.

The murder of Brian Barrett at the hands of factory worker Thomas Montgomery represents another cyber crush that ended in tragedy. In 2005, husband and father of two Thomas Montgomery posed on an internet chat room as a bullet-scarred 18-year-old marine. Tommy, as he called himself, was looking for romance and had just got back from a tour in Iraq;

it wasn't long before the handsome marine had struck up a relationship with 'TalHotBlondbig50', a 17-year-old long-legged blonde from West Virginia whose real name was Jessie. Romance bloomed.

A few months later, the couple was sending each other letters in the post. To whet her hot young marine's appetite, Jessie sent him photos of herself in a bikini lounging by the pool and posted him a G-string. The affair quickly became so intense that the couple were spending almost every waking hour online chatting to each other. Even though they had never actually met, after only eight months the marine proposed – an offer that his blue-eyed blonde sweetheart immediately accepted.

But when Montgomery's wife stumbled upon an email between the two and learned of her husband's cyber romance, she immediately wrote to Jessie, telling her the truth. Along with the letter she included a picture of her pot-bellied, balding husband, along with his two children.

Jessie had been so drawn into the romance, though, that she wasn't sure who to believe at first, so she went online and managed to track down a co-worker of Montgomery's, a 22-year-old called Brian Barrett. Barrett was only too willing to confirm that her marine fiancé was not a marine at all but his middle-aged work colleague.

It wasn't long before Jessie had struck up a new online romance, though this time with the much more suitable Barrett. That made Montgomery mad. Not only had he been outed as a cyber predator stalking teenage girls, the love of his life was now flirting online with a co-worker.

Insults began to fly as Barrett and Jessie continued their cyber romance and Montgomery was left out in the cold. To make matters worse, Barrett would often brag about his new 17-year-old girlfriend to his colleagues at work. At the same time, however, Jessie seemed unable to completely break off her relationship with Montgomery and continued to keep in contact – only adding to Montgomery's sense of miserable frustration.

Matters reached a head on 15 September 2006. Montgomery waited for Barrett to finish his shift at the factory. As Barrett was sitting in his pick-up truck in the car park, Montgomery shot him with a .30-calibre rifle three times, at close range, killing him instantly.

It turned out, however, that Montgomery's so-called lover was as different from her online profile as he had been from his. When police went to find Jessie to interview her, they discovered that Jessie was not a 17-year-old blue-eyed blonde at all… but a frumpy, middle-aged housewife who had been sending Montgomery pictures of her teenage daughter.

# CHAPTER FIFTEEN
# DIG TWO GRAVES: TERRIBLE REVENGE

'Before you embark on a journey of revenge, dig two graves.' (Confucius)

Payback can be a very nasty affair, as the following tale of crazed revenge proves. From the enraged psychologist who murdered his own patient to the henpecked husband who slaughtered his entire family, revenge is without exception a very bloody business that leaves only further misery in its wake. 'Revenge is a dish best served cold', according to an old saying; these killings suggest that it is a dish probably best not served at all.

## UNHAPPY FAMILY: RONALD SHANABARGER

Perhaps the most harrowing revenge plot of all time was devised by Ronald Shanabarger. In 1998, Shanabarger got his wife pregnant so that he would one day be able to kill their baby and get some payback on her. The reason? In October 1996, Shanabarger's wife had refused to cut short a cruise and attend his father's funeral. According to the murder charge affidavit: 'He married her, got her pregnant, allowed time for her to bond with the child and then took its life.'

Once the pair were married, they had a son, whom they named Tyler. Seven months later, Shanabarger sprang his trap. On the evening of 20 June 1999, Amy Shanabarger came back from the local supermarket where she worked and found Tyler lying dead in his cot. The child was taken to the Indiana University Medical Center where an autopsy was performed and the pathologist ruled that Tyler had been a victim of sudden infant death syndrome. On the night of Tyler's funeral, however, Ronald Shanabarger confessed to his wife that he had killed their only son.

As she later testified in court, 'He said, "I killed Tyler." I said, "How?" And he said, "With Saran wrap."' After he had killed his son, Shanabarger told his wife, he had gone into the kitchen and made himself a sandwich. All the same it didn't take Shanabarger long to realise the enormity of what he had just done.

Shortly after his son's funeral, Shanabarger turned himself in to police at the Johnson County Sheriff's Office, where he confessed to his crime and begged police officers to shoot him where he stood. Shanabarger was handed down a life sentence in May 2002. Since then he has tried to appeal his sentence, an appeal that was summarily rejected in May 2006 by the Indiana Court of Appeals.

## PORNOGRAPHY AND PAYBACK: LI YIJIANG

When student Li Yijiang was gang raped in Beijing in December 2002, he sought out a terrible revenge on the six men who had assaulted him. The 25-year-old had made initial contact with the men through a homosexual, pornographic website and all concerned had agreed to meet at a local disco. There the six men got Li Yijiang drunk and took turns raping him. Almost immediately after his ordeal was over, Li Yijiang began plotting his revenge. Within six months he had managed to lure each one of his attackers away individually to isolated spots, where he murdered them and then cut off their genitals.

When it was discovered that the six murders had all been subscribers to the same pornographic internet site, police managed to track down Li Yijiang, who was arrested in August 2003. He promptly confessed to the six murders, for which he showed not the slightest trace of remorse.

The fact that the murders stemmed from an internet porn site was yet another justification for the Chinese government's recent crackdown on internet pornography and adult cinemas countrywide, especially near universities and schools. Apparently, Li Yijiang had been an excellent student until he had become addicted to pornography, or at least so his defence team had argued. But there was to be no mercy for Li Yijiang, or the 'Penis Slasher' as he had quickly but briefly become known the world over. Shortly after being found guilty, he was executed by firing squad.

## REVENGE OF A DYING MAN: MICHAEL LUPO

When ex-army commando-turned-Chelsea fashion boutique owner Michael Lupo learned that he had AIDS in March 1986, he decided to wreak revenge on the entire gay community, whom he blamed for his impending death. His first victim was 37-year-old James Burns, a railway worker he met in a gay bar. Lupo, who boasted that he had slept with at least 4,000 men during his lifetime, bit off his victim's tongue, strangled him to death, smeared the corpse with excrement and then mutilated the body with a razor.

He continued his quest for vengeance in the course of a two-month murder spree, strangling to death a homeless man, a waiter and a hospital worker, all of whom he picked up in gay bars. Lupo (or the 'Wolf Man' as he preferred to call himself) was finally brought to justice when one of his victims managed to escape after being very nearly strangled to death in a car park.

This victim was later instrumental in Lupo's capture. Soon after agreeing to help police track down the killer, he spotted Lupo in a gay bar in Brixton; Lupo was apparently scouring for his next potential victim. When arrested and taken in for questioning, the 33-year-old Lupo immediately admitted the killings and a further two attempted murders and was sentenced to life terms by the Old Bailey. He spent the last seven years of his life on a hospital ward in prison before finally succumbing to an AIDS-related illness in February 1995.

## DOING HUMANITY A FAVOUR? MARIO POGGI

In 1986, a serial killer called Angel Diaz Balbin was arrested and charged with the murder of over 20 prostitutes in Peru's capital city, Lima. Balbin, it was suspected, had raped and then dismembered his victims, dumping the remains in trash cans all over the city. His final capture was, of course, a huge relief to the citizens of Lima, who had been living under the shadow of the serial killer for several months, but to begin with Balbin refused to confess. In fact, he steadfastly refused to say a single word to police at all.

Unsure if Balbin was faking some kind of psychological disorder, police requested the help of famed psychologist Dr

Mario Poggi to try to get Balbin to talk and hopefully get a confession. As well as being a psychologist, Poggi had been a child prodigy, was a famous eccentric and had gained national fame as a pundit and outspoken TV personality; he also sported trademark dyed-green hair. To add to his CV, Poggi spoke five languages fluently, had studied in eminent universities all over Europe; he was also a notorious womaniser, hypnotist, sculptor, writer, journalist and even ventriloquist.

Eager as always for the media spotlight, as soon as he was asked to participate in the case, Poggi went to the magazine with the largest circulation in Peru and offered them an exclusive interview. Three days later, the story made the front page of the magazine, which ran a picture of Poggi examining the patient, while inside there was a three-page spread describing how the doctor had attempted to hypnotise his patient and get him to confess to his hideous crimes. Balbin, though, much to Poggi's annoyance, hadn't said a single word.

Poggi was absolutely certain of Balbin's guilt but was also sure that the killer would be released to a mental hospital, where he would be treated and perhaps released once again back into society. Certain that Balbin would kill if he ever got the chance, Poggi decided to take matters into his own hands. A few days after his interview with the magazine, Poggi requested that he be left alone with his patient, a request that was granted.

According to Poggi's later confession, Balbin had been left handcuffed with his hands tied behind his back in his cell. On entering the cell, Poggi removed the killer's clothes and his own in order to try to get the killer sexually aroused so that he would finally break and show him how he raped his victims before cutting them up and killing them. Yet the utterly impassive killer remained silent. In a rage, Poggi put the killer face down on the floor, removed his belt from his trousers and strangled him to death.

Appearing on national television as he was being taken away by police, Poggi was seen weeping uncontrollably and screaming, 'I saved humanity! I finished the monster.' Later, after his release from prison, Poggi said in an interview, 'I had to eliminate him. He was a bad element in society. I had to do it. My sacrifice was not a crime. All of the world flattered me for it. The whole world wanted to shake my hand and say, "Well done." I feel rewarded by society for what I have done. After all, what does it mean to sacrifice oneself? I gave everything to society, my diploma, my titles, my prestige... society has rewarded me for the loss of all these things, but I did it with a lot of love.'

Poggi recently claimed in an interview that he had not killed Balbin at all, that instead he had willingly taken a fall for the Peruvian police. According to this version of events, the police had lost their temper with the killer because he had refused to talk and so had kicked him to death in his cell; they then faked the autopsy to make it look like he had been strangled. Poggi claims that he had agreed to take the blame so that he would be able to study the psychology of prisoners in Peruvian jails after being told that he would only get a sentence of four months. In fact, he ended up serving five years. Poggi received a hero's welcome on his release, appeared regularly on chat shows and wrote an autobiography called *I'm the Only One Who Knows I'm a Jerk*.

Although there is no real solid evidence either way, many journalists and law-enforcement officials in Peru hold firmly to the belief that Poggi might well have strangled the wrong man, as prostitutes continued to suddenly disappear off the streets of Peru long after Balbin's arrest and vigilante-style murder.

## THE MAD MARINE: STEPHEN SCHAPS

One revenge murder case is so bizarrely grotesque that it is often taken wrongly for an urban myth. In 1993, when serviceman Stephen Schaps found that his wife had been cheating on him with buddy and fellow soldier Sergeant Glover – and that, worse still, his wife was pregnant with his friend's child – he went well and truly berserk. The furious GI hacked off his friend's head with an army knife and promptly drove off to the hospital where his wife was scheduled to give birth. He then showed his wife her boyfriend's head, which he took out of a bag.

Completely covered in blood, the marine told her, 'Look, Diane – Glover's here! He'll sleep with you every night now. Only you won't sleep – because all you'll see is this!'

When doctors arrived at the scene, Schaps had laid the head on a nightstand so that the decapitated head was looking straight at his wife.

Just so there is absolutely no doubt that this did actually happen, here is the account according to court transcripts:

'Placing the severed head into an athletic bag, appellant took it to the hospital where his wife had been admitted when it was feared she might be suffering a miscarriage (of a child by the deceased). To the horror of his wife and hospital personnel, appellant burst into her room, pulled the head out of the bag, deposited it on her bedside tray table, and physically forced her to look at it.'

One of the German doctors who rushed to the room described the killer as talking 'logically' about what he had just done while they waited for the police to arrive. The doctor recalled, 'And the context of what he talked about to us was that he felt humiliated and betrayed by his wife. I remember that he told us that he found a list in her car with several names. And he repeated some times, all of this. And then he told us that he had learned how to disconnect a head from a human body.'

During his trial, his wife stated that she recalled her husband saying, 'Don't underestimate me. I'm very skilled at what I do. I studied this, I planned this, I calculated this.'

## REVENGE FOR A TRAGEDY: VITALI KALOYEV

Whether architect Vitali Kaloyev had actually intended to kill air-traffic controller Peter Nielsen all along will never be known for sure, because to this day Kaloyev claims that he does not remember stabbing Nielsen to death. Instead, he insists he tracked down the air-traffic controller to his suburban home in Gloten in Zurich simply because he had wanted an apology, or at least some kind of explanation, for the death of his entire family in a plane crash in July 2002.

Danish-born Nielsen had been on duty when the Bashkirian Airlines passenger plane had crashed into a DHL cargo plane above southern Germany. Nielsen had wrongly ordered the passenger plane to descend when he should have ordered it to climb. Seventy-one people had died in the resulting crash. The majority of the victims were schoolchildren from the village of Ufa en route via Moscow to a school outing in Madrid and among the victims had been Kaloyev's wife and two young children. Three executives of the air-traffic control company SkyGuide had been handed down 12-month suspended sentences for manslaughter, but Nielsen had never been prosecuted.

## DIG TWO GRAVES: TERRIBLE REVENGE

On 11 November 2003, Kaloyev received a letter in which SkyGuide offered him 60,000 Swiss francs (£29,000) for the death of his wife and a further 50,000 Swiss francs (£23,000) for the death of each of his two children, in return for his promising to make no more legal claims against the company. The way the life of his family was apparently being haggled over further infuriated Kaloyev, who decided to meet with the company director in person.

Kaloyev arrived in Zurich in February 2004 in an attempt to receive an official apology from SkyGuide's director, Alan Rossier. As he was unable to meet with him, he travelled instead to Nielsen's home. He arrived at the house, carrying a knife with a 14cm blade, stood in Nielsen's front garden and waited.

When Nielsen came outside and demanded to know what he wanted, they began to argue. Kaloyev claimed later that Nielsen had refused to apologise to him. 'He murmured something to me,' Kaloyev later testified in court. 'Then I showed him some pictures of my children and said, "They were my children. What would you feel if you saw your children in coffins?"... He hit me on the hand, when I was holding the envelope with the photographs of my children. I only remember that I had a very nasty feeling, as if the bodies of my children were turning in their graves.'

Kaloyev stabbed Nielsen repeatedly, threw the knife away and fled the scene, leaving Nielsen to bleed to death. He was arrested the next day and later handed down a sentence of eight years for premeditated murder, for which he only served five years and three months. On his return to Russia, Kaloyev received a hero's welcome and was mobbed at the airport by well-wishers; the streets were lined with banners showing the killer their love and support.

## CULT KILLER: RICKY RODRIGUEZ

The 'Children of God' was a free-love hippie Christian cult, founded by self-proclaimed prophet Ricky Berg in Huntington Beech, California, in 1968. In order to raise membership for his new group, Berg promoted a novel new Christian recruitment practice known as 'flirty fishing', whereby cult members would use sex in order to recruit new members. As well as bringing in cash in return for sex, many new members were persuaded to join the cult for good.

Ricky Rodriguez was one of the estimated 300 'love babies' that were born as a direct consequence of flirty fishing. In fact, Rodriguez was cult royalty, being the son of Karen Zerby (Ricky Berg's favourite consort) and a hotel waiter in Tenerife. The free-loving cult founder had no problem with the fact that the boy's mother was having sex outside the relationship and when the boy was two years old Zerby and Berg would claim that he would one day be a prophet and deliver humanity 'out of great sorrow and bondage'. But the boy, whom they would raise as the holy prince and saviour of the Children of God, would in later life turn crazed avenger and killer, hunting down one of the key members of the cult before turning the gun on himself.

The cult's message of free love had for a long time had horrific connotations. Many ex-members have since claimed that the free love message extended to children and that minors were passed around among cult members for sex – a practice that extended as far as the cult leader and his consort's own son. Rodriguez often claimed to have suffered sexual abuse at the hands of the nannies who reared him and, he later said, also at the hands of his own mother.

Not only this, but, when he escaped the cult and tried to make a life of his own, he found himself hopelessly unprepared to make his way in the world. Deciding to wreak revenge on the cult that had ruined his life, he resolved to track down his mother and kill her.

His mother, though, had long disappeared without a trace. Having posted complaints about his upbringing in the family on several internet sites, and unable to discover his mother's location, he apparently settled for murdering Angela Smith, whom he also hoped might be able to give him his mother's address. Ex-cult member Smith had been personal secretary to David Berg for almost 20 years.

On the eve of his short-lived revenge spree against the cult, Rodriguez videotaped his confession while loading his Glock .23 handgun and later posted the video to friends, asking them to pass it on to the media. In the video, he seems pretty calm, listening to music and sitting at his kitchen table. As he drinks a beer, he debates with himself the pros and cons of different handguns. He also wields his K Bar knife, which he says is his 'weapon of choice', which he wants for 'taking out scum' and 'taking out the fucking trash'. And, as he talks, glimpses of undisguised rage rise, with increasing frequency, to the surface.

'Fucking animals,' he says at one point, when talking about the abuse other children suffered at the hands of cult members. 'I hate those fuckers. They are going to fucking get it too if I have anything to do with it… Anger does not begin to describe how I feel about these people and what they have done… It's going to feel so fucking good… liberating.'

Then, Rodriguez starts talking about his mother. 'I'm going to keep going until I get her or someone else gets her. Justice will be done… Maybe fate will smile on me. The God of War. The God of Revenge. Maybe they will grant me happy hunting.'

Rodriguez duly invited Angela Smith to go to dinner with him. When she arrived at his apartment in Tucson, he stabbed her three times and slit her throat with his K Bar knife. Revenge was hardly sweet for Ricky Rodriguez, though. After it was all over, he then drove across the Californian border to a small desert town and blew his brains out.

## 'IT WAS THEM OR ME': RICARDO BARREDA

On a warm, pleasant Sunday morning in November 1992, Ricardo Barreda went downstairs for breakfast. His two daughters, 26-year-old Adriana and 24-year-old Cecilia Barreda, had already eaten, as had his mother-in-law and his wife, Gladys. The impeccably neat and apparently mild-mannered dentist told his wife that he planned to do some chores around the house, such as cleaning some cobwebs from the ceiling in the hall. He was feeling pretty relaxed, he later recalled, until his wife replied, 'Go and do that. Go and clean. Jobs for little pussies like you suit you the best. It's the only thing you're good for.'

Barreda was used to being talked to that way by his wife, and by the rest of his family for that matter, so he simply turned on his heel and walked out. He then started looking for a crash helmet. (The ultra-careful Barreda always wore a crash helmet if he was going to climb a ladder.) It was while he was rummaging around for it in a cupboard upstairs that he saw the shotgun. It had been in the cupboard for many years and usually he didn't notice it. That day, for some reason, was different. The cartridges were on the floor by the side of the gun.

'And, well, it was odd,' he later testified. 'I felt a force that made me take it. I was sick of their jokes, their hatred, their

186

indifference and their lack of love towards me. I went back downstairs and started shooting.'

He shot his wife, Gladys, and then his youngest daughter. He then killed his mother-in-law as she came downstairs. When his eldest daughter saw the bodies lying on the floor, she screamed, 'What have you done, you son of a bitch?' He killed her too. It was 9.15 a.m.

In jail, Barreda remained unrepentant. 'Seeing them on the floor and thinking that they were dead, I felt relief and a sense of liberation because justice had been done,' he told reporters. 'I would do it again,' he added, 'because it was a living hell and they were driving me crazy. It was either them or me.'

According to Barreda, his murderous rampage was an act of vengeance for years and years of mental abuse at the hands of his wife, his two daughters and his mother-in-law, who together constantly plotted against him and mocked him under his own roof. His wife, he claimed, had often threatened to kill him with the help of her two daughters. He also claimed that he had been a victim of physical as well as mental abuse.

'Once I wanted to give one of my daughters a slap and she caused a huge commotion. She hurt my face and she hit me... My wife used to say terrible things to me, like, "You make me sick, you are nothing but a piece of shit."... I told them once. I said, "Look, this family is sick, why not seek help?" And they said that I was the one that was making them sick. The fact is that I lived alone. My wife didn't want to sleep with me. We did not have any sexual contact. So I had wet dreams at night. One day I called her over and I showed her the stained sheets and she just laughed at me.'

At his trial, Barreda claimed that he had been driven to an act of temporary insanity in the face of constant and systematic abuse. The judge didn't buy it, however, and he was sentenced to a life of incarceration. He was asked to sign autographs while on trial, though, and received a warm welcome when he entered prison. And, incredible as it may sound, today Ricardo Barreda has become something of a national hero to many henpecked Latin American men.

## CHAPTER SIXTEEN

# BIZARRE BODY DISPOSAL

Body disposal at the hands of some of the most infamous killers of all time.

By utterly destroying a body, or concealing it in a place where it will never be found, many killers may have believed that they have committed the perfect murder: police are far less likely to launch an investigation if they don't have a dead body to go on, and without a body the case is invariably categorised as a missing person's inquiry. In their attempt to get away with murder, killers have subjected their victims' bodies to every kind of indignity imaginable. They have buried them under the floorboards, stuffed them into freezers, thrown them from planes into oceans and crushed their bones into dust.

## MURDER ON THE FARM: ROBERT PICKTON
Perhaps the most sickening way to keep a murder 'bodiless' was demonstrated recently by Canadian serial killer Robert Pickton. Pickton was found guilty in December 2007 on six counts of second-degree murder and is now serving a 25-year

sentence without the possibility of parole. But Pickton, police suspect, could well be responsible for at least a further 40 disappearances.

Pickton preyed on prostitutes in the downtown eastside area of Vancouver, picking them up and bringing them back to his isolated farm in Port Coquitlam in British Colombia. There, after giving them alcohol and drugs, he strangled them. According to witness testimony at his trial, Pickton then skinned his victims on a meat hook, gutted them and then fed them to the pigs on his farm. What the pigs didn't eat went into 45-gallon drums filled with industrial waste.

Witness for the prosecution Andrew Bellwood, who stayed on Pickton's farm for six weeks, told jurors that Pickton had told him how he had strangled his victims and then disposed of their bodies. 'He told me that he'd kill them and take them into the barn and bleed them and give them to the pigs,' Mr Bellwood told sickened jurors at the killer's trial.

When Pickton's farm was searched in February 2002, investigators found human skulls and teeth in his freezer as well as human blood in the slaughterhouse and in the pig troughs. This led local health officials to issue a frantic warning to anyone who might have bought pork from the farmer, as the pigs could well have feasted on human remains. Luckily, though, the meat was never distributed commercially. That said, about 40 friends and neighbours of Pickton ate meat from the farm during barbecues, or were given some to take home with them to eat later.

Pickton was by no means the first killer to feed his victims to pigs. Joseph Brigand killed at least 12 homeless men and fed them to the prize-winning hogs on his California ranch. He was arrested and sent to San Quentin jail in 1902. And, as terrible as it may seem, other depraved killers in the past have shown absolutely no qualms at all about feeding their victims to animals.

Joe Ball, variously known as the 'Bluebeard of Texas', the 'Butcher of Elmendorf' and the 'Alligator Man', worked in a similar fashion. Born to an affluent family in Texas, Ball had money and a university degree but chose instead to spend much of his adult life bootlegging and gambling before finally opening a rowdy roadside bar called the Sociable Inn, which soon became a popular hotspot among the locals. Especially popular was the alligator pit that Ball built out back. There, he invited customers to watch as he fed the alligators live cats and dogs.

Things got really out of hand, though, once the bar doors were closed and he shut up shop for the night. Ball murdered an estimated 15 waitresses and then disposed of their bodies by feeding them, bit by bit, to his three pet alligators. If asked where his waitresses had suddenly gone, Ball would claim that they had upped sticks and gone to work elsewhere. Their relatives, though, were not convinced.

Police finally questioned Ball's long-suffering handyman who confessed that at gunpoint he had been forced to help Ball get rid of two bodies and led the authorities to the remains of two ex-waitresses: Hazel Brown (she had been shot and then dismembered) and Minnie Gotthard (pregnant at the time, with Ball's child). It later turned out that a neighbour, who had actually seen Ball feed one of the girls to his alligators, had been so terrified that he had fled to California and had never been seen since. In September 1938, as he was about to be arrested, Ball took a gun from a drawer in his bar and shot himself. The alligators were donated to the San Antonio zoo.

The most harrowing addition to this grisly category came only recently. In October 2007, an ex-convict was found guilty of feeding a five-year-old girl live to alligators. Harrel Franklin Braddy assaulted Shandelle Maycock, whom he had met through the local church, and choked her in a field in the Everglades. She survived the attack but Braddy, believing she was dead, drove off with Maycock's daughter, Quatisha, who had witnessed the attack. He then left her to die in a swamp known as 'Alligator Alley'.

Braddy was found guilty of first-degree murder and the jury voted 11 to 1 in favour of the death penalty. Circuit Judge Leonard Glick upheld the jury's recommendation that Braddy should die by lethal injection. In his sentencing, he grimly summed up the deeds of the defendant: 'The defendant caused this five-year-old to die, alone in the wilderness, and to be mutilated by monsters of the swamp,' he said. 'Adults are supposed to protect children from monsters. They are not supposed to be the monsters themselves.'

## HOUSE WITH A HISTORY: DR SAMSON PERERA

In February 2004, while watching a crime documentary called *Arrest and Trial* on Channel Five, a couple realised with growing horror that the programme was actually about a gruesome murder that had been committed in their own house. The previous tenant had been dental biologist Dr Samson Perera, who had murdered his 13-year-old adopted daughter and then cut her into pieces. Police had found 105 pieces of flesh and bone secreted around the suburban home in Wakefield, Sheffield. Perera had hidden his victim's remains under floorboards, in coffee pots and in the garden; a police search even revealed an entire human spine curled up at the bottom of a plant pot.

At the time of the murder, Perera had claimed that his daughter had gone home because she had been homesick and missed her native country of Sri Lanka. But, when police flew out there to meet with her birth family, they were able to confirm that she had never flown back home at all. Perera claimed that the body parts were pork before changing his story and telling police that they were in fact body parts from a cadaver he had brought back with him to experiment on at home. Police were able to prove that the parts they had found in his home did not belong to a cadaver from a lab and Perera was sentenced to life imprisonment in March 1986.

After watching the documentary, the couple immediately put the house on the market and sold it for a loss of £8,000. They then sued the previous owners for damages, though ultimately they lost their case in the Appeals Court. Lord Justice Peter Gibson summarised by saying that, while he sympathised with the couple's case, he could not rule in their favour as the previous owners were under no legal obligation to inform the buyers about the house's grisly past, even though he added, 'There is the possibility parts of the victim's body might still lie undiscovered in this house.'

## LIVING WITH THE DEAD: DENNIS NILSEN

The most famous killer in this gruesome category has to be Dennis Nilsen, who disposed of his victims in his North London flat: 195 Melrose Avenue. Nilsen was reluctant to part with the bodies straight away. He would sometimes fetch them from beneath the floorboards, bath them, prop them up on his living-room sofa and talk to them or have sex with them.

When he was tired of the bodies, Nilsen, who had been a cook and a butcher while serving 11 years in the army, invariably dismembered his victims on the floor of his kitchen, boiled the heads of his victims in saucepans and then burned the bodies in bonfires at the end of the garden. He then dumped the internal organs in the rubbish or down the drains, or just over the fence for animals to eat. At the height of his killing spree, Nilsen had three bodies in his flat: one under the floorboards, another stuffed in a wardrobe and a third crammed in a cupboard under the kitchen sink.

In fact, Nilsen soon became convinced that if he moved home then it would stop him from killing – as getting rid of the bodies in his own home had just been too easy. Despite the frequent bonfires and terrible stink emanating from his house, his activities had not even raised the faintest of suspicions among his neighbours. Once he had moved to his new flat at 23 Cranley Gardens, Muswell Hill, he killed three more times before he managed to block the drains with the internal organs of his victims, which he had flushed down the toilet. When police searched his flat, they found the remains of three young men stashed in bin bags in cupboards throughout his home.

## INFAMOUS ADDRESSES

Rather than dismembering their victims at home, many other infamous killers have simply stashed the bodies in their own house. John Wayne Gacy, convicted murderer of 33 men, would sometimes keep his victims for days, either under his bed or in the attic, before putting them in the crawlspace under his two-bedroom ranch house on the outskirts of Chicago. Police found a total of 27 corpses hidden there and in their search for more bodies they destroyed the entire property, finding in the process a further two male victims buried in the concrete of his patio. Gacy invariably handcuffed his victims, sexually assaulted them and then strangled them, stuffing their mouths with socks or their own underwear to muffle their screams.

When serial killers are targeting drifters or picking up men or women at random, they can often get away with murder for years on end if they can stomach living in close proximity to the corpses of their victims. Theirs are invariably the addresses that we remember, such as 10 Rillington Place (Reginald Christie), 25 Cromwell Street (Fred and Rosemary West) or The Oxford Apartments (Jeffrey Dahmer).

A less-well-known killer with the same modus operandi was Frederick Bailey Deeming, who killed his entire family and then buried them under the floorboards in his living room in August 1891. Indeed, using a false name, Bailey had rented the house – in Rainhill, near Liverpool – expressly for that purpose. He waited until his family was asleep and then, having knocked his four children and wife, Marie, unconscious with the blunt end of an axe, he slit their throats.

After burying them under the floor, he left the house – indeed, he left the country, travelling to Australia, where he soon married 27-year-old Emily Mather. He then did exactly the same thing to her. Authorities were alerted to Mather's body when the owner of the house noticed a strong smell coming from beneath the floorboards while showing a prospective tenant his property. A journalist in Liverpool traced Deeming's previous home and, on learning that Deeming's family had suddenly disappeared, persuaded the authorities to dig up the floorboards, uncovering the remains of his first wife and children. Deeming was caught and arrested in March 1892 in Perth, Australia, and was hanged two months later.

## YOUR VERY OWN HELL HOLE

American serial killer Herman Webster Mudgett (known more commonly under the pseudonym HH Holmes) famously built his very own murder hotel in 1893, specifically designed so that he could entice, kill and then dispose of his victims all on the premises. Holmes started building the hotel in 1888 so that it would be ready for the Chicago World Fair, where he planned to lure young women to their deaths. The World Fair also provided him with cover, as he believed (rightly, as it turned out) that the women would not be missed among the millions of guests flocking to Chicago each day to attend the fair. He later confessed to 27 murders, but is suspected of killing at least 50 women.

Holmes designed the layout of the hotel himself, ensuring that not one contractor stayed on long enough to realise that they were actually building an enormous murder machine on a busy street corner in Chicago. So that builders were unaware of the wider context of the building, and to save money at the same time, Holmes simply refused to pay them, telling them that their work wasn't up to scratch, and contracted new ones.

Holmes kept his apartment on the third floor, guests stayed on the second floor and on the first floor he built shops. Below that was a basement with a walk-in vault and ostensibly a kiln designed for producing sheet glass. But the kiln was actually a crematorium, where Holmes could turn a body into ash in a matter of minutes. Also in the basement, Holmes kept an acid vat in which police would later find eight human ribs, pits filled with quicklime and a bloodstained dissecting table.

Another killer to purposefully go about creating his very own hell hole was Gary Heidnik. Over a four-month period, beginning in November 1986, Heidnik kidnapped six women from the streets of Philadelphia and chained them to water pipes in his basement. There, he brutally raped and tortured them at his leisure. After weeks of abuse, his first captive, Sandra Lindsay, was handcuffed to a beam and left hanging there for days. When she died, Heidnik dragged her upstairs and dismembered her with a power saw. He then blended parts of her flesh in the blender and mixed it up with 'Alpo' brand dog food. He fed this hideous concoction to his dogs and then made his five remaining 'slaves' eat it too; he put the limbs in the freezer and labelled them 'dog food'.

Heidnik was able to kill another of his 'sex slaves', Deborah Dudley, before he was finally arrested thanks to the resourcefulness of Josefina Rivera. Rivera, his second kidnap victim, managed to gain Heidnik's confidence over a period of time, to the extent that he agreed to let her go as long as she promised to come back with a new 'slave'. Once free, she told horrified police of her ordeal; they immediately went to his house and, on seeing the dungeon below, arrested him. Heidnik, an investment whiz who had made a small fortune on the stock market, went for an insanity plea during his trial to avoid the death sentence. The jury didn't buy it, though, and Heidnik was sentenced to death on 3 July 1988. He was finally put to death 11 years later.

## BODILESS MURDERS

When a killer manages to make a body disappear completely, the case is called a 'Bodiless' murder by police officials. These are notoriously tough cases to crack and investigators must be absolutely convinced that a crime has been committed before bringing any charges against a possible suspect. The problem is that there is always a very real possibility that the police have got it wrong and that the victim will later show up somewhere unscathed.

This happened quite recently in Queensland, Australia. In April 2003, Natasha Ryan, who was believed to have been abducted and murdered by a serial killer, was found to be alive and well and living in her boyfriend's house just a few blocks from her parents' home. She had been hiding there for almost five years and had failed to appear even when her family had held a memorial service in her honour. Ryan, who was 14 when she had disappeared, had run off to go and live with her boyfriend, who was eight years her senior and, afraid that her parents would disapprove of the relationship, had remained in hiding ever since. She was found halfway through her supposed 'murderer's' trial after an anonymous tip-off.

But often foul play is most certainly involved and thankfully police don't need a body to secure a murder conviction. The first successful conviction in a 'bodiless' murder case in the UK was that of James Camb. Camb murdered Eileen Isabella Ronnie Gibson on 18 October 1947 onboard a ship, and then stuffed her body out of a porthole and into the ocean. Camb claimed that Gibson had suddenly died during sex and that he had thrown the body overboard in a panic. However, scratches on his arm as well as traces of blood and urine on Gibson's bed pointed to an attempted rape, during which Camb had strangled Gibson to death. It took the jury 40 minutes to find Gibson guilty of first-degree murder.

All the same, without a body, justice can be a long time in coming for killers who manage by their own ingenuity to make a body disappear. Plastic surgeon Dr Robert Bierenbaum managed to get away with murder for almost 15 years because there was no body to serve as evidence of his crime.

# BIZARRE BODY DISPOSAL

According to Bierenbaum, on 7 July 1985, his wife had walked out of their Manhattan apartment after a violent argument and had never come back. Neighbours later testified that the couple often argued; as police dug further, they discovered that the couple's marriage was on extremely rocky ground and had been for some time. Not only had Gail Bierenbaum been seeing several other men behind her husband's back, she had also been planning to leave him for many months. There were even some bizarre reports (which were never actually confirmed) that Dr Bierenbaum had at one point attempted to flush his wife's cat down the toilet because he was jealous of the attention she paid it and had started choking his wife just because he had caught her smoking a cigarette.

Police suspicions were aroused almost immediately because on the day Gail Bierenbaum had gone missing her husband, a qualified pilot, had taken a two-hour flight in a rented Cessna 172 aircraft over the Atlantic Ocean – something he had failed to tell police about when first questioned. He had also tried to alter the flight log. Police believed that his wife had never left the apartment at all – or, at least, not alive. Instead, during the argument he had choked her to death. He had then dismembered her body, put it in a large duffel bag and dumped it into the sea.

Because the body had never been recovered, Dr Robert Bierenbaum remained a free man for the next 15 years, during which time he started a new family and began a successful plastic surgery practice in Las Vegas and North Dakota. However, the prosecution team was able to convince the court that Gail Bierenbaum had no reason to kill herself or simply make herself vanish off the face of the earth. They were also able to prove that her husband had a motive and the opportunity to kill his wife and dispose of the body. In October 2000, Dr Robert Bierenbaum was finally found guilty of second-degree murder and sentenced to 20 years in jail.

# CHAPTER SEVENTEEN
# BLOODY PACKAGES

Be careful before opening that slightly
damp package delivered unexpectedly on your
doorstep. You might be in for a very nasty
surprise.

Confronted with the problem of how to remove a whole body from a house without alerting the neighbours, many killers in the past have taken the corpse piecemeal through the front door and then disposed of it all over town. For the person who has the bad luck to actually come across one of these packages, it can be a very traumatic and nasty surprise; what's more, it can often prove an almost impossible task for the police to identify the body.

Perhaps the most infamous bloody parcel case in the UK is that of the Brighton Trunk Murder, which for a while earned Brighton the name 'The Queen of Slaughtering Places' – a twist on its much older nickname, 'The Queen of Watering Places'.

On 17 June 1934, a stationmaster noticed a bad smell coming from a trunk at Brighton railway station; when he opened it, he found the torso of a woman wrapped in brown paper. Other train stations were alerted and three days later police found another foul-smelling parcel, this one wrapped inside a suitcase at King's Cross station. The case contained the body's legs and feet, but the head and arms were never located. All police were able to discover was that the body belonged to a pregnant woman of around 25 years of age.

This wasn't the first time that a body had been put in a trunk and left at a London train station, though. On 6 May 1927, retired army sergeant John Robinson murdered prostitute Minnie Bonati, dismembered her body, wrapped it into five parcels and put the body in a large black trunk. He then hailed a cab and deposited the trunk at Charing Cross station at the left luggage office.

Two days later, an attendant noticed a strong smell coming from the trunk and alerted Scotland Yard. Because the trunk had been so heavy, Robinson had enlisted the help of a taxi driver to help him carry it to his taxi and the driver had remembered picking him up and taking him to Charing Cross station. Robinson immediately confessed when he was picked up by policemen. 'I want to tell you all about it,' he told them. 'I done it and cut her up.'

Robinson was hanged at Pentonville jail on 12 August 1927.

Both of these cases are quite well known. A far less familiar case (in fact, this is the first account of it ever to appear in English) is the story of the Barrancas Ripper, who only killed one woman, but still managed to cause a city-wide panic when he left a number of neatly wrapped parcels filled with his handiwork all over Buenos Aires in the very hot summer of 1955.

The first person unlucky enough to spot one of his parcels was priest Juan Andrés Smolen, who saw a large, rather oddly shaped package in a ditch as he was leaving a train station. Something about the parcel bothered him, though he was never able to say exactly why. It looked like... well, just to be sure he went back to the station, found a policeman and asked him to come with him and have a closer look. When the policeman bent over and undid the string he immediately recoiled: inside the parcel, and carefully wrapped up in brown paper, was a woman's torso.

Six days later, a housewife was on her way to the park with her two children when she spotted a parcel that had been dumped in a ditch at the side of the road. She immediately covered her children's eyes and told them to look the other way while she went running for help; she was sure she had seen what appeared to be a foot sticking out of the paper wrapping. Again, the foot had been quite carefully wrapped up in brown paper and lying next to it police found a human thigh.

That same afternoon, a sailor on guard duty in Buenos Aires harbour heard a scream from a member of a ship's crew. When he rushed over, he saw that the crewman was pointing wildly at the water. There, among a pile of newspapers, was a human hand. When police went out to have a closer look, they found a thigh as well as a bundle of papers containing a hand, two arms and a severed human head.

The Argentine press had a field day. The body had been cut up with a pretty steady hand, it seemed, and quite expertly too. At the same time, every single scrap of clothing had been removed, along with the woman's fingertips, making it impossible to identify the body. The press postulated wildly that they were dealing with a mad surgeon or perhaps a butcher and were soon making comparisons between the recent discoveries and the past activities of Jack the Ripper. More bodies, the press hinted, were imminent.

By February 1955, no less than a hundred police officers were working full-time on the case and trying to identify the body. The problem was, they had next to nothing to go on. All police were actually able to say for sure was that the torso belonged to a woman in her early twenties and the only real lead they had was a very recent surgical scar just below her collarbone.

Acting on the only lead they had, detectives sent photos of the scar to every hospital in Buenos Aires in the hope that a local surgeon might recognise his own handiwork. The scar was fresh, so the operation was recent. Perhaps they might get lucky. To begin with, nobody came forward. Indeed, it soon began to seem so hopeless that a district judge decided to try a very different tack altogether and ordered that the head be put on display at the local morgue. That way, all of those who had reported missing female relatives could go and try to identify it.

On 1 March, the morgue doors opened. Thirty-nine women and 11 men waited grimly to see the head. Nobody recognised it. Then, on the second day, police finally got the break that they needed. A surgeon had finally recognised the scar on the back of the torso as bearing his handiwork and remembered that he had performed an operation of that type only recently. The woman, he remembered, had been hit by a truck. She had been lucky, though, and only suffered a fractured collarbone.

From hospital records, police were able to obtain the exact date of the operation and the name of the woman. The surgeon was then shown photos of the woman's head, to see if he recognised her. He did. The woman he had performed the operation on was called Alcira Methyger. She had been 28 years old, worked as a maid and lived in Buenos Aires.

Police immediately went to talk with her employers, a

wealthy family who lived on Chacabuco Street in the capital. They told them that after her accident Methyger had spent the summer working for the family in their holiday home in the coastal resort town of Mar del Plata, but during that time she had received numerous telegrams from one of her many suitors, a 38-year-old travelling salesman called Jorge Burgos. Just before the summer was about to end, Methyger announced to her employers that she was quitting for good and that she was leaving for Buenos Aires on the next train. They hadn't heard from her since.

Next, police went to talk to Alcira's sister. Had she seen Alcira since she had got back to Buenos Aires? Her sister said that she had not. She did know, though, that Alcira had left her job and that she had come back to Buenos Aires to see Burgos, but she had not seen her or talked to her since then. When she had gone looking for her in Buenos Aires at Burgos's apartment, where Alcira told her she would be staying, Burgos had told her that Alcira had won a considerable sum of money on the roulette wheel while in Mar del Plata. She had used the money, he had told her, to buy a bus ticket north to the city of Cordoba, where she planned to settle down.

By this time, police were convinced that Burgos was their man and on 2 March they went to arrest him at his home. But Burgos had just taken the train to Mar del Plata, where he apparently had some important business to attend to, and his family didn't know when he would return. A patrol car raced out of the city and managed to get to the next station just in time to intercept the train en route as it approached Mar del Plata. They found Burgos sitting alone in a cabin and when they searched him they found that he was carrying Methyger's diary, along with a few scraps of her clothing. He immediately confessed to the crime. In fact, as one of the detectives in the case later recalled, he seemed relieved that it was all over.

Burgos was from a middle-class family and lived with his parents and younger sister in an affluent neighbourhood called Barrancas in Buenos Aires (hence the popular nickname for the crime). Apparently, he spent much of his free time reading detective novels. He had graduated from high school, had studied several languages, was proficient in English and French and had been a well-behaved student. One policeman later remembered the moment that Burgos had been brought into the station for questioning. Every policeman in the station came to have a good look at the 'Butcher of Barrancas', one of the most famous murderers in Argentina's history: 'He was sitting there trembling like a little boy with his eyes shut and his teeth shut tight together,' the policeman later recalled. 'I was sent to keep watch over him as the police were afraid that he might kill himself. Police from all over came over to catch a glimpse of this curious example of a caged man. I suddenly felt sorry for him. He touched my arm lightly. A tear ran down his cheek. Burgos whispered to me, "Mum and Dad… they were so happy. Look now. What a mess."'

When the press learned who Burgos was and that he had confessed, it made a strange final twist to the story. The apparently inoffensive, harmless-looking, slightly chubby and balding middle-aged man who still lived with his parents – this was the so-called 'Barrancas Ripper'?

What had really happened that night? What had driven this well-educated and seemingly gentle young man to kill? According to Burgos, it had all begun with a terrible and violent argument after he had finally learned that Alcira had been using him all along and didn't love him at all. For ten years, Burgos had been in love with her but she had never once returned his affections. She had seemed to warm to him lately, though – or, at least, that's what he had thought. When she had finally accepted his offer to come to Buenos Aires and stay with him while his parents were away on holiday, he had been overjoyed.

But when Alcira arrived in Buenos Aires, Burgos soon found out that he had been mistaken. She had been seeing someone behind his back and it turned out she had no intention of living with him or marrying him. He had even found some love letters from another man hidden in the pages of a book she gave him. But he went ahead anyway and asked her to marry him. She laughed in his face. During the violent quarrel that had ensued, Burgos called her 'a lying whore'. She lashed out. He punched her and then throttled her.

He told police that he had tried to revive her but it was no good. She was dead. He put her on the bed in his bedroom. From the crime novels he loved reading, Burgos knew that if the body was never identified he stood a much greater chance of getting away with murder. So, he took off her clothes and carried her to the bathroom. He cut off her head first and spent the rest of the night cutting the body into pieces in the bath, drinking a bottle of whisky as he did so. Then he went to the stationers and bought wrapping paper and string; he spent the next few days travelling firstly by train and then by bus, dumping his parcels all over town.

According to one detective who was involved in the case, Burgos was deeply regretful about what he had done. 'He cried like a baby,' the detective remembered, 'and did not stop repeating that it had never been his intention to kill her. I tried to explain to him that Alcira hadn't really been the kind of girl you would have wanted to marry anyway but there was nothing you could say to him. He kept on crying and saying that he loved her.'

Judge Cesar Black handed Burgos a sentence of 14 years in jail, which was reduced by appeal to 11 years and then reduced again to nine years and seven months for good behaviour. The murder became so infamous that soon after Burgos's imprisonment a book appeared called *I Didn't Kill Alcira*, with Burgos credited as the author. (In fact, it had been written by his lawyer, as a way to earn his fee back from the sales of the book.) It was a bestseller in Argentina.

In a final bizarre twist to this case, Burgos's parents died while he was in prison and left him the apartment in their will. Having nowhere else to go, the Barrancas Ripper moved straight back in and he lived there until he died, presumably sleeping in the same bed where he had stripped Alcira's lifeless corpse and washing in the same bath where he had dismembered her all those years earlier.

## GOING POSTAL

Incredible as it may seem, while some killers like Burgos dump the body parts themselves, other killers have actually used the postal service to get rid of the bodies of their victims, mailing them bit by bit to different addresses. In fact, it seems to be quite a popular tactic today, with frequent accounts in the press of people receiving bloody and totally unexpected parcels all over the world.

Usually when someone receives a human body part in the post, it is not the result of foul play but the result of a mix-up made by hospital administrators, the postal service or sometimes both. As hospital researchers and doctors regularly send body parts in the post, it is inevitable that the odd human limb or internal organ gets sent to the wrong address.

For instance, three years ago in Missouri, FedEx workers opened up a package that seemed to be leaking and discovered two legs and an arm that had been sent by a donor research company in Las Vegas. In 2007, another parcel delivery service, DHL, made a mistake and delivered a bubble-wrapped liver and part of a human head to a horrified couple in Michigan. The body parts had been sent from a lab in China and should have been on their way to a research laboratory in the States. Most recently, a human eyeball was accidentally delivered to a hotel in Hobart, Australia; when the receptionist saw what was in the parcel, she wisely decided to put it in the fridge.

But sometimes there is a far more sinister explanation for a bloody package, and by far the most famous bloody package of all time has to be the one that arrived during the evening mail on 16 October 1888 and was addressed to a certain Mr George Akin Lusk in London.

## FROM HELL

George Akin Lusk was a builder by trade and had recently been elected Chairman of the Mile End Vigilance Committee – a group of well-to-do businessmen and merchants who were offering a reward for information on a killer who was stalking prostitutes in Whitechapel and had been dubbed 'Jack the Ripper' by the press. Lusk and his associates had put posters up all over the city and announced their award in the London papers.

The package that arrived at Lusk's house on that October evening contained a letter and a three-inch-square cardboard box containing half a kidney that had been preserved in wine. The note read as follows:

> From hell.
> Sor
> I send you half the Kidne I took from one women prasarved it for you tother piece I fried and ate it was very nise I may send you the bloody knif that took it out if you only wate a whil longer
> Signed Catch me when you can Mishter Lusk

Although it has never been ascertained whether any of the other 600 so-called 'Ripper letters' are genuine, the 'From Hell' letter is adjudged to be the real thing by many Ripper experts. True, it could have been a hoax, perpetrated by medical students from the London Hospital, and Lusk, who had received plenty of prank letters since becoming Chairman of the Vigilance Committee, certainly thought so. But, erring on the side of caution, he put the kidney (which he thought belonged to an animal) along with the note in his desk drawer and decided to mention it at the next meeting, just in case.

At the next session of the committee, which took place four days later, he showed the kidney and the letter to the other members. Several members immediately decided to take it to the Curator of the Pathology Museum at London Hospital, Doctor Thomas Horrocks Openshaw. Dr Openshaw examined the kidney and declared that it was a portion of a left adult human kidney. Consequently, the letter and package were taken to Leman Street police station.

The package had arrived three weeks after the gruesome murder of Catherine Eddowes, who had been found dead in

## BLOODY PACKAGES

Mitre Square, Aldgate, on Saturday, 29 September 1888. The killer had cut her throat, mutilated her face, repeatedly stabbed her and removed part of her womb. Crucially, he had also carefully removed her kidney and taken it with him – presumably as a souvenir.

More recent bloody packages definitely involve foul play and are no ruse or prank. For instance, in 2002 in Bangalore, India, a man working in a video shop received a parcel in which he found the palm of a right hand and part of a left leg. The sender of the body parts was never discovered, nor was the identity of the body.

The year before that, in 2001, in the Czech city of Brno, postal workers found a grisly bundle in a neatly wrapped package that had been sent from Prague four days earlier. Inside, they found a badly decomposed severed human arm and leg. The parcel had been returned to the postal office as the address written on it was non-existent and the parcel had been lying among the piles of undelivered mail ever since.

Two weeks later, a second package arrived with similar handwriting on the front and addressed to the same location. This time, postal workers immediately called the police, who discovered yet more body parts. The body, however, was never identified. In fact, an autopsy was unable to determine whether the victim was a man or woman. Although the police did not release any information as to what body parts were contained in the second package, a spokesman told journalists that tests had shown they belonged to the same person, believed to be either an adult or a teenager.

The most recent case of a killer couple going postal was in China in 2007. According to the newspaper *China Daily*, in

January of that year a young man and a prostitute murdered a 50-year-old man, chopped him into pieces and then shipped his body to three different cities in China in cardboard boxes labelled 'medicine and machine fittings'. The first parcel was intercepted by police in Qingdao city, in China's eastern Shandong province, after postal officials reported that it was dripping blood. Inside, police found a human torso; two days later, they intercepted two other parcels containing the remaining limbs and head. The couple had been captured on closed-circuit television as they signed the release of the parcels in the shipping company under the fake name 'Song Deyuan', which means 'sent far away' in Chinese.

## CHAPTER EIGHTEEN
# WEIRD SCIENCE

Meet ten of the most notorious scientists
in the world.

## TEN

### Giovanni Aldini

Twenty years before Frankenstein's monster was kick-started
into life with a lightning bolt, Giovanni Aldini was putting
massive currents of electricity into human bodies and watching
them twitch. Nephew and disciple of Luigi Galvani, who
investigated the effect of electricity on dissected animals in the
1780s, Aldini took a show on the road that involved cutting off
the heads of cattle and making them roll their eyes. He also
demonstrated, before packed and often horror-struck
audiences, moving human limbs and making severed human
heads grimace and wink.

In 1803, Aldini applied an electric current to hanged
criminal George Foster before the distinguished guests at the
Royal College of Surgeons in London. Foster's face twitched
horribly when Aldini attached a current to it, but he really

started to move when Aldini electrocuted his rectum. His movements, according to once spectator, 'so much increased as almost to give an appearance of reanimation'.

Aldini wasn't the only reanimator. Carl August Weinhold beheaded several kittens, then zapped them and made notes as they flopped about, and Dr Andrew Ure experimented on the corpse of hanged murderer Matthew Clydesdale in Scotland. So impressive was this show that two gentlemen in the audience became convinced the murderer was going to make a second reappearance and ran for it; another fainted.

# NINE
## Dr Robert J White

In 1908, Charles C Guthrie grafted the entire head of one dog on to the neck of a larger dog whose own head remained intact. Result: a two-headed dog. But in the 1970s, neurosurgeon Robert J White went much further. After creating his own dog with two brains, he carried out the first successful mammalian head transplant on to a rhesus monkey. As surgeons are yet to devise a way to reconnect severed spinal nerves, the monkey was paralysed from the neck down. Understandably furious, the monkey tried to bite one of the surgeons the moment it came to. It survived for eight days with another monkey's head attached to its body (or another body attached to its head, depending on which way you look at it).

In 1999, White and his team developed a blood-cooling system, which could extend the life of a severed human head while it was being surgically connected to another body. By claiming that the same procedure could be carried out on a human being, White got himself branded as a Dr

Frankenstein by the press and invoked the fury of many fellow surgeons, who claimed that his actions were both grotesque and unethical.

Dr White's motivations for the bizarre experiments, though, were entirely humane. It was his belief that his head-swapping experiments will one day give many quadriplegics a longer life. In an interview with the *New York Times*, Dr White explained, 'For a quadriplegic who is already paralysed, the main cause of death is generally the eventual failure of several organs. If such a person were to be given a new body, it would be a new lease on life, even though he or she would still be paralysed.'

## EIGHT

### Paracelsus

Born Aureolus Philippus Theophrastus Bombast von Hohenheim, Paracelus (as he preferred to call himself) was a child prodigy already deeply into the complex arts of alchemy as a 14-year-old; by the age of 34, he was the most celebrated man of learning of his day. Born in Austria in 1493, Paracelsus is still highly regarded by the scientific community for founding the science of medicinal chemistry. He is also remembered for carrying out one of the most bizarre experiments of all time – and in the process telling one of the biggest fibs in scientific history.

Paracelsus claimed that he had put human sperm in a sealed container to putrefy and then buried it in the depths of a stinking pile of rotten horse manure. He claimed that he had carefully maintained the temperature of the manure so that it equalled the temperature of a mare's womb and fed the sperm rotten human blood from time to time so that the sperm first became 'agitated' and began to move. After 40 weeks, he reported, he opened the container and had, through his careful efforts and patience, created his very own 16th-century 'mini me', which he called a 'homunculus'. The homunculus, he said, was around a foot tall and he was able to educate it like any other child until it reached maturity, when it promptly left home and never returned.

The concept of the homunculus was later taken up by occultist Aleister Crowley. In his novel *The Moonchild*, Crowley defined it as 'a living being in form resembling man, and possessing those qualities of man which distinguish him from beasts, namely intellect and power of speech, but neither begotten and born in the manner of human generation, nor inhibited by a human soul'. The homunculus, he went on to say, was 'the great idea of magicians of all times to obtain a messiah by some adaptation of the sexual process'.

Rocket scientist-turned-occult spiritualist Jack Parsons, a disciple of Crowley, later became intent on creating an homunculus himself. Crowley and his acolytes believed the homunculus (which they called a 'moonchild', in a reference to Crowley's book) would signal the end of Christianity and usher in a new era unfettered by outdated Christian values. It is believed that it could have been while Parsons was trying to create a homunculus in his lab that he accidentally mixed fulminate of mercury with explosives and blew himself up.

## SEVEN
### Dr Larry Ford
A devout Mormon, Sunday-school teacher and family man, Dr Larry Ford seemed harmless at first sight. He lived in a

big, comfortable house in a quiet suburb of Irvine, California, and was married with three children. A biotechnology entrepreneur by trade, Ford had graduated with honours from Brigham Young University and was a trained gynaecologist, microbiologist and ex-faculty member of UCLA in Los Angeles.

For the last ten years of his life, Ford had run a successful biotechnology company called Biofem Inc., with entrepreneur and marketing expert Patrick Riley. For much of that time, Ford had been working on a radically new type of female contraceptive: a suppository that would kill germs transmitted through sex and which would be capable of preventing every known sexually transmitted disease – including AIDS. Together, the two men planned to market the product under the name 'Inner Confidence'.

The potential of the project was, of course, huge. Ford and Riley believed that, once testing was complete and the product was in the marketplace, it would generate $400 million a year in profit. But Ford had become increasingly aggravated by the fact that, under his contract with Riley, half of all the profits made from every single one of his inventions went automatically to his business partner. It was for that reason that, in 2000, he decided to get rid of Riley for good and hired a hit man to shoot him dead in the company's car park.

Riley survived the hit, however, and Ford immediately became a prime suspect in the case. Three days later, after a meeting with his lawyer, Ford realised that the police were fast closing in on him, went into his bedroom, locked the door and blew his brains out with a double-barrelled shotgun. But, as police were to find out, there was much more to Ford than the apparent absent-minded and well-meaning façade he had projected to his community and his peers. In fact, Larry Ford was a real-life Dr Jekyll and Mr Hyde.

Ford had a number of shotguns and rifles in his home, all of which he had a licence for, but when police searched his house more thoroughly they discovered thousands of rounds of illegal machinegun ammunition hidden under the floorboards. They then received an anonymous telephone tip-off that Ford might have stockpiled weapons and biological materials in his garden.

This was confirmed when police found six white cylinders buried beneath a concrete slab near his swimming pool. Every single resident within a 300ft radius of the Ford home was immediately evacuated. The cylinders were found to contain C4 plastic explosive and machineguns. In all, gun nut Ford had enough C4 plastic explosives, guns and ammunition to take out the whole block.

But that was nothing compared to the biological substances Ford had in his fridge. Police found 266 vials of lethal toxins and cultures of botulism, typhoid fever, salmonella and cholera, most of it stored in the fridge in his garage, and also one of the most deadly substances known to man – ricin – standing in a jar next to a salad dressing in the fridge in his office. Ricin is 6,000 times more toxic than cyanide and 12,000 times more poisonous than rattlesnake venom.

But why? Who was Ford really working for and what was he afraid of? Even seven years after his death, many parts of Larry Ford's story still simply don't add up. Ford often claimed that he had been part of the CIA's bio-warfare research programme, but recent evidence has emerged of several trips that he made to South Africa in the 1980s, suggesting that he met the controversial Wouter Basson from South Africa. (See number four below.)

In fact, soon after his suicide, South African military officials confirmed that Ford had worked from time to time as an 'informal consultant', providing advice on how their personnel could protect themselves from a biological attack. Some newspaper sources in South Africa, though, have since claimed that Ford was deeply involved in 'Project Coast', the apartheid government's plan to eliminate all opposition via biological warfare.

## SIX

### Dr Sidney Gottlieb

During the Korean War, Director of the CIA Allen Dulles had heard several reports of mind-control techniques being successfully used on American prisoners of war. According to one of the reports, the Czechs, under Russian orders, had built a hospital in North Korea in which they had housed a hundred prisoners of war and brainwashed them via the use of mind-control drugs. It suggested disturbing possibilities.

Could Soviet scientists really erase someone's memory and reprogramme them to kill on command? And, if so, was it possible that in the future communist scientists would be able to manufacture a drug that could make entire populations susceptible to their will? It seemed to Director Dulles that American progress in this field was woefully and dangerously inadequate. In order to catch up with the Soviets, he created a mind-control research programme called Project MKULTRA and put it under the leadership of talented chemist Sidney Gottleib, then head of the chemical division of the Technical Services Staff .

Gottlieb was actually very skilled in the use of poisons and had in the past come up with a great many suggestions for getting rid of Cuban premier Fidel Castro, including contaminating his shoes with thallium so that his beard fell out and poisoning his cigars. During his career, Gottlieb once sent a lethal handkerchief to an Iraqi colonel in the post and in 1960 personally delivered a deadly bio-toxin in a tube of toothpaste to a CIA agent in Leopoldville in the Congo, to be used in an attempt to assassinate Prime Minister Patrice Lamumba. But as head of MKULTRA, Gottleib was interested in one thing in particular and that was the possible uses of LSD, which had been discovered by accident in 1943 in Switzerland.

While universities, hospitals, prisons and military bases took CIA money in the search for a way to break down the subconscious mind completely, Gottlieb focused on the effects of LSD on unsuspecting American citizens. In order to study its effects, Gottlieb tested it on himself and his unwitting associates in the CIA. Then, in 1953, he started using it out in the field, leaving in his wake a long trail of permanently ill patients and one suicide. The latter was Frank Olsen, a member of the Army Chemical Corps' Special Operations Division and an expert in biological warfare. Gottlieb spiked Olsen's Cointreau with LSD during a conference in November 1953 and then asked him how he felt. Olsen became gripped by depression and increasing paranoia over the next few days and jumped from the tenth floor of a hotel just a week later. (It is worth noting here that some historians argue it was not suicide at all and that Olsen was in fact murdered because he was about to blow the whistle on elements of the CIA's bio-warfare programme.)

What is known for sure is that, under Gottlieb's orders,

agents drugged homeless vagrants, mentally unbalanced individuals, drug addicts and criminals, and also dished the acid out to hookers and their clients in three CIA-sponsored brothels. They also sprayed LSD from canisters, disguised as insect repellent and deodorant, in public places such as bars and restaurants. As part of 'Operation Midnight Climax', hookers were also paid $100 to slip LSD Mickey Finns and then have sex with unsuspecting customers, while CIA operatives watched through one-way mirrors.

The activities of MKULTRA remained classified until 1974, when the press finally began to report that the CIA had experimented on American citizens as test subjects. By this time it had had become painfully obvious to the CIA that none of the mind-control techniques actually worked anyway; on the recommendation of the Inspector General's office, MKULTRA had scaled back its operations in the early 1960s, then terminated them altogether.

Sidney Gottlieb was called before the Congressional Committee, where he confirmed that the CIA under MKULTRA had illegally drugged at least 40 American citizens without their knowledge. The true scale of MKULTRA's activities will remain a secret, though, as many of the documents related to it were destroyed by Gottlieb himself in 1972, under orders from then CIA Director Richard Helms.

# FIVE
### Dr Ewen Cameron
For 21 years, Scottish-born neurologist Ewen Cameron headed the Allan Memorial Psychiatric Institute in Montreal, Quebec. Highly ambitious and hungry for a Nobel Prize,

Cameron was ostensibly searching for a cure to schizophrenia. But in his search for a cure, he created something called 'psychic driving', one of the most hideous psychological techniques ever devised.

Convinced that there had to be a way to utterly break down a person's mind and then reprogramme it, over nine years Cameron zapped his unsuspecting patients (the majority of whom had come in for minor psychological disorders) with unprecedented, bone-breaking levels of electricity and then combined it with injections of LSD as well as the occasional lobotomy. Having been subjected to this horrific psychological technique, the vast majority of the 500 or so patients who survive today remain in permanent care.

In his attempt to establish 'lasting effects in a patient's behaviour', between sessions Cameron placed his human guinea pigs in the notorious 'sleep room', where they were drugged with Thorazine and Seconal. There they were made to sleep – in some cases, for up to 85 days in a row. When they awoke, they could hardly walk, frequently soiled themselves and had to be spoon-fed. Their earliest memory was invariably walking through the doors of the clinic.

Psychic diving soon reached the attention of Sidney Gottlieb of the CIA, because if it worked it could prove very handy for manipulating foreign leaders. Starting in 1959, the CIA under MKULTRA secretly donated $69,000 a year to Cameron's clinic, to take research beyond memory loss. In order to create desired character traits, once patients' minds had become 'depatterned' speakers were placed under their pillows or football helmets with speakers attached to them were strapped to their heads. A fragment of their therapy session was then replayed for up to 22 hours a day, six days a week. Simply unable to stand it any more, many patients lost their minds completely.

And it didn't even work. After one test, Cameron noted grimly, 'Although the patient was prepared by both prolonged sensory isolation (35 days) and by repeated depatterning, and although she received 101 days of positive driving, no favourable results were obtained.'

## FOUR

### Dr Wouter Basson

South African cardiologist Dr Wouter Basson headed 'Project Coast' – apartheid South Africa's chemical and biological warfare programme – for ten years. After the fall of the apartheid regime, Basson stood trial for 46 charges of murder, conspiracy and drug trafficking. In court, he was accused of spearheading research into a whole array of weird 'smart' poisons and viruses that were aimed specifically at the black population. These included a beer poisonous to blacks only and a toxin that would make black women infertile. At the trial, it was alleged that chemists from his lab, Roodeplaat Laboratories, also produced cigarettes laced with anthrax and bottles of whisky spiked with paraoxon and even devised a scheme to poison pornographic magazines and leave them lying around enemy barracks.

Basson was also accused of being involved in several assassination attempts on anti-apartheid leaders. These included, in once case, placing a lethal nerve poison in an activist's underwear. According to one witness, he also supplied drugs used to knock out about 200 Marxist guerrillas in neighbouring Namibia. Once unconscious – so the allegations went – they were hurled into the ocean from an aeroplane. The same witness claimed that Basson had once ordered that three prisoners be chained in a secluded wood and then smothered with an experimental toxic substance and left to die.

However, in 2002 Basson was declared innocent of all charges against him by the South African Supreme Court and cleared. After his trial, Basson reiterated his innocence, claiming, 'I did many things, but not one of them was illegal and not one of them led to the death or bodily harm of a single person... The US and Britain do all these things on a daily basis. Whatever we did is peanuts by comparison.'

Three years later, however, the Constitutional Court of South Africa ruled that he should face trial on charges of crimes against humanity after the State argued that the judge who had presided over the original trial, Judge Willie Hartzenberg, was biased and had refused to listen to the testimony of many key witnesses. For the moment, though, Basson is a free man and runs a cardiology practice in Cape Town and Pretoria.

## THREE

### Dr Theodore Kaczynski

Kaczynski had a genius IQ, was fast-tracked to Harvard when he was only 16 and had shown outstanding brilliance during his post-graduate studies, where he specialised in geometric function theory. He was soon offered a teaching post at the prestigious Berkeley Faculty of Maths, but after becoming increasingly withdrawn and isolated from staff and students, Kaczynski abruptly quit in 1969 and went to live the life of a hermit in a one-room plywood shack in the wilds of Montana. The hut, which cost just over $2,000, had no running water and no electricity and Kaczynski lived off a small allowance provided for him by his parents along with the money he earned from odd jobs. After living there for some time, he had become adept at hunting, identifying edible herbs and vegetables and was in the end living off less than $400 a month.

It was while he was living in his shack that he wrote his 35,000-word anti-technology manifesto and started building homemade bombs.

Kaczynski had a pathological hatred of technology. With a severely warped logic – he thought that through his actions we would all be able to live happier lives, closer to nature. Kaczynski therefore targeted scientists and technology professionals during an 18-year-long reign of terror, leaving three individuals dead and 23 others maimed. He mixed his own powders and made most of the components painstakingly by hand, including the trigger mechanisms. By using everyday household materials such as wood, string and nails, and then filing away any telltale marks, his devices were impossible to trace. His precision-made bombs were packed with razor blades, metal shards and nails and were designed to withstand heavy handling; they were triggered, in most cases by opening a sealed package, lifting a lever or, in one case in 1985, opening a three-ring binder.

In 1995, Kaczynski demanded that the *New York Times*, the *Washington Post* and *Penthouse* magazine print a manifesto he had drawn up, promising to stop his activities if they did so. When Kaczynski's brother recognised some of the ramblings in the writing, he reported his suspicions to the police and Kaczynski was finally traced. When police investigated his shack, they discovered a sophisticated, ready-to-go letter bomb.

While awaiting trial, Kaczynski was examined by a psychologist, who diagnosed him as a paranoid schizophrenic but ruled that he was competent to stand trial. Kaczynski claims that his murders were essentially political in nature, as outlined in his manifesto, but he also kept a journal between 1969 and 1996 that points to a different story altogether. Unfortunately, the whole content of the journal has not been made public and only snippets have been released to the press as part of the psychological assessment.

Of what is known from Kaczynski's journals, his motivations were not political at all but revenge for being ostracised and hated at school and at university and also for being ignored by women – all of which makes him not that different to the majority of serial killers. In his journal, Kaczynski remembers the 'gradual increasing amount of hostility I had to face from the other kids. By the time I left high school I was definitely regarded as a freak by a large segment of the student body.' In 1971, before he started killing people, he wrote, 'My motive for doing what I am going to do is simply personal revenge.'

In January 1998, two weeks after an attempted suicide in his cell, Kaczynski declared that he was the Unabomber, as part of a plea-bargain agreement with state prosecutors. The agreement allowed Kaczynski to avoid death by lethal injection in return for life without the possibility of parole. The judge sentenced him to four life sentences, to run consecutively, plus a further 30 years in jail, stating that: 'The defendant committed unspeakable and monstrous crimes for which he shows utterly no remorse.'

# TWO

## Dr Josef Mengele

Josef Mengele graduated in medicine from the University of Munich and went on to earn further degrees from universities in Bonn, Vienna and Frankfurt – where he studied genetics and anthropology. Of particular interest to Mengele were the theories of eugenicist Otmar von Verschuer at the Institute of Hereditary Biology and Racial Hygiene in Frankfurt. Verschuer's hypothesis that the Nordic race had to be protected from weaker genetic influences had found favour with Adolf Hitler, who had ordered the sterilisation of the mentally ill in 1934 and one year later prohibited unions between Aryans and Jews as well the 'eugenically' unfit.

The theory that the Nordic race was genetically superior to other races also fitted in perfectly with Mengele's ideas of German racial superiority; he had been a fervent Nazi supporter since its beginnings, a member of the Nazi Party since 1936 and a member of the SS since 1937. The outbreak of war, however, put a temporary stop to Mengele's academic ambitions and he spent the next three years with the Waffen SS seeing active service on the Russian front, during which time he had shown quite considerable bravery in the face of enemy fire and earned four medals.

Injured and removed from the front, Mengele seemed quite happy with his new post at Auschwitz, which gave him the opportunity to continue with his research. He became obsessed with unlocking the genetic cause for the birth of twins: it was his belief that, if German mothers could give birth to twins, then the Third Reich would soon be populated with perfect Aryan specimens. As the trains rolled into Auschwitz, Mengele was guaranteed an endless supply of live subjects for his bizarre and brutal genetic experiments; he became the arbiter of life or death there.

Separated from their parents and housed in special barracks (nicknamed 'The Zoo'), twins selected for his work would receive sweets and special treatment before they were experimented on and then murdered. In attempting to create the Aryan look, Mengele injected their eyes with blue dye, causing severe pain and in some cases blindness. (Mengele had his own collection of human eyeballs, which he pinned to the wall of his office.) He also amputated limbs without anaesthetic, carried out castrations, induced incestuous pregnancies and injected patients with infectious diseases, each time meticulously noting the results. In one case he even sewed the veins of two twins together in order to create Siamese twins, and, when a one-year-old triplet fell into Mengele's hands, he had the child cut open and autopsied while still alive.

In all, 800 pairs of twins died a hideous death under his supervision. In addition to these unspeakable crimes, Mengele also had a sideline in dwarves and hunchbacks. After studying them, he boiled the flesh off their bones and sent them express delivery to the Anthropological Museum in Berlin.

Mengele, of course, was not the only Nazi involved in research of this kind. In all, it is estimated that the Nazi scientists murdered more than 7000 men, women and children in the course of their research. They froze their prisoners to death, gave them malaria, infected them with mustard gas, streptococcus, gas, gangrene and tetanus and secretly poisoned their food, all the while calmly noting down the results in their notebooks. Mengele's experiments, however, remain some of the most bizarre and cruel.

Like many Nazi mass murderers, Mengele managed to escape justice. In 1949, using the name Helmut Gregor, he arrived in Argentina and stayed there for ten years before moving to Paraguay just before the Israeli secret service, Mossad, came to Buenos Aires and kidnapped fellow murderer Adolf Eichmann (who was tried and promptly hanged). After a very short stint in Paraguay, Mengele moved to Brazil and died there at the age of 73; he was pulled out of the sea just outside Sao Paulo. It was the height of summer and, after reminiscing about his native Germany, he had gone in to cool off. Not a bad way to go, all things considered.

## ONE

### Dr Ishii Shiro

Brilliant army physician Ishii Shiro first shot to fame after inventing a water filter that helped bring about the end of an outbreak of meningitis in the Japanese province of Shikoku. When appearing before Emperor Hirohito to show off his new invention, Shiro urinated in it and then kindly offered it to the Emperor to drink – an offer the Emperor politely declined. So Shiro drank it himself.

A notorious boozer, Shiro spent much of his free time chasing whores around the local geisha houses but he was ambitious, short-tempered and ruthless, and had shot through the ranks to become a major. He was also convinced that biological warfare was the way to defend and further spread the glory of the Japanese Empire and soon became the country's foremost bacteriologist. As such, he was given the task of building and overseeing a series of secret research facilities designed to develop biological weapons.

In order to test his pet plagues, Shiro needed human guinea

pigs and during the Sino-Japanese War (1937–45) and World War II he had access to no end of live subjects on which to experiment. As the majority died within two weeks, troops were regularly sent out to the nearest occupied village to restock. In fact, the 3,000 men under his supervision, known collectively as Unit 731, experimented on and killed 10,000 prisoners in territories it occupied during the war – mainly in its 6 sq. km facility in Pingfan, Manchuria.

While most of his research examined the effects of diseases such as typhoid, tetanus, the bubonic plague and anthrax on human beings, Shiro also observed and minutely charted the levels of human endurance. Prisoners were hung upside down to see how long it would take for them to choke to death; they were frozen and their limbs were hacked off one by one to measure the effects of frostbite. Military researchers also tied their prisoners to posts and bombed them (in order to chart the impact and distribution of bomb fragments), roasted them with massive volts of electricity and injected their kidneys with horse urine. Many of the prisoners, after being injected with plagues, were then autopsied while still alive and without anaesthetic.

One medical assistant who had worked under Shiro during World War II later recalled in an interview with the *New York Times*: 'The fellow knew that it was over for him and so he didn't struggle when they led him into the room and tied him down. But when I picked up the scalpel, that's when he began screaming. I cut him open from the chest to the stomach and he screamed terribly and his face was all twisted in agony. He made this unimaginable sound, he was screaming so horribly. But then finally he stopped. This was all in a day's work for the surgeons, but it really left an impression on me because it was my first time.'

As well as these truly hideous crimes, Shiro also managed to spread anthrax, the bubonic plague and cholera to Chinese villages, raising his body count by another astounding 250,000 men, women and children.

After the defeat of the Japanese by the Allied forces, MacArthur secretly offered Shiro immunity in return for information gathered from his research into bio-warfare. He was never prosecuted and died of throat cancer in 1967.

# CHAPTER NINETEEN

# SERIAL-KILLER GROUPIES: MEET THE WOMEN WHO LOVE KILLERS

For some women only the ultimate bad boy will do.

When serial killers are caught and go to trial, they often receive fan mail, love letters and marriage proposals. Brooding Richard Ramirez, convicted of 13 murders, found love in the arms of a freelance magazine editor, Doreen Lioy, who had to compete with hundreds of fellow admirers for his affections. They married in San Quentin jail in 1996 and in fact Lioy is rumoured to be planning on suicide when her Satanist husband is finally executed. Even the infamous Jeffrey Dahmer, a homosexual who was convicted of killing 15 men, left a flock of heartbroken female admirers in his wake. Serial killer poster boy Ted Bundy confessed to over 30 murders, but hordes of women vied for his attention at his trial. He even proposed to Carole Ann Boone, a former colleague, just before he was sentenced to death for the second time – an offer she accepted.

The most notorious serial-killer groupie of all time was

Veronica Lynn Compton. Kenneth Bianchi and Angelo Buono Jr – who killed several Los Angeles women in the 1970s – were facing murder charges when Compton approached Bianchi, claiming she wanted his opinion on a play she was writing about serial killers. Soon the pair were exchanging letters, prompting Bianchi to ask Compton to copycat his crimes in an effort to clear his name. She was to leave evidence at the murder scene, leading police to believe that the real killer was still at large.

Bianchi was a non-secretor, meaning that (in those days) his blood type could not be determined by seminal fluid or saliva. He collected his sperm in a rubber glove, stashed it in a book and gave it to Compton when she visited him in prison. Compton travelled to Washington, where she tried (unsuccessfully) to strangle a woman she met in a bar.

Convicted of attempted murder and sentenced to prison, Compton soon sparked up a postal relationship with another serial killer, Douglas Clarke, a.k.a. 'The Sunset Strip Slayer'. In 1983, Clarke was found guilty on six counts of murder and sentenced to death. Compton and he soon began exchanging letters, discussing the delights of necrophilia and wondering 'why others don't see the necrophiliac aspects of existence as we do' (Compton to Clarke). Clarke also sent Compton a Valentine's card with a drawing of a headless corpse. He had, on at least one occasion, had sex with a victim's decapitated head.

So who are these women who throw themselves so willingly at lunatics? To find out, I talked to groupies, pen-pals, frequent Death Row visitors and women engaged to Death Row inmates.

## IGNORING THE MONSTER

While killer groupies are by no means a new phenomenon, the way they befriend murderers today is changing. Numerous prisoner websites and online pen-pal services now help groupies search for their chosen criminal.

Sally (not her real name) works as a desk clerk in Santa Fe in California, and belongs to a group that sends books to Death Row prisoners. She's been a pen-pal to several prisoners, and is a regular visitor on Death Row. 'I find condemned convicts to be basically very nice and polite,' she says. 'Actually, I feel more comfortable writing them than I do with the jerks out here. I even went to visit one every Sunday for ten months. He's the nicest guy I ever met.' The nice guy turns out to be Robert Consalvo, who stabbed a woman to death in 1991 when she found him trying to rob her apartment. 'We get along great. We were writing for several months, so it was like visiting a friend.'

Sally also writes regularly to Charles Ng, one of the most notorious serial killers of all time. In 1998, Ng was sentenced to death on 11 counts of murder (including the murder of two baby boys) and now awaits the gas chamber in San Quentin. Ng teamed up with his best pal Leonard Lake to abduct, rape and torture female victims while videotaping the atrocities in the basement of Lake's cabin in the Sierra Nevada foothills.

Like many groupies, Sally is quick to defend her deranged pen-pal. 'I think, if Charles hadn't run into Leonard Lake, he'd never have killed anyone. He's a nice guy, but on the emotionally needy side. He doesn't talk about his case as he's still in the appeal process. He talks about his family – growing up in Hong Kong and what's happening in prison. He likes to do origami.'

Sally is a member of a web list called Killer Groupies. The owner of the list, Kimba D'Michi, began tracking current serial killers' cases in the media eight years ago via online list services. 'Our news list began to attract members who held a strange sympathy for serial killers and in some cases a sensual attraction,' D'Michi says. 'While I was curious about what makes a person a serial-killer fan, these folks were not appropriate for our news list and, to be frank, were often attacked by other list members who just didn't understand how anyone could admire a serial killer. So we started the groupies list.

'Groupies come from all walks of life. We seem to have groupie mums, teenagers, and most seem to be young, under-25-year-old women. These people seem to find the human side of these monsters, and are able to ignore the ugly monster within. They often feel that the killer is misunderstood, was abused, was driven to commit their crimes by circumstances of their upbringing and lives. The key word is they *excuse* the crimes due to circumstance.

'They want to see a nice man, so they see one. To gain closeness in such an interpersonal way with someone who's committed heinous acts, and to blind themselves to that person, also makes them co-dependent. They need the positive interaction with this killer to quantify themselves in some way.'

D'Michi uses Ian Brady as an example of how a groupie's mind might rationalise the attraction. 'They would think I can make Brady out to be a nice man. See, if the right woman were there for him instead of Myra Hindley, then he'd never have committed those crimes. I can see the real him even if no one else can. They are looking to be the Madonna, the one woman in the world who can turn these men around.'

One of the members of D'Michi's list is girlfriend to Melinda

Loveless. In 1992, the aptly named Loveless, then aged 16, stabbed, beat and tortured to death 12-year-old Shanda Sharer. In fact, Sharer's murder represents one of the most harrowing crimes in recent memory (certainly one of the worst this writer has come across). Along with fellow psychopath Laurie Tackett, Loveless spent hours torturing the helpless 12-year-old, whom Loveless blamed for stealing her girlfriend. After smashing her repeatedly in the head with a tyre iron in the boot of Tackett's car, they dumped her in a field, poured petrol on her and burned her alive. Loveless, who lit the match, will be released in 2052.

Incredible as it may seem, since then, Loveless has found someone on the outside who is head over heels in love with her and who says she will be waiting for her when she gets out.

D'Michi explains, 'The girl met Melinda Loveless through her aunt, who volunteers at a Christian prison outreach programme. They started out writing letters and fell in love. Loveless's girlfriend makes no excuses for her relationships and she says that her family is non-appreciative about her closeness with Melinda Loveless, but they tolerate it all the same.

'She also seems to glow in the fact she knows things about Melinda that she can share with the list. It made her a celebrity to be Melinda's girlfriend. I don't think this type of attention was her motivation, though. I believe it's a side effect that the groupies embrace and flaunt when it suits them, because the audience on the Killer Groupies website are interested in each other and are nice to each other. They are not criticising them for their ties to killers.'

## BAD BOY FANTASIES

Many psychologists and sexologists believe that falling for a killer is a result of a psychological disorder called hybristophilia, otherwise known as the 'Bonnie and Clyde syndrome'. Famed sexologist John Money coined the term and describes hybristophilia as a condition that can cause women to become attracted, or even sexually aroused, by 'marauding or predator type partners'.

According to his definition, 'Sexuerotic arousal and facilitation and attainment of orgasm are responsive to and contingent on being with a partner known to have committed an outrage or crime, such as rape, murder or armed robbery.'

Serial-killer groupies openly mock the term, saying that it completely misses the point. This isn't about sex, they argue, as there is absolutely no sex involved at all.

There are, of course, other psychological explanations for the phenomenon, all of which are dismissed equally out of hand by groupies. Some theorists say that the groupies are simply after the notoriety a bad-boy killer boyfriend can give them, while others argue that groupies find purpose and meaning in their lives by taking on a killer lover. A groupie, particularly if they are religious, can devote themselves entirely to taking their man away from the path of wickedness on to which he has inadvertently strayed.

Having said that, the reasons for dating a killer behind bars are usually far more mundane. At first sight, it might not seem practical to actually be involved with someone whom you might never meet outside visiting hours, but the arrangement is actually quite sensible if seen from a certain angle. Besides their notoriety, captured bad-boy killers make curiously perfect partners. After all, they can't cheat (not with another woman, at least) and you always know where they are. You don't have to live with them day in day out, so they won't get on your nerves and destroy any idealised fantasy you have of them. And if you're afraid of sexual intimacy, that's another problem solved.

Moreover, there's inevitably an element of high drama associated with a killer on Death Row. If you believe (as most groupies do) that their boyfriend is innocent, the situation can give rise to a thrilling sense of righteous anger – 'We're in this together!' Even if the groupie does recognise that their killer boyfriend is guilty, they quickly become convinced that he has repented and is now a reformed character, that they are in love with a completely different person to the person who committed that terrible crime all those years ago.

Those who take it beyond the pen-pal stage and have become romantically involved with killers can share their experiences through other websites, such as Prisontalk.com. Here they can discuss issues of sex (or lack of it), share notes on how hard it is to carry on a relationship through letters and infrequent visits, chat about how their family and friends 'just don't get it', and exchange sickly sweet anecdotes on how cute and attentive their killer was in their last letter or phone call.

In almost all cases, the relationship seems to begin with a letter; they become pen-pals; it moves on to a jail visit. Suddenly, the groupie can't believe what is happening: she feels as if she has known this guy forever. Some of them are already involved in a serious relationship. But the killer and the groupie just have so much in common. He's so sensitive and such a good listener too. He knows all of her secrets. She can tell him *anything*. He's her best friend in the world *ever*. Before you know it, love blooms.

Do they intentionally set out to fall in love with a killer? According to the numerous groupies I talked to, the opposite is true. Many claimed they fought very hard not to. Falling in love with a killer is apparently something that 'just happens'.

## THE MAN OF MY DREAMS

Frank and Suzy, who is 38 (both names have been changed), met through a pen-pal ad. He's been on Death Row in the US for ten years and has had two death warrants signed, both of which were stayed. Suzy was watching a programme on TV about women who love men in prison when they mentioned a site where you could contact a prisoner (Prisonpen-pals.com). Now the couple are engaged.

'Out of complete boredom and curiosity I looked at the site,' she says. 'I went through a hundred or so ads, just curious, and I came across Frank's. I can't explain it, but I felt compelled to write to him. We wrote for a few months and it became clear he was really special. It didn't take long for me to fall in love with him. In December I went and saw him for the first time, and I knew then there was no going back. Now I see him every two months as he lives in Georgia, and I live in Minneapolis.'

Although Suzy didn't want to go into the details of her fiancé's crime or give his proper name, she does admit he stands accused of murdering a young girl. But she believes he's innocent. 'I have to believe this for my own sanity. The crime was horrific. I know my man's heart, and there's no way he could have done it.'

Suzy certainly doesn't fit the mould of the typical clinging, insecure and obsessed Death Row fiancée. She has a degree, a busy life and no fear of men or intimacy in any way. Before she met Frank, she'd had several 'normal' relationships and was even married. 'It just turned out that the man of my dreams happens to be sitting on Death Row,' she says. 'We have a connection I've never experienced before. I've never been treated so well, or with so much respect. When he asked me to marry him I had no doubts – there was no hesitation at all.'

While Suzy has found love with one convicted murderer, the undisputed queen of serial-killer groupies is the crime writer Sondra London, who dated future serial killer Gerard Schaefer when she was 17. Later, in 1973, Schaefer was found guilty of murdering Susan Place and Georgia Jessup, and is suspected of slaying another 30 women at least. Shaefer (who used to be a policeman) was murdered in his cell by fellow inmate Vincent Rivera.

London contacted her childhood sweetheart in prison 16 years after his arrest and helped him publish *Killer Fiction* – a gruesome series of short stories and drawings found in Schaefer's house after his arrest, all of which feature the savage torture and murder of women and clearly reflect his fantasies and suspected crimes. In 1991, the two were engaged. Soon afterwards, however, London met a younger killer, Danny Rolling, and got engaged to him instead. (See Chapter Five for more on Rolling, the Gainesville Ripper.)

London also flirted with Keith Hunter Jesperson, known as the 'Happy Face Killer'. Jesperson committed eight murders in five states, dumping the bodies in woodlands. He got his nickname because of the smiling faces he drew on taunting letters he sent to the police, in which he boasted of his crimes. Like most serial killers, Jesperson started out on harmless animals. When he was 20, he was choking cats and dogs in the middle of a field near his home. He would later say that strangling a human being and strangling an animal gave him much the same feeling.

For dating and falling in love with such notorious killers,

as well as providing all three with an outlet to publicise their views, London attracted a lot of bad publicity for herself. So what does she think about being called a serial-killer groupie? 'There are things going on the public is not aware of. It's all inexplicable, yet I can't be the one to explain it,' she told me, somewhat mysteriously. 'I don't choose to publicly analyse and explain what's been or is being done to me. There's no percentage in that, and there are so many reasons to remain silent. I'm content to walk away from the deconstruction of my good name, considering the alternatives. At this time I have no purpose or ambition. I am inactive and non-participatory.'

With such figures as London on the scene, 'serial-killer groupie' is a term most women involved with imprisoned murderers utterly despise. Keshia lives in New York and is close pals with Kendall Francois, a former school caretaker who killed eight women in Poughkeepsie. Branded the 'Black Pillsbury Doughboy' by Fred Rosen in his account of the case, *Body Dump*, Francois targeted prostitutes, whom he strangled and then left to rot in his house.

'The term "serial-killer groupie", it's like someone trying to say we are, like, obsessed or in love with serial killers,' says Keshia. 'Not that I care – let people think what they like. My friends and family tend to think I have this strange fascination with killers, like a fetish or whatever.' Keshia has been writing to Francois for a few months now. She hasn't visited him yet but plans to do so as soon as she gets the chance.

'He's an awesome person and a very caring guy, and tends to put a lot of thought into what he has to say. He's a good friend and we don't really talk about the fact he killed eight people – it's not something he likes to bring up, and nor do I. It's not something he really likes to remember. I mean, you have to understand that he's locked up.

'This guy doesn't have the same rights we do and he doesn't get treated with the same respect we do. And… someone like me writes to him just to tell him that, even though I don't understand why he did what he did and I can't ever understand what he's going through, I still want to be his friend, even if he never wants to tell me why he did what he did.

'I just want to be there for the bad days when a prison guard treats him like crap or a fellow inmate treats him like crap, or the days when he's sick and he doesn't have his family there to take care of him and all he can do is sit in his cell all day and feel like crap. I just want him to know that I'm thinking about him and hoping that he gets better.'

## CELEBRITY PSYCHOS

The groupies are an organised bunch. They remind each other to send the killers Christmas and birthday cards, and are always happy to forward a killer's address. I discovered that many girls write to six or seven killers on a regular basis. With the proliferation of websites dedicated to contacting convicted murderers and Death Row inmates, the phenomenon of the serial-killer groupie is likely to continue.

Death Row inmates are often in their cells for 23 hours a day, and so have an awful amount of time on their hands. Chances are, if you take the time to write to them they will write to you. But the more notorious the killer the more letters he will receive, so befriending one of the 'big catches' takes more persistence. Indeed, some of the killers are so well known that establishing contact with them is not dissimilar to becoming a close friend with a celebrity. Perhaps some of us feel impulsively drawn to contact people in the public eye because fame is at such a premium these days – no matter how gruesome the process through which that fame was achieved.

# CHAPTER TWENTY
# SEVEN

Seven Deadly Sins. Seven Final Tales of
Bizarre Murder and Mayhem.

## LUST

Romantic story of a man defying the terrible inevitability of death, or a sordid tale of a dirty old man with a taste for necrophilia? Either way, the story of Count Carl Von Cosel has to be one of the most bizarre tales of all time. According to research carried out by Ben Harrison for his fascinating book *Undying Love: The True Story of a Passion That Defied Death* (2001), German immigrant and self-appointed aristocrat Count Carl Von Cosel had left Germany behind in 1927 to look for a new life in Florida's Key West. There, he managed to get work as a radiologist at Marine Hospital, where he met Cuban beauty Elena Hoyos. But Hoyos was dying of tuberculosis, and, while the good doctor did everything in his power to save her, he could not do so. She died soon afterwards.

While the love had been one-sided (she was only 22 when she died; Cosel was 56), the family knew that the grief-stricken doctor had genuinely cared for her and allowed him to construct a mausoleum in memory of his lost young love. Cosel hadn't given up on her quite yet, though. Every night, without fail, he would go down to the mausoleum where, he later claimed, the ghost of Elena would declare her undying love for him and beg the good doctor to get her out of her tomb.

This went on for a year and then, rather strangely, his nightly jaunts to the mausoleum suddenly stopped. This seemed rather out of character to the dead woman's sister. All the same, she didn't actually do anything about it for seven years; when she finally went to the mausoleum, she was told that the body wasn't there any more. She had a pretty good idea where to look, though...

To her horror, she discovered that Cosel had removed her sister's body and had been happily living with it for seven long years. As well as subjecting the corpse to huge amounts of electricity through a Tesla coil specifically designed for the purpose of trying to bring Hoyos back to life, Cosel had also tried to completely reconstruct it. But legend has it that things hadn't exactly got off to a great start for the reunited couple: Cosel, in his excitement, had dropped the body as he carried it over the threshold for the first time and it had promptly fallen to pieces.

From then on, Cosel kept the bones from slipping off the decaying flesh with piano wire, replaced the rotting eyeballs with glass ones (ordered months apart in order to avoid suspicion) and made a wax death mask out of the face. As for her hair, that was less of a problem as a lot of it had fallen out years ago while he had been zapping the corpse with X-rays (naturally he had kept the hair as a souvenir). Then, in order to give the body some kind of shape, he stuffed it with formaldehyde-coated rags.

As well as dressing the corpse up in a wedding dress and sleeping beside it each night, he talked with it and played it music. He was also regularly having sex with it.

Incredibly, Cosel was never prosecuted for his crime and the doctors concerned made no mention of their grisly findings at the time in order to spare the feelings of the public, who had strangely found the whole thing rather romantic. It was for this reason that the body had to suffer one final indignity before being laid to rest. As the story had caused such a stir and as so many people had been so moved by this tale of 'endless love', the corpse was put on display at the Lopez Funeral Home so that rubberneckers could have a nice long look at the corpse bride. Her body was then buried at last – in a secret location so that the doctor would never be able to find her and dig her up again.

## PRIDE

Whether anyone has actually committed the perfect murder is, of course, unknown, but we do know that an attempt to actually carry it out has proven the downfall of more than one self-titled master criminal. For a classic example, let us turn to the case of 19-year-old clerk Herbert Leonard Mills, who killed someone just to prove that he could get away with it.

On 2 August 1951, Mills invited 50-year-old Mabel Tattershaw on a date after spotting her outside a cinema in Nottingham. Flattered by the young man's attentions, she agreed and the next day the two went to a secluded orchard two miles from her home. Once there, Mills immediately strangled her and then dumped the body in some nearby bushes.

Mills waited and waited, but nobody seemed to notice that Tattershaw was missing. It was no good committing the perfect murder if nobody actually realised that a murder had taken place, so the annoyed Mills phoned the *News of the World* from a payphone and told the astonished reporter on the other end of the line that while he had been out reading poetry he had found a body; the police were contacted immediately and Mills took them to the orchard.

Although he was immediately a suspect in the case, Mills was not charged with the murder and so, emboldened by his initial success, he went further, assuring a reporter from the *News of the World* that the police would never catch the killer who was, he told them, far too clever for the bungling cops. Mills also claimed that it was pretty obvious to anyone who cared to look that the woman had been strangled – something that the police had yet to establish.

Actually, as Mills boasted to reporters, police were fast closing in on the self-professed genius, because Mills had left fibres from his coat under her nails and strands of his hairs on her coat. Still he persisted with his boastful behaviour, seemingly eager to do the authorities' work for them until, unable to contain himself any longer, he eventually felt compelled to confess to the murder. After writing a long account of the crime, which he gave to (you guessed it) the *News of the World*, he turned himself in to the police. In his confession, Mills wrote: 'I had always considered the possibility of the perfect crime… I am very much interested in crime. Seeing an opportunity of putting my theory into practice I consented to meet her on the morrow… I put on a pair of gloves. I knelt, my knees on her shoulders… I was very pleased. I think I did it rather well. The strangling itself was quite easily accomplished.

'I have been most successful, no motive, no clues,' he wrote. 'Why, if I had not reported finding the body, I should not have been connected in any manner whatsoever. I am quite proud of my achievement.'

It took the jury less than half an hour to sentence Mills to death.

Incidentally, another excellent example of a killer's warped sense of pride came courtesy of chubby serial killer Rudolf Pleil. Pleil was accused of killing nine women in Germany from 1946 to 1947 but insisted on telling the jurors that the body count was actually much higher. He was 'the best death-maker' in Germany, he told them, and boasted that he had claimed 25 victims in total. Germany's self-professed greatest killer strangled himself in his own cell in February 1958.

## GREED

One game show contestant in Colombia was so keen to win a $25,000 cash prize that she admitted being involved in an attempted murder live on national TV. The contestant was appearing on the controversial lie-detector game show *Nada Mas Que la Verdad* ('Nothing But the Truth') when she made the stunning confession – and walked off with the prize.

The admission was aired in May 2007 before an estimated five million viewers – and the woman's visibly shocked son, who was sitting in the studio audience. In the show (which has also screened in the UK under the name *Nothing But the Truth*, hosted by Jerry Springer), contestants are hooked up to a polygraph machine and asked increasingly intrusive and embarrassing questions. The more answers the contestants answer truthfully, the more money they win. The incredible confession immediately caused the TV station to pull the plug on the show for good after the channel was inundated with complaints by horrified viewers.

The show had just started when the host, who had previously been tipped off about the incident, asked, 'Did you pay a hit man to kill your husband?'

'Yes,' the woman replied.

Seated in the audience, the woman's shocked son piped up, 'I didn't know that.'

Quickly, the woman added, 'The crime was never carried out, though. The hit man warned my husband and he ran away for ever and never came back.'

During previous episodes of the show, other contestants had confessed to fraud, drug-dealing and bribery, but owning up to an attempted murder was too much for the TV channel and police immediately began investigating the incident. The confession was particularly shocking in Colombia because hit men are known to carry out a murder for as little as $500 and according to local press are responsible for a great many of the estimated 17,000 murders committed each year in the crime-stricken country.

## WRATH

Here, we are in the realm of the spree killers who, in a fit of rage, set out to wipe out as many people as they can in a single day. That day invariably ends with them turning the gun on themselves and blowing their own brains out. A spree killer's fury can be invoked by a myriad of seemingly mundane reasons. They are angry because they have been, or are about to be, fired: postal worker Patrick Henry Sherril killed 14 people in Edmond, Oklahoma, in 1986 – hence the term 'going postal'. They have just been jilted: sheriff deputy Tyler

Peterson used an AR-15 rifle to kill six people at a party in Crandon, Wisconsin, in 2007, after failing to get back together with his girlfriend. Or they believe their fellow workers are plotting against them: lab technician Leo Held killed six people in Loganton, Pennsylvania, in 1967.

One of the most deadly spree killings of all time occurred in 1982 in South Korea when policeman Woo Bum-kon went berserk after he had an argument with his girlfriend. After the quarrel – which, according to some reports, began because his girlfriend had swatted a fly off his chest and awoke him during his afternoon nap – Woo Bum-kon got drunk and headed to the armoury at his local police station. There he grabbed two carbines, 18 rounds of ammunition and as many grenades as he could carry.

Using his position as a police officer to gain entry into people's houses, he then embarked on an eight-hour murder rampage through five villages, leaving a staggering 53 people dead and a further 36 injured. It all ended in the early hours of 27 April when police finally cornered him, whereupon he strapped two hand grenades to his chest and blew himself up. Tragically, he killed a further three hostages in the process.

Cuban-born Julio Gonzalez was another killer who did away with a great many people after a lover's tiff. On 25 March 1990, Gonzalez was thrown out of the Happy Land Social Club in the Bronx because he had an argument with his ex-girlfriend, who worked there. Minutes later, he came back with a dollar's worth of petrol in a can, which he poured on the stairs, effectively sealing up the only entrance and exit to the club. He then lit two matches, set the petrol alight and calmly walked across the street, where he watched the ensuing blaze. A total of 87 people died in the bloody inferno that followed.

There were only five survivors; among them was Lydia Feliciano, his ex-girlfriend.

## SLOTH

Pulling off a murder typically requires considerable effort, but in one highly unusual case a murder was committed that stemmed not from aggravation over someone else's supposed laziness, but from the slothfulness of the murderer herself.

In May 2000, 36-year-old Alison Firth poisoned 84-year-old Alzheimer's sufferer Alice Grant with an overdose of the sedative drug heminevrin while working in an old people's home in Gateshead. Grant had suffered two strokes in the previous year, was barely able to do anything for herself and needed frequent attention and care. Fellow nurses later testified that on the day before the murder they had heard Firth complain about her patient, expressing the wish that she would 'hurry up and die'. On the next morning, when Grant was dead, Firth apparently commented that there was now 'one less patient to get up in the morning'. One detective involved in the case told the press that Firth 'would rather spend her time asleep on duty rather than care for patients and she set about, in what can only be described as an evil manner, to sedate Alice Grant with what was an overdose of the drug heminevrin'.

Judge Mr Justice Bell agreed, telling the court that Firth had committed murder 'largely because she didn't want to be put to the trouble of caring for [Alice Grant] in the future'. He sentenced her to a minimum term of 14 years in jail.

## ENVY

Petty officer Alan Grimson, a fire drill instructor in the Royal Navy, wasn't the best-looking guy in the world. In fact, his friends in the navy called him 'Frank' – short for Frankenstein. Grimson seemed to take the jibes on the chin. He had been in the navy for 22 years, travelled all over the world and was actually well liked and respected by his colleagues. But, although he hid it well, Grimson was extremely sensitive about his looks. So sensitive, in fact, that psychologists later suggested it may well have been envy for other men's good looks that caused him to kill.

In December 1997, Grimson invited 18-year-old naval rating Nicholas Wright to his flat, but became incensed when the good-looking Wright spurned his advances. Grimson punched him to the ground then hit him with a baseball bat, cut off his ear and slit his throat. When it was all over, Grimson punched the air in triumph. 'It was such a feeling. I have never had that feeling. It was a feeling of power, a good feeling. I felt good about it,' he told police later. It was, he added, 'better than sex'. The next morning, he wrapped the body in plastic sheeting and dumped it by the side of an isolated country lane in Hampshire.

A year later, he killed again. After spending hours torturing and raping his second victim – 20-year-old Sion Jenkins – he handcuffed him to the bath, covered his head with a towel and beat him to death with a baseball bat.

At his trial, a psychiatric report described Grimson as having a 'severe personality disorder of a psychopathic type'. Grimson, it stated, 'was a loner who wore a charming mask'. In his sentencing, Judge Mr Justice Cresswell told Grimson, 'You are a serial killer in nature if not by number. You are a highly dangerous serial killer who killed two young men in horrifying and appalling circumstances.'

As a fire officer in the navy, Grimson had travelled all over the world and is now a suspect in a number of missing-person cases – many of them involving sailors who were thought at the time to have jumped ship.

## GLUTTONY

No collection of bizarre murders would be complete without a mention of what has to be the oddest murder in recent memory. In 2001, after several months of searching the internet, 41-year-old cannibal Armin Meiwes found somebody who wanted to be eaten. The message Meiwes had posted online was: 'Seeking young, well-built 18- to 30-year-old for slaughter.' His victim was 43-year-old engineer Bernd-Jurgen Brandes, who on 9 March 2001 willingly went to meet his killer at the main train station in Kassel. Meiwes then drove him to his farm in Rotenburg, where the two had sex.

Brandes had actually wanted to be eaten alive, but Meiwes wasn't strong enough to literally rip the flesh from his bones as Brandes had wanted. So, instead, as per prior agreement, Meiwes plied him with booze and pills and then chopped off his penis. He then seasoned it, fried it and fed it to Brandes and ate some of it too. In a recent interview that was shown on Channel Five, Meiwes – or 'the Master Butcher' as he is sometimes referred to in Germany – went into harrowing detail of the events of that night. 'I was relatively quick preparing it,' he recalled, 'as I thought that, because he had such a massive wound, he'd feel faint quite quickly.'

After letting Brandes bleed unconscious in the bath for three hours (during which time his killer lay on his bed and read a *Star Trek* novel), Meiwes cut his throat and killed him. He then hung Brandes's body on a meat hook in the larder. The next day, he cut the body into pieces and froze the hunks of flesh in the freezer in pizza boxes. As it was a special occasion, Meiwes got out his best tableware and made a steak out of human flesh, which he ate with potatoes and sprouts. Over the ensuing months, Meiwes managed to consume over 20kg of flesh, which he ate lightly fried in olive and garlic, until police were alerted to the fact that a man in an internet chat room was boasting that he had eaten someone and was apparently looking for his next victim.

During the investigation and the consequent probe into the connection between the internet and cannibalism, German police discovered that there were well over 200 Germans who expressed their desire to be killed and fed to a cannibal, while a further 30 said that they would like to eat a fellow human being if the opportunity ever arose.

These disturbing findings were borne out two years later when a second, similar case surfaced in Germany, this time in Berlin. In October 2004, 41-year-old musician Ralf Meyer walked into a police station in Berlin and announced, 'I have killed a man. Help me, there's a man in my fridge.'

When police entered Meyer's house, they found that he had indeed killed and then dismembered 33-year-old music teacher Joe Ritzkowsky.

Like Armin Meiwes and Bernd-Jurgen Brandes, the two had met via an internet chartroom. After a masochistic sex session, Meyer had stabbed Ritzkowsky in the neck with a screwdriver and then spent the rest of the night dismembering his victim. He ripped out the lungs, which he fed to his cat, and sliced off the man's penis, which he prepared with spices and popped into the fridge. He then hacked off the arms and limbs and left them by the side of the torso on the bed.

When Meyer had finished dismembering the body, he

wrapped the internal organs in clingfilm and then carefully placed them in the fridge too. Detectives believed that Meyer had planned to eat his victim as a continuation of his violent, sado-masochistic murder binge, but had resisted the temptation to do so.

Meiwes claimed that Brandes had been a willing victim and that therefore no murder had been carried out. His lawyers argued for a conviction on the charge of 'killing on demand'. The prosecution though wanted him to be charged with murder for 'sexual pleasure' and also for the crime of 'disturbing the peace of the dead', due to the fact that he hacked up and ate parts of the body. In the end Meiwes was convicted of manslaughter and was handed down a sentence of eight-and-a-half years. However, the German Supreme Court of Appeal ruled in 2006 that the sentence was too lenient and Meiwes should be retried for murder. He was convicted for murder and sentenced to life in prison.

## CHAPTER TWENTY-ONE

# HOW TO SPOT A NATURAL BORN KILLER

Is a killer's real nature written all over his face?

Today, we still associate evil with a certain type of person – just look at all those ugly-looking villains out there in movies. So, while common sense tells us that a killer can look like anyone else, we still somehow expect them to *look* like murderers. Unfortunately for us, they very rarely do. The reality is that killers almost always look and act (in public, at least) just like you or I. Take Ted Bundy, for instance – he murdered an estimated 37 women and wasn't a bad-looking guy at all. Then there was 'Cross-Country Killer' Glen Rogers, a real lady's man suspected of murdering at least 70 women (including OJ Simpson's wife).

But imagine if you could actually identify a killer just by looking at his face. It may seem incredible to us today, but, from the 16th century up until the 1950s, hordes of scientists and scholars were convinced that there could well be a way to discover a killer in a crowd and stop him before he ever committed a crime. They visited jails and lunatic asylums, photographed thousands of prisoners, carried out endless autopsies on dead convicts and made extensive studies of every single part of the human body. Then, in order to back up their research, they examined some of the most celebrated killers of their time.

Once published, their discoveries were eagerly lapped up by the public. The idea that you really could spot a killer just by looking at him was incredibly seductive. If he could be identified at birth, so much the better. You could just wipe him off the face of the earth.

Problem solved.

## THE MURDER ORGAN

The first scientists to equate physical characteristics with inborn depravity were the phrenologists. Swiss physician Franz-Joseph Gall (1758–1828) claimed that there were some 26 'organs' on the surface of the brain that could be identified by examining the skull, including the so-called 'murder organ'.

Phrenology is considered a bit of a joke today, but it represented an unprecedented attempt to provide a scientific explanation for murder. Dr Nicole Rafter, who runs a graduate course in Biological Theories of Crime at the College of Criminal Justice at Northeastern University, explained to me that phrenologists 'could even explain the behaviour of criminals whom we today would call serial killers and psychopaths'. Although phrenology was largely discredited by the 1850s, it resurfaced in dramatic fashion when phrenologist Dr Edgar Beall was asked to examine murderess Ruth Snyder and report his findings to the jury in one of the most sensational court cases of the early 20th century.

In 1927, Snyder had persuaded her weak-willed lover, Judd Gray, to bash her husband's head in with a sash weight while he was asleep. As Gray turned chicken, she grabbed the weight and finished the job herself. By the time Beall was called to testify, the evidence against the two was already overwhelming, but the phrenologist's report made sure that their fate was well and truly sealed. Snyder, concluded Beall, had all 'the character of a shallow-brained pleasure seeker' and the jury agreed, condemning the star-crossed lovers to squirm in the chair at Sing Sing. Incidentally, photographer Thomas Howard from *The Daily News* took a photograph of Snyder as she died in the chair. It made the front page of the paper and was so popular that 75,000 extra copies had to be printed immediately. The murder case also inspired, arguably, two of the best film noirs ever made: *Double Indemnity* and *The Postman Always Knocks Twice*.

## CRIMINAL MAN

Soon after the conception of phrenology, scientists started looking elsewhere on the body for signs of inborn evil – particularly the face. The most famous figure in this field was Italian anthropologist and father of criminology Cesare Lombroso, whose *Criminal Man* (1876) was a bestseller in its day, going through five editions and expanding from just 200 pages in its first edition to 3,000 in its fifth.

Lombroso would devote 50 years of his life attempting to body-map the evilness in man's soul. He argued that criminals were remnants of man's more murderous past and labelled them 'atavistic'. The atavists, he argued, were throwbacks to the Stone Age and he defined them as 'murderer savages living in the midst of a flourishing European civilisation'. They were less evolved than the rest of us, according to Lombroso, and as such retained various animalistic 'stigmata'. Thus, rodent-like people were stealthy, while ape-like people were crafty and not to be trusted at all.

As Lombroso's fame grew, he appeared as an expert witness in countless trials. Rebecca B Fleming wrote an award-winning study of Lombroso (*Scanty Goatees and Palmer Tattoos: Cesare Lombroso's Influence and Popular Opinion*) and discovered that in 1908 the French courts, unable to decide if a woman accused of murdering her children was guilty, sent a photo of the accused killer to Lombroso. He immediately declared that she was guilty just by looking at the picture. She had, he claimed, a round small skull, a flat forehead and a virile expression on her face – all bad signs of innate inborn depravity. She was convicted on the basis of the photo alone, although all the evidence pointed to the fact that the children had died of natural causes. On another occasion, Lombroso was asked to decide which of two brothers had murdered their stepmother. Lombroso picked one, claiming that he was 'the most perfect type of born criminal', and the man was promptly convicted.

In order to support his findings, Lombroso examined some of the most famous murderers of his time, including a vampire-type killer called Vincent Verzeni. Verzeni strangled two women to death in 1871, wallowed in their internal organs, drank the blood of one of his victims and carried the intestines around in his pocket to touch and sniff on the way back to his mother's house. He also took part of a thigh so that he could roast it when he got home (but then hid it because he thought his mother might find it). Verzeni, Lombroso claimed, was a perfect example of 'primitive humanity'.

## BODY TYPE

The process of body-mapping evil continued in the 1920s with the work of Ernst Kretchmer, who worked in a mental asylum. Noticing that the different varieties of schizophrenics appeared to have different body shapes – for example, paranoids were slight and slim, manic-depressives larger and fatter – Kretchmer launched a series of studies and published his findings in 1921.

Perhaps the widest and most ambitious study to find a correlation between body shape and crime was undertaken by Earnest Hooton, a Harvard anthropologist, in 1927. Determined to prove that Lombroso's theory was fundamentally sound, Hooton undertook the massive task of studying 14,000 criminals over 12 years in ten states. At the end of this mammoth exercise, he declared that there was 'a well nigh incredible relationship of body build to nature of offence'.

Dr Hooton became so convinced of the importance of his findings that, during the American Association for the Advancement of Science Fair in Pittsburgh in 1938, he outlined a plan to cleanse the human race of evil: 'What we must avoid is a progressive deterioration of mankind as a result of the reckless and copious breeding of protected inferiors,' he proclaimed. 'We have not the knowledge to breed supermen, but we can limit the reproduction of criminals and mental defectives. Let us cease to delude ourselves that education, religion or other measures of social amelioration can transform base metal into gold. Public enemies must be destroyed – not reformed.'

The concept that body type could be an indicator of criminality was taken up yet again in the 1940s, this time by

American psychologist Dr William Sheldon. Sheldon spent 30 years taking photographs of prison inmates and categorising them into three distinct body types. 'Endomorphs' were fat and round, liked luxury and were lazy. 'Ectomorphs' were frail, gangly and thin, and were introverted, cunning and stealthy, while 'mesomorphs' were large, strong, tough, active, dynamic and extremely assertive in their dealings with others. Through his hundreds of visits to prisons all over the United States, Sheldon concluded that criminals were predominantly mesomorphic.

Although criminology may have moved on since those days, criminal physiognomy has never actually been discredited. Dr Candland, Professor of Psychology and Animal Behaviour at Bucknell University, explained to me that 'few ideas in social science are truly discarded or found to be invalid: rather, they fade out, often enough to return again under a different guise. Criminal physiognomy is not disproved, for no one has tried seriously.'

In fact, a handful of recent studies have persisted with a search for the link between physical looks and a propensity to commit crime. So, if you've got your doubts about a certain someone, here are a few things to watch out for. You never know, it might just save your life.

## HAIR

The hair of criminals tends to mimic the hair of the opposite sex, argued Lombroso, while Hooton argued that red-brown hair was a common trait among born criminals. Thin hair or baldness, though, was regarded as absent among criminals, as was white or grey hair. Murderers had dark hair. Swindlers had curly hair. Arsonists had ash-blond hair. Burglars and second-degree murderers had golden hair and robbers sported long, wavy hair.

## FACIAL AND BODY HAIR

Facial hair was significant too. It was believed that bushy eyebrows were a bad sign, as were eyebrows that met across the bridge of the nose. Another bad trait was a soft down on the forehead and a scanty beard – a sure sign of a pickpocket – while prostitutes, Lombroso discovered, generally tended to be hairy.

## THE SKULL

Phrenologists believed that a slight protuberance above the ears was the sign of the 'murder organ'. This was also known as the organ of 'Murder to Destructiveness', suggesting an inborn propensity not only to kill, but also to 'pinch, scratch, bite, cut, break, pierce, devastate'. It was said to be larger in men than in women.

## THE FACE

According to Lombroso, the protrusion of forehead and jaw was 45% greater in criminals than in non-criminals. Look out for people with asymmetrical faces and also those with projecting cheekbones and a predominance of wrinkles. According to Hooton, those individuals with compressed facial features and narrow jaws were best avoided. Helpfully, James Bruce Thomson, resident surgeon for a Scottish prison in the late 19th century, wrote in *The Hereditary Nature of Crime* that a criminal is 'marked by a singular stupid and insensate look'.

## NOSE

A high nasal bridge was a very bad sign for Hooton. According to Lombroso, in thieves the nose was often twisted, upturned or flattened, while in murderers it was aquiline 'like the beak of a bird of prey'.

## MOUTH

Fleshy lips, but a thin upper lip and 'a depression in the jaw where the canine muscle is to be found. This muscle is commonly found in the dog where it serves, when contorted, to draw back the lip leaving the canines exposed.' (Lombroso)

## CHEEKS

'Folds in the flesh of the cheek which recall the pouches of certain species of mammals' – this was a sign for murderers (Lombroso).

## TEETH

Strong canine teeth are often present in murderers, as are enormously developed middle incisors, and tread lightly around those with a double row of teeth. Criminals had sharp teeth like predatory animals and gigantic canines. Lombroso noticed also that the middle incisors were often absent, 'a peculiarity which recalls the incisors of rodents'.

## EARS

Handle-shaped ears were another bad sign – 'Ears of unusual size, or occasionally very small, or standing out from the head as do those of the chimpanzee'. This too was a sure sign of a natural born killer (Lombroso).

## EYES

Eye defects and peculiarities such as the asymmetry of the iris were bad signs, as were large eye sockets. The eyes often show a 'hard expression' and 'shift glance' and are hooded by oblique eyelids. According to Havelock Ellis, in *The Criminal* (1890), 'The eyes of assassins resemble those of the feline animals at the moment of ambush or struggle.'

## BODY SHAPES

Hooton divided body types into types of criminals. So, short-slender individuals were burglars. A short-medium frame suggested an arsonist. Short-heavy individuals were rapists. Tall-slender types were murderers in all degrees, while tall-heavy men with large chests and heads were cold-blooded first-degree murderers.

## TATTOOS

Lombroso associated tattoos on the body with criminality, especially among women. They were, he argued, an emblem of a man 'still living in a savage state'. A criminal's ability to take the pain of getting a tattoo was also given as evidence that he or she was less sensitive to pain.

## BACK

An enlarged coccyx that could be mistaken for a stump of a tail, especially if it has hairs on the end of it, meant that the individual was without any doubt a remorseless killer.

## HANDS

Long hands were prevalent in pickpockets, whereas pointy or snubbed fingers were prevalent in criminals in general. Extra fingers or a diminished number of lines in the palms of one's hands were further signs of innate evil.

## FEET

Flat footed. Too many toes. Mobile big toes. Pointy, webby, stubby toes. All were regarded as signs of innate criminality. Prostitutes, according to Lombroso, possessed a very large big toe that was unusually separated from the other toes.

## CHEST

A large chest was more prevalent in murderers – and watch out for an extra nipple, which was a sure sign that its possessor was a natural born murderer.

# BIBLIOGRAPHY

## CHAPTER ONE

- Abos, Alvaro. 'El Petiso Orejudo: primer asesino serial argentino'. *La Nacion*, 15 January 2006.
- Cuneo, Carlos. *Las Carceles*. Centro Editor de America Latina, 1971.
- Cuneo, Carlos and Gonzales, Abel. *La Delinquencia*. CentroEditor de America Latina S.A., 1971.
- Gonzalez, Gustavo and Barcia, Jose. *Testimonios y experiencias de un cronista porteno*. Historia Press, 1979.
- Staff. 'La saga del Petiso Orejudo'. *Clarin*, 31 August 2005.
- An excellent variety of primary sources are available online thanks to the work of Milton Javier Contreras, who wrote the definitive account of the case in his book *Santos Godino El Petiso Orejudo*, Dunken Press, 2000.

## CHAPTER TWO

- Kamiyama, Masuo. 'Paris "Cannibal" Sagawa Still hungers for Attention'. *Mainichi Daily News*, October 2007.
- Ramsland, Katherine. 'The Cannibal Celebrity Issei Sagawa'. *Crime Library*. (www.crimelibrary.com)
- Ryall, Julian. 'Taste in Women that Takes Some Swallowing'. *Scotsman on Sunday*, 18 July 2004.
- Sagawa, Issei. *Into the Fog*. Tokyo: Hanashi No Tokusyu, 1983.
- Schreiber, Mark. *The Dark Side: Infamous Japanese Crimes and Criminal*. Relié Publishing, 2000.
- Schreiber, Mark. 'Japan's own "Cannibal" tries his hand at comics'. *Japan Today*, 20 February 2001.
- Staff. 'The real Hannibal Lecters'. *BBC News*, 16 February 2001.
- Whipple, Charles T. 'The Silencing of the Lambs'. 4 March 2008. (www.charlest.whipple.net)
- Wright, Evan Alan. 'Death of a Hostess'. *Time Magazine*, 7 May 2001.

## CHAPTER THREE

- Azevedo, Solange; Dantas, Edna. 'Marcelo de Andrade – O sadismo tinha subido à minha cabeça'. *Epoca Magazine*, 22 September 2003.
- Casoy, Ilana. *Serial Killers: Made in Brazil*. Editora Arx, 2004.
- Mendoza, Antonio. *Serial Killer Hit List Part II Marcelo de Andrade*, Internet Crime Archives. (www.mayhem.net)
- Morrison, Helen. *My Life Amongst The Serial Killers: Inside the Minds of The World's Most Notorious Murderers*. Harper Collins, 2004.

- Staff. 'Brazil "serial killer" on trial'. *BBC News America*, 24 October 2006.
- Staff. 'Mad Cow Disease In The U.S.? Don't Panic, But One Version's Already Here'. *Newsweek*, 8 April 1996.

## CHAPTER FOUR

- Chacón, Daniel. 'Mystery persists as sailor laid to rest'. *The San Diego Union Tribune*, 14 August 2005.
- Kraft, Randy. Randy Kraft's memoirs are published online via: *Voices from Death Row*, which is sponsored by the Canadian Coalition against the Death Penalty (www.ccadp.org). Some of Kraft's memoirs used in the chapter are: 'The Old Homestead'; 'Working the Soil'; 'Midway City Elementary School'; 'Kindergarten'; 'First Grade'; 'Planting with Dad'; 'The Helm's Bakery Man'; 'The Crowded Hole'; 'Dad and the Fire'; 'Mom's Bible'; 'My Friday The 13'. Definitely not recommended reading. Supreme Court of California decision. The People Plaintiff and Respondent vs. Randy Steven Kraft Defendant and Appellant Filed 08/10/2000.
- Maloney, J. 'Randy Kraft: The Southern California Strangler'. *Crime Magazine*. (crimemagazine.com)
- McDougal, Dennis. 'Life After Death Penalty'. *Beach The Magazine of Long Beach*, April 2000.
- McDougal, Dennis. *Angel of Darkness: The True Story of Randy Kraft and the Most Heinous Murder Spree.* Grand Central Publishing, 1992.
- Newton, Michael. 'All about Randy Kraft'. *Crime Library*. (www.crimelibrary.com)
- Court Transcripts. 'The People of the State of California vs. Randy Steven Kraft'. *Case Number 52776*.

## CHAPTER FIVE

- Crabbe, Nathan. 'Florida killers sell "murderabilia"'. *The Gainesville Sun*, 11 December 2007.
- Crabbe, Nathan. 'Rolling execution closes chapter of area history'. *The Gainesville Sun*, 31 December 2006.
- Fisher, Lise. 'Danny Rolling executed for five student murders'. *The Gainesville Sun*, 28 October 2006.
- Rolling, Danny and London, Sondra. *The Making of a Serial Killer. The Real Story of the Gainesville Student Murders in the Killer's Own Words*. Feral House, 1996.
- Staff. 'Danny Rolling's Execution Just Hours Away'. *Local 10*, 25 October 2006. (www.local10.com)
- Staff. 'Rolling Execution Set For Wednesday'. *Wesh News*, 23 October 2006. (www.wesh.com)
- Staff. 'Serial Killer Rolling Executed in Florida'. *The Washington Post*, 26 October 2006.
- Staff. 'Victim's Family Calls Killer's Execution Final Chapter: Serial Killer Executed For 1990 Gainesville Student Murders'. *News4Jax*, 25 October 2006. (www.news4jax.com)
- Staff. 'Louisiana Drifter Became Known As "Gainesville Ripper"'. *News4Jax*, 23 October 2006. (www.news4jax.com)
- Staff. 'Victim's Family: Execution Will Not Bring Closure'. *News4Jax*, 24 October 2006. (www.news4jax.com)
- Staff. 'Florida Serial killer died singing a hymn'. *CNN* and *Associated Press*, 26 October 2006.
- Staff. 'Rolling executed for murders of 5 Florida college students'. *News4Jax* and *Associated Press*, 26 October 2006. (www.news4jax.com)
- Staff. 'Victim's Brother Talks About Execution Of Mass Murderer'. *WFTV* and *Associated Press*, 24 October 2006. (www.wftv.com)

- Tisch, Chris. 'Rolling executed: 47 people pack room to watch Rolling's execution'. *St Petersburg Times*, 25 October 2006.
- For an excellent resource of the case, including primary sources such as Rolling's letters and poems, as well as the transcripts of the audiotape he made just before he killed Sonya Larson and Christina Powell, go to *The Independent Florida Alligator* 'A Killer's End'. (www.alligator.org/pt2/specials/rolling/)

## CHAPTER SIX

- Barker, Mayerene. 'Ninja story not credible murder trial jurors told'. *Los Angeles Times*, 4 May 1989.
- Lozano, Carlos. 'Man Who Killed Actress Mother Gets Probation'. *Los Angeles Times*, 30 November 1989.
- Lerner, Patricia. 'Son accused of killing actress tells court she attacked him'. *Los Angeles Times*, 6 October 1989.
- Lerner, Patricia. 'Actress in deep despair on day she was slain'. *Los Angeles Times*, 5 October 1989.
- Lerner, Patricia. 'Man accused of killing his mother changes plea'. *Los Angeles Times*, 28 September 1989.
- Lozano, Charles. 'Cabot slaying new defence readies case for trial'. *Los Angeles Times*, 23 June 1989.
- Quinn, James. 'Jurors Hear Tape of Police Interrogation Defendant Sobs But Remains in Control Under Intense Questioning in Death of Actress Mother'. *Los Angeles Times*, 12 May 1989.
- Staff. 'Son testifies on actress death'. *Los Angeles Times*, 6 October 1989.
- Staff. 'Manslaughter Verdict for Susan Cabot's Son'. *Los Angeles Times*, 11 October 1989.

- Staff. 'The Bizarre Death of Susan Cabot'. *Find a Death.* (www.findadeath.com)
- Weaver, Tom. 'The Life and Tragic Death of Susan Cabot'. The Astounding B Monster Cult. (www.bmonster.com)
- Weaver, Tom. 'Lost Souls Susan Cabot'. *The Irish Journal of Gothic and Horror Studies,* November 2007 (www.irishgothichorrorjournal.homestead.com). All of the quotes from Tom Weaver are taken from this article and used with his kind permission.

## CHAPTER SEVEN

- Daquilante, Paul. 'McMinnville woman's murderer dies in prison'. *Associated Press News-Register,* 30 March 2006.
- King, Gary. *Blood Lust: Portrait of a Serial Sex Killer.* Onyx, 1992.
- McCarthy, Linda. 'A History of the Oregon's Sheriff's Office 1841 to 1991'. *The Oregon State Sheriff Association.*
- Ramsland, Katherine. 'Jerome Brudos The Fetish Killer'. *Crime Library.* (www.crimelibrary.com)
- Rule, Anne. *Lust Killer.* Signet True Crime, 1983.
- Turvey, Brent. 'Building a Career in Forensic Science'. *Young Forensic Scientists Forum Newsletter.* July 1998.
- Turvey, Brent. 'The Impressions of a Man: An Objective Forensic Guideline to Profiling Violent Serial Sex Offenders'. *Knowledge Solutions, LLC,* 1995.

## CHAPTER EIGHT

- Altimari, David. 'Remains not Tolland Girl's'. *The Hartford Courant,* 31 March 2001.
- Altimari, David. 'Case Raises Chilling Suspicions'. *The Hartford Courant,* 23 May 2002.

## BIBLIOGRAPHY

- Belkin, Douglas. 'Accused killer's account of deeds shocks city'. *Boston Globe*, 28 December 2000.
- Emey, Theo. 'Interstate finger pointing erupts over sex offender killing, cooking boy'. *Batesville Daily Guard*, 21 June 2001.
- Gallagher, Susan. 'Cannibalism Charges Stun Montana Town'. *ABC News*, 21 December 2002.
- Hanchett, Doug. 'Bar-Jonah's Life History Full of Tales of Violence'. *The Boston Herald*, 1 July 2001.
- Laceky, Tom. 'Suspect in Montana child slaying gets 130 years for separate assaults'. *Berkeley Daily Planet*, May 2002.
- Laceky, Tom. 'Police Challenged in Bar-Jonah Trial'. *AP Online*, 22 February 2002. (www.ap.org)
- Murphy, Kim. 'Sex Cannibalism Allegations Shake Town'. *Los Angeles Times*, 17 February 2002.
- Skornogoski, Kim. 'Prosecutor goes after conviction in cold case'. *Great Falls Tribune*, 14 November 2005.
- Skornogoski, Kim. 'Convicted molester maintains innocence'. *Great Falls Tribune*, 16 October 2005.
- Staff. 'Accused Cannibal Pleads Not Guilty: Nathaniel Bar-Jonah Pleads Innocent To Murder, Kidnapping'. *CBS News*, 11 January 2001.
- Staff. 'Latest Attempt to Find Conn. Child's Body Futile'. *Boston Globe* and *Associated Press*, 9 November 1980.
- Staff. 'State woman says she was victim of Montana predator'. *Record-Journal*, 22 January 2001.
- *Janice Pockett The Charley Project* – a web page that profiles over 7,000 'cold case' missing people, mainly from the United States. (www.charleyproject.org)
- *The National Centre for Missing & Exploited Children (NCMEC)* .The Nation's Resource Centre for Child Protection.

(www.missingkids.com)

- Court transcript No. 02-769.
- In the Supreme Court of the State of Montana 2004 MT 344.
- State of Montana Plaintiff and Respondent, vs. Nathaniel Bar-Jonah Defendant and Appellant. Appeal From: District Court of the Eighth Judicial District, In and for the County of Cascade, *Cause No. ADC* 2000-273(c).
- The authority on the Bar-Jonah case is staff reporter Kim Skornogoski at *The Great Falls Tribune* in Montana. As mentioned in the text, Skornogoski first began covering Nathan Bar-Jonah in March 2000 and continues to write stories about him as they develop. In all, Skornogoski has written around 200 stories on Bar-Jonah and a lot of what is known about him, especially regarding his troubled youth in Lake Webster, is thanks to her research.

## CHAPTER NINE

- Graysmith, Robert. *Auto Focus: The Murder of Bob Crane.* Berkeley, 2002.
- Hirschberg, Lynn. 'First came the sitcom. Then came the murder. Then came the pornographic web site. Now here comes the Hollywood biopic'. *New York Times,* 29 September 2002.
- LaRue, Jan. 'Porn, Sex and Murder – Bob Crane's Fatal Focus'. *Concerned Women for America,* 26 November 2002. (www.cwfa.org)
- Mt Clarke, Denis. 'Cold Case: The Murder of Hogan's Hero'. *Crime Magazine.* (crimemagazine.com)
- Noe, Denis. 'The Bob Crane Case'. *Crime Library.* (www.crimelibrary.com)
- Olsen, Eric. 'Sex, Death and Videotape'. *Blog Critics Magazine,* 16 October 2002. (The blogcritics.org)

# BIBLIOGRAPHY

- Rubin, Paul. 'The Bob Crane Murder Case'. *Phoenix New Times*, 21 April 1993.
- Scott Royce, Brenda. *Hogan's Heroes: Behind the Scenes at Stalag 13!* Renaissance Books, 1998.
- Staff. 'Seedy World of Bob Crane, TV's Colonel Hogan'. *Franks Reel Reviews*. (www.franksreelreviews.com)
- Staff. *Find a Death*. February 2005. (www.findadeath.com)
- Thoreson, Tyler. 'Death of a Salesman; or How the Sexual Revolution Killed Col. Hogan. The life and death of Bob Crane'. *Gadfly Magazine*, January 1999.

## CHAPTER TEN

- Douglas, John. 'What I Do, Hunting the Hunter'. *MindHunter*. (www.johndouglasmindhunter.com)
- Du Clos, Bernard. *Fair Game*. St Martins Press, February 1993.
- Gilmour, Walter and Hale, Leland. *Butcher Baker*, Onyx 1991. It was in their account that the Hansen interviews with the police were first published.
- Lohr, David. 'Hunting Humans'. *Crime Library*. (www.crimelibrary.com)
- Lundberg, Murray. 'Robert Hansen: A Serial Killer in Alaska'. *Explore North*. (explorenorth.com)
- Mitchell, Alex. 'Police raid Milat family home for clues to unsolved murder'. *Sydney Morning Herald*, 20 August 2006.
- Staff. 'Troopers try to identify victim of serial killer'. *Kenai Peninsula* and *Associated Press*, 21 February 2003.
- Staff. 'Milat a suspect in teen's cold-case murder'. *Fairfax Digital*, 27 January 2005.
- Toomey, Shelia. 'Bad Bob: The Butcher Baker Story of Anchorage Serial Killer Robert Hansen'. *Anchorage Daily News*, 24 November 1991.

- Toomey, Shelia. 'Escape Plan Prompts State to Move Killer'. *Anchorage Daily News*, 8 March 1990.
- Toomey, Shelia. 'Troopers seek real name of slain Eklutna Annie'. *Anchorage Daily News*, 20 February 2005.
- Wellner, Andrew. 'Valley is city killers' body dump'. *Anchorage Daily News*, 10 October 2007.
- Wellner, Andrew. 'Trooper left behind legacy of solving tough cases'. *Anchorage Daily News*, 8 August 2007.
- Almost all of the quotes from this chapter are thanks to Mary Katzke, documentary filmmaker and playwright. While researching her play *Dancing for the Hunter*, she interviewed a great many prostitutes at the time of the Hansen murders. Katzke changed the names of the girls whom she interviewed, for their own protection. All of the quotes attributed to Hansen and the prostitutes are thanks to the kind assistance of Mary Katzke, who collected a great many documents during her research, including court transcripts.

## CHAPTER ELEVEN

- Bragg, Rick. 'Quest for Beauty Went Awry at Hands of a Fake Surgeon, Miami Police Say'. *New York Times*, 7 October 1999.
- Cabrera, Javier. 'Cubre silencio historia de los Carrillo Fuentes'. *El Universal*, 6 July 2005.
- Ciotti, Paul. 'Why Did He Cut Off That Man's Leg? The Peculiar Practice of Dr John Ronald Brown'. *LA Weekly News*, 15 December 1999.
- Dotinga, Randy. 'Out on a Limb'. *Salon*, 29 August 2000. (www.salon.com)
- Dotinga, Randy. 'Murder Case Canters on Amputation Fetish'. *APB News*, 30 September 1999. (www.apbnews.com)

# BIBLIOGRAPHY

- Ellison, Michael. 'Ex-doctor faces life for botched fetish amputation'. *The Guardian*, 7 October 1999.
- Henig, Robin. 'At War With Their Bodies, They Seek to Sever Limbs'. *New York Times*, 22 March 2005.
- Hill, Vicki. 'True Desire of the Pervert Devotees'. *Daily Record*, 7 October 1999.
- Horn, Francie. 'A Life For A Limb: Body Integrity Identity Disorder'. *Social Work Today*, 24 February 2003.
- Jones, Harry. 'Ex-doctor found guilty of murder of leg amputee'. *The San Diego Union-Tribune*, 6 October 1999.
- Potter, Tony. 'How to get your rocks or legs off'. *The Sunday Star-Times*, 10 October 1999.
- Reaville, Gil. 'The Butcher of South Beach'. *Maxim Magazine*, February 2002.
- Staff. 'Suddenly, facelift fatality looks like a 30-year grudge'. *Associated Press*, 27 October 2006.
- Staff. 'Prosecutors: Nurse May Have Sought Revenge'. *ABC News*, 25 September 2006.
- Staff. 'Nurse Arrested In 2001 Death Of Former High School Rival Cold Case Unit: N.C. Nurse Administered Fatal Dose Of Painkiller'. *The Denver Channel*, 26 September 2006.
- Staff. 'Sex Change Doctor on trial for Murder'. *Associated Press*, 1 July 2000.
- Staff. 'Sex-change practitioner convicted of murder in botched amputation'. *Associated Press*, 6 October 1999.
- Staff. 'Surgeon defends amputations'. *BBC News*, 31 January 2000.
- Staff. 'Trust bans "private" amputations.' *BBC News*, 1 February 2000.

- Williams, Michelle. 'Murder Trial Opens for Fetish M.D.'. *Associated Press*, 29 September 1999.

## CHAPTER TWELVE

- Barbano, Rolando; Caneletti, Ricardo; Gambini, Hector. *Crimenes Argentinos Grandes Casos Policiales Que Conmovieron Al Pais*. Planeta 2001.
- Dahl, Roald. *Completely Unexpected Tales*. Penguin, 1986.
- Davish, Francisco García. 'Yo sabía que no existe el crimen perfecto'. *Mi Morelia*, 21 April 2004. (www.mimorelia.com)
- Davish, Francisco García. 'Capturan a presunto tamalero descuartizador'. *Mi Morelia*, 20 April 2004. (www.mimorelia.com)
- Davish, Francisco García. 'Consignan al tamalero'. *Mi Morelia*, 22 April 2004. (www.mimorelia.com)
- Davish, Francisco García. '"El tamalero", sin alteraciones mentales'. *Mi Morelia*, 21 April 2004. (www.mimorelia.com)
- Enriquez, Mariana. 'Todos tus muertos'. *Pagina 12*, 15 August 2004.
- Grinstein, Maria. *Mujeres Asesinas*. Editorial Sudamercana, 2005.
- Kidd, Paul. 'Katherine Knight Australia's "Hani Lector"'. *Crime Library*. (www.crimelibrary.com)
- Marshall, Anne. 'Extreme Domestic Violence – after sex killer stabs, skins, beheads victim cooks body parts'. *Australia New Commentary*, 3 July 2006.
- Mendoza, Antonio. 'Nikolai Dzhurmongaliev'. *Serial Killer Hit List Part III*, Internet Crime Archives. (www.mayhem.net)
- Staff. 'Tamales mexicanos con carne humana'. *Univision Online*, 21 April 2004.

- Staff. 'Investigan a cocinero mexicano por usar carne humana'. *Terra and Reuters*, 21 April 2004.
- Staff. 'Cocinó el cuerpo de compinche y salió a vender frente a hospital: Ambulante cuate se hacía el pino con tamales rellenos con carne humana'. *La Cuarta*, 22 April 2004.
- Staff. 'Hacia Tamales con carne humano'. *Terra*, 22 April 2004.
- Staff. 'Sentencian a 30 años de prisión a "tamalero" en Michoacán'. *Motimex news agency*, 25 August 2006.
- Court Case in the Supreme Court of New South Wales Criminal Division at Newcastle No:70094/00 Coram O'Keefe J vs. Regina Katherine Mary Knight, 8 November 2001.

## CHAPTER THIRTEEN

- Costa, Pedro. 'La vampira del carrer Ponent'. *El Pais*, 1 January 2006.
- Grinstein, Maria. *Mujeres Asesinas*. Editorial Sudamericana, 2005.
- Knowles, George. 'Murder by Witchcraft'. (www.controverscial.com)
- Pengelly, Adrian. 'Charles Walton Fifty Years on'. White Dragon, 1995. (www.whitedragon.org.uk)
- Staff. 'The Correggio Soap Maker'. From the online archives of The Criminology Museum in Rome. (www.museocriminologico.com)
- Staff. 'A Copper Ladle'. *Time Magazine*, 24 June 1946.
- Staff. 'Warwickshire's Sinister Secret. Was there a link between murder and witchcraft in Lower Quinton in the 40s?' *BBC Warwickshire and Coventry News*, 17 August 2007.

## CHAPTER FOURTEEN

- Austreng, Sue. 'Blaine teen pleads guilty to murder'. *ABC News*, 3 February 2006.
- Carlton, Sue; French, Thomas; Hull, Anne. 'The Great Divide'. *The St Petersburg Times*, 9 April 2000.
- Carlton, Sue; French, Thomas; Hull, Anne. 'Mad Love'. *The St Petersburg Times*, 10 April 2000.
- Carlton, Sue; French, Thomas; Hull, Anne. 'Valessa in the Tower'. *The St Petersburg Times*, 11 April 2000.
- Carlton, Sue; French, Thomas; Hull, Anne. '"Dear Journal. It's me, Valessa"'. *The St Petersburg Times*, 25 April 2000.
- Holewa, Lisa. 'Daughter Gets 20 Years for Mom's Murder: Woman Disapproved of Girl's Relationship With Drifter'. *APB*, 30 May 2000.
- Labi, Nadya. 'An IM Infatuation Turned to Romance. Then the Truth Came Out'. *Wired Magazine*, 21 August 2007.
- Labi, Nadya. 'The Internet Chatroom Murder'. *BBC World Service* radio report. First broadcast November 2007.
- Lewis, Leo. 'Schoolgirl blogger poisons mother in homage to killer'. *The Times*, 3 November 2005.
- Maag, Christopher. 'A Hoax Turned Fatal Draws Anger but No Charges'. *New York Times*, 28 November 2007.
- Moharib, Nadia. 'Accused Killer in Court'. *Calgary Sun*, 2 May 2006.
- Staba, David. 'Pretend Web Romance, Then a Real-Life Murder'. *New York Times*, 7 January 2007
- Staff. 'Judge: Murder Hearing Most Painful Case He's Had'. *CBS Broadcasting*, 28 February 2006.
- Staff. 'Pauline Parker Found'. *Daily Mail*, 6 January 1997.
- Staff. 'Sweet Spinster Who is one of the World's Lost Killers: Grey-haired schoolteacher unmasked 43 years after

battering her mother in Heavenly Creatures murder'. *The Express*, 6 January 1997.

- Staff. 'Solved: Hulme's greatest secret'. *The Press*, Saturday, 6 August 1994.
- Staff. 'Woman's body found'. *Press*, 23 June 1954.
- Staff. 'Two teenagers face charge of killing woman. Trial of city girls opens today in Supreme Court'. *Star-Sun*, 23 August 1954.
- Staff. 'The Enemy Within. Exploring A Murder Close To Home'. *CBS News*, 9 August 2002.
- Staff. 'Ruling on Japan poison-diary girl'. *BBC News*, 1 May 2006.
- Staff. 'Parents: Cyber Bullying Led to Teen's Suicide. Megan Meier's Parents Now Want Measures to Protect Children Online'. *ABC News*, 19 November 2007.
- Staff. 'MySpace Mom Linked to Missouri Teen's Suicide Being Cyber-Bullied Herself'. *Fox News*, 6 December 2007.
- Staff. 'Jeremy Allan Steinke and Jasmine Richardson'. *People You'll See in Hell*. (pysih.com)
- Staff. 'Teen killer to be sentenced today'. *CanWest News Service*, 7 November 2007.
- Stevenson, James. 'Accused in Alta Family Slaying Likely to Wait Until 2008 for His Murder Trial'. *The Canadian Press*, 4 January 2007.
- Stevenson, James. 'Alberta girl admits stabbing her brother'. *The Canadian Press*, 3 July 2007.
- Zickefoose, Sherri. 'Medicine Hat prepares for shocking trial'. *CanWest News Service*, 26 March 2007.
- Zickefoose, Sherri. 'Murdered family "gutted like fish", court told'. *CanWest News Service*, 27 June 2007.

## CHAPTER FIFTEEN

- Barbano, Rolando; Caneletti, Ricardo; Gambini, Hector. *Crimenes Argentinos Grandes Casos Policiales Que Conmovieron Al Pais*, Planeta 2001.

- Bennetto, Jason. 'Serial killer with HIV virus dies in jail'. *Independent*, February 1995.

- Bird, Paul. 'Man confesses to killing infant son who lawmen believed died of SIDS'. *Indianapolis Star*, 24 June 1999.

- Bird, Paul. 'Man says he killed son to get back at his wife'. *Indianapolis Star*, 25 June 1999.

- Callahan, Rick. 'Suspect says he fathered child with intent to kill him'. *Topeka Capital-Journal*, 28 June 1999.

- El Buho. 'El loco Poggi'. *Trome*. (www.trome.com)

- Harding, Nick Paton; Walsh, Luke. 'Nothing left to lose: grief-crazed murder suspect haunted by family's air deaths'. *The Guardian*, 28 February 2004.

- Kawamura, Eiko. 'Mario Poggi no es imbécil, se hace'. *Entrevistas*, February 2002. From the online archive of el Universidad de Peru de ciencias aplicadas (www.upc.edu.pe/home_upc.aspx).

- Lar, Rodolfo. 'Asesinadas a sangre fría Ricardo Barreda eliminó a su familia el domingo Todo terminó antes del mediodía'. *Clarin*, 15 November 1992.

- Monique, Doctor (pen name). 'Una Velada con Poggi'. *Cronicas de la faradala kitch*. (es.geocities.com/doctor_monique/susy/susy.htm)

- Potesta, Orazio. 'Ya, Pues, ¿Cómo lo Hiciste? Psicólogos de la Policía pueden hacer hablar hasta al delincuente más peligroso y descubrir cómo se convirtió en un criminal'. *Carretas Magazine*, 28 October 1999.

# BIBLIOGRAPHY

- Mancinelli, Leopoldo. 'El crimen del odontólogo, diez años después'. *La Plata*, 10 April 2004
- Nash, Carlos. *Locura resignada – Entrevistas*, February 2002, from the online archive of Universidad de Peru de ciencias aplicadas. (www.upc.edu.pe/home_upc.aspx)
- Staff. 'Penis Slasher put to death in China'. *iol*, 27 August 2004. (www.iol.co.za)
- Staff. 'Michael Lupo case summary'. *Murder in the UK*. (www.murderuk.com)
- Staff. 'Uni Dropouts Grisly Revenge'. *China Daily*, 27 August 2004.
- Staff. '50 Años De Policiales. Los casos más sonados del medio siglo de Caretas. Del Monstruo de Armendáriz al caso Succar, dramas íntimos que captaron la atención de multitudes'. *Caretas Magazine*, 9 November 2000.
- Staff, 'Beheaded for Trouble'. *Snopes Urban reference page*, 28 December 2005. (www.snopes.com)
- Staff. 'Barreda loco?' *El Dia*, 14 November 2004. (www.eldia.com.ar)
- Staff. 'Swiss court orders release Vitaly Kaloyev, air traffic controller murderer'. *Pravda* and *Associated Press*, 11 August 2007.
- Shmelev, Ivan. 'Swiss court finds Russian man guilty of revenge killing SkyGuide's employee'. *Pravda*, 27 October 2005.
- Staff. 'Free Love Religious Sect Child Sex Allegations Haunt Group Known For Biblical Prophecy, Sexual Freedom'. *ABC News*, 27 January 2005.
- Wilkinson, Peter. 'The Life and Death of the Chosen One'. *Rolling Stone Magazine*, 30 June 2005.

- Zogg, Jeff. 'Shanabarger found guilty in son's murder'. *Indianapolis Star*, 8 May 2002.
- United States, Appellee vs. Stephen J. SCHAP, Sergeant U.S. Army, Appellant *CASE No. 96-1058*.
- Ronald Shanabarger vs. State of Indiana. Appeal from the Johnson Superior Court *Case No. 41D01-0402-PC-1*, 3 May 2006

## CHAPTER SIXTEEN

- Charter, David; Watson, Rory. 'Dinner guest discovers bodies in freezer'. *The Times*, 6 July 2007.
- Dorsey, Christine. 'Bierenbaum Sentencing: Former LV doctor gets 20-to-life'. *Las Vegas Review-Journal*, 30 November 2000.
- Donrey, Tony. 'Doctor on Trial: Wife had vowed to ruin husband's career'. *Las Vegas Review*, 11 October 2000.
- Donrey, Tony. 'Murder trial for ex-Las Vegan set to begin'. *Las Vegas Review*, 4 September 2000 .
- Finkelstein, Katherine. 'Doctor Gets 20 Years to Life For the Murder of His Wife'. *New York Times*, 30 November 2000.
- Finkelstein, Katherine. 'A New Life Re-examined; After Murder Verdict, Town Questions Doctor'. *New York Times*, 30 October 2000.
- Finkelstein, Katherine. 'Minimum Sentence Sought For Doctor Who Killed Wife'. *New York Times*, 23 November 2000.
- Glendinning, Lee. 'Pig farmer jailed for six murders'. *The Guardian*, 10 December 2007.
- Godl, John. 'The Life and Crimes of Frederick Bailey Deeming'. *Simply Australia*, Issue 10. (www.simplyaustralia.net)

# BIBLIOGRAPHY

- Hickey, Brian. 'Return to the House of Horrors'. *Philadelphia Weekly*, 13 March 2002.
- Larson, Erik. *Devil in the White City Murder, Magic and Madness At the Fair that Changed America*. First Vintage Books, 2003.
- Leonard, Tom. 'Death sentence for alligator child killer'. *The Telegraph*, 20 October 2007.
- Lohr, David. 'All about Joe Ball'. *Crime Library*. (www.crimelibrary.com)
- Masters, Brian. *Killing for Company: Case of Dennis Nilsen*. Arrow Books Ltd, 1995.
- Matas, Robert. 'Week 24: Pickton demonstrated how he strangled prostitutes, witness says'. *Globe and Mail*, 30 November 2007.
- Roberts, Greg. 'TV grabs Natasha's story in $200,000 deal'. *Sydney Morning Herald*, 16 April 2003.
- Senley, Rick. 'Lovely home. Shame about the homicidal former tenant'. *The Observer*, 19 June 2005.
- Shimo, Alexandra. '"Horror movie" trial begins of pig farmer accused of killing 26 prostitutes'. *The Independent*, 22 January 2007.
- Staff. 'Joe Ball The Alligator Man'. Frances Farmers Revenge. (www.francesfarmersrevenge.com)
- Staff. 'Justice For Girl Eaten Alive By Alligators: Ex-Con Who Abandoned 5-Year-Old In Everglades Gets Death Sentence'. *CBS News* and *Associated Press*, 16 October 2007.
- Staff. 'Gary Heidnik and His Cellar of Death'. *New Criminologist*, 14 September 2007.
- Staff. 'Couple lose house of horror case'. *BBC News*, 27 February 2004.

- Staff. 'Pickton appeal hearing scheduled for 2009'. *The Canadian Press*, 3 March 2008.
- Staff. 'Pickton gets maximum sentence for murders'. *CBS News*, 12 December 2007.
- Staff. 'Alleged Australian murder victim found alive'. *The Guardian*, 11 April 2003.
- Usborne, David. 'Canada gripped by lurid case of "serial killer" pig farmer'. *The Independent*, 15 January 2003.
- Waugh, Rob. 'Monster left victim's spine in a plant pot'. *Yorkshire Post*, 27 February 2004.
- Waugh, Rob. 'Yorkshire couple who found from a TV programme their home was scene of horrific killing to hear verdict on damages. Gruesome past of a house of horror'. *Yorkshire Post*, 27 February 2004.

## CHAPTER SEVENTEEN
- Abós, Álvaro. 'Burgos: el descuartizador de Constitución'. *La revista del diario La Nacion Cronicas rojas*, 19 February 2006.
- Barbano Rolando; Caneletti Ricardo; Gambini, Hector. *Crimenes Argentinos Grandes Casos Policiales Que Conmovieron Al Pais*. Planeta, 2001.
- Caixiong, Zheng. 'Two held for killing & chopping man in "love triangle"'. *China Daily*, 15 January 2007.
- Canaletti, Ricardo. 'El misterioso caso del torso de mujer'. *Clarin*, 7 July 2005.
- DiGrazia, Christopher-Michael. 'Another Look at the Lusk Kidney'. Jack the Ripper Casebook (www.casebook.org). The dissertation originally appeared in *Ripper Notes* ed. Norder, Dan. and Vanderlinden, Wolf.
- Diaz, Roberto. 'Yo no maté a Alcira'. *La Cuidad*, 27 December 2007.

- Gonzalez, Gustavo; Barcia, Jose. *Testimonios y experiencias de un cronista porteno.* Historia Press, 1979.
- Manning, Gregg. 'Trunk Murders'. *Real Crime UK.* (www.real-crime.co.uk)
- Mead, Geoff. 'Brave new city, same mean streets. Changing face of Brighton and Hove'. *My Brighton and Hove,* 22 March 2006.(www.mybrightonandhove.org.uk)
- Pilkington, Ed. 'A human ear and a liver but no table legs'. *The Guardian,* 5 March 2007.
- Sassone, Martín. 'Un asesinato macabre'. *Clarin,* 4 October 2003.
- Staff. 'Body parts delivered to Michigan home'. *Associated Press,* 4 March 2007.
- Staff. 'Postal Workers Find Human Limbs in Parcel'. *Reuters,* 24 August 2001.
- Staff. 'Man gets parcel with human body parts'. *Times of India,* 11 January 2002.
- Staff. 'Two held after body parts found in mail'. *Reuters;* appeared also in *China Daily,* 15 January 2007.

## CHAPTER EIGHTEEN

- Allen, Arthur. 'Mad scientist: A grand jury is looking into the double life of Larry C. Ford, a brilliant doctor who killed himself before others learned about his dark side'. *Salon,* 26 June 2000. (www.salon.com)
- Atack, Jon. 'A Piece of Blue Sky Scientology Dianetics, and L. Ron Hubbard Exposed'. Published online: www.cs.cmu.edu/~dst/Library/Shelf/atack/contents.htm.
- Bell, Rachael. 'The Mysterious Dr Ford'. *Crime Library.* (www.crimelibrary.com)

- Brittain, Victoria. 'After The Apartheid Truth and reconciliation in South Africa'. *Le Monde Diplomatique*, December 1998.
- Carter, John. *Sex and Rockets: The Occult World of Jack Parsons*. Feral House, 1999.
- Chase, Alston. 'Harvard and the Making of the Unabomber'. *The Atlantic Monthly*, June 2000.
- Cockburn, Alexander; St Clair, Jeffrey, ed. 'CIA's Sidney Gottlieb: Pusher, Assassin & Pimp US Official Poisoner Dies'. *Counter Punch*. (www.counterpunch.org)
- Collins, Anne. *In the sleep room: The story of the CIA brainwashing experiments in Canada*. Key Porter Books, 1988.
- Conlogue, Ray. 'The Sleep Room's Missing Memories'. *The Globe and Mail*, 1 October 1998.
- Crowley, Aleister. *Moonchild*. Mandrake Press, 1929.
- Foster, Sarah. 'Meet Sidney Gottlieb – CIA dirty trickster: He's the target of more than one lawsuit'. *WorldNetDaily*, 19 November 1998. (www.worldnetdaily.com)
- Gould, Chandré. 'More Questions Than Answers: The Ongoing Trial of Dr Wouter Basson'. *The Acronym Institute for Disarmament Diplomacy*, November 2000.
- Harris, Sheldon. *Factories of Death: Japanese Biological Warfare, 1932–1945, and the American Cover-Up*. Routledge, 15 August 1995.
- Humes, Edward. 'The Medicine Man'. *Los Angeles Magazine*, July 2001.
- Jackson, David. 'Man Behind the Mask. The accused Unabomber's lawyers says he's schizophrenic, but can they use that as a defence?' *Time Magazine*, 17 November 1997.
- Jackson, David. 'He's Not Crazy, He's Our Neighbour In

# BIBLIOGRAPHY

Montana. Ted Kaczynski's acquaintances insist he was normal'. *Time Magazine*, 3 November 1997.

- Kristof, Nicholas. 'Unmasking Horror – A special report: Japan Confronting Gruesome War Atrocity'. *New York Times*, 17 March 1995.
- Lee, Martin and Shlain, Bruce. *Acid Dreams: The Complete Social History of LSD: The CIA, the Sixties, and Beyond*. Grove Press, 1994.
- Lifton, Robert Jay. 'What Made This Man? Mengele'. *New York Times*, 21 July 1985.
- Lindseth, Shawn. 'Awesome Or Off-Putting: Dr White's Monkey Head-Transplants'. *Heckler Spray*, 8 October 2007. (www.hecklerspray.com)
- MacDonald, Helen. 'Human Remains: Dissection and Its Histories'. Yale University Press, 2006.
- Marks, John. *The Search for the Manchurian Candidate: The CIA and Mind Control*. W. Norton & Company, 1991.
- Martelle, Scott; Leonard, Jack; Reza, H.G. 'Suspicious Canisters, Clues Unearthed in Orange County, California'. *Los Angeles Times*, 10 March 2000.
- Parent, André. 'Giovanni Aldini: From Animal Electricity to Human Brain Stimulation'. *The Canadian Journal of Neurological Science*, November 2004.
- Reed, Christopher. 'The United States and the Japanese Mengele: Payoffs and Amnesty for Unit 731 Scientists'. *Japan Focus*, 1 August 2006. (A shorter version of the same article first appeared in *Counterpunch* under the title 'The Pentagon and the Japanese Mengele. The Abominable Dr Ishii'. 27 May 2006.)
- Segel, Lawrence. 'To die in Unit 731'. *Free Republic*. (www.freerepublic.com)

- Staff. 'The Memory Thief: The Story of Dr Ewen Cameron'. *BBC News*, December 2004.
- Staff. 'The Frankenstein Factor'. *Cleveland Scene*, 9 December 1999.
- Staff. 'Live Brains in the Lab'. *Time Magazine*, 19 June 1964.
- Staff. 'Doctor Death implicates west'. *BBC News*, 31 July 1998.
- Staff. 'Kaczynski gets life, says government lied Unabomber, victims speak in court before sentencing'. *CNN*, 4 May 1998.
- Staff. 'Who was Josef Mengele?' *The Holocaust History Project*. An online archive of documents, photographs, recordings, and essays regarding the Holocaust. (www.holocaust-history.org)
- Sidley, Pat. 'Dr Wouter Basson cleared of murder of apartheid opponents'. *British Medical Journal*, 20 April 2002.
- Tsuneishi, Kei-ichi. (Translated by Orr, James.) 'New Facts about US Payoff to Japan's Biological Warfare Unit 731'. Japan Focus. (www.japanfocus.org)
- Wu, Tien-wei. 'A Preliminary Review of Studies of Japanese Biological Warfare and Unit 731 in the United States'. *Century China*. (www.centurychina.com)

## CHAPTER NINETEEN

- Allison, Ralph. 'Difficulties Diagnosing The Multiple Personality Syndrome In a Death Penalty. Case'. *The International Journal of Clinical and Experimental Hypnosis* Vol. XXXII, 1984.
- Boren, Roger (Justice). 'The Hillside Strangler Trial'. *Loyola Law Review*, Volume 33.
- Crary, David. 'Manipulation, self-deception often involved

when women fall for hard-core criminals'. *Police One*, 11 August 2005. (www.policeone.com)

- Fimrite, Peter and Taylor, Michael. 'No Shortage of Women Who Dream of Snaring a Husband on Death Row: Experts ponder why deadliest criminals get so many proposals'. *San Francisco Chronicle*, 27 March 2005.
- Leon, Harmon. 'Women Who Love Murderers Too Much'. *Harmon Sacramento News and Review*, 10 July 2004.
- Ramsland, Katherine. 'Serial killer Groupies'. *Crime Library*. (www.crimelibrary.com)

## CHAPTER TWENTY

- Boyes, Roger. 'Cannibalism Copycat Who Kept a Man in His Fridge'. *The Times*, 4 May 2005.
- Davey, Pauline. 'Operation Thornhill Revealed the Sinister Life of a Sadistic Killer Who Longed to Kill Again'. *Frontline Newspaper*, Issue no. 79; April/May 2001.
- Hall, Allan. 'This is What We Wanted'. *The Sun*, 4 December 2003.
- Harding, Luke. 'Victim of Cannibal Agreed to be Eaten'. *The Guardian*, 4 December 2003.
- Harrison, Ben. *Undying Love: The True Story of a Passion That Defied Death*. St Martin's True Crime Library, 2001.
- Huwash, Ali. 'Woman Tortured, Killed Maid for Being "Lazy"'. *Arab News*, 8 June 2007.
- O'Shaughnessy, Patrice. '17 years don't diminish fire tragedy'. *New York Daily*, 20 March 2007.
- Robins, Derek. 'Cannibal Shocker on Five'. *The Sun*, 10 October 2007.
- Roman, Silvia. 'El aprendiz de caníbal'. *El Mundo*, 6 May 2005.

- Smith, Martina. 'Shooter killed after Wisconsin gun rampage'. *The Telegraph*, 2 October 2007.
- Staff. 'Sad Misfit Who Chose Victim and Killed in Cold Blood'. *This is Nottingham*, 5 December 2007. (www.thisisnottingham.co.uk)
- Staff. 'A Murder of Small Significance'. *The Times*, 27 August 1951. Posted on *Ain't No Way to Go*. (www.aintnowaytogo.com)
- Staff. 'Nurse convicted of murder'. *BBC News*, 19 June 2001.
- Staff. 'Nurse accused of murder at nursing home'. *Northern Echo*, 8 June 2001.
- Staff. 'Murder trial nurse "bored and lazy"'. *Northern Echo*, 12 June 2001.
- Staff. 'Fin de un Reality'. *El Universo*, 12 October 2007.
- Staff. 'The Revolt of Leo Held'. *Time Magazine*, 3 November 1967.
- Staff . 'Sale del aire Nada más que la verdad'. *El Colombiano*, October 2007.
- Stanley, Alessandra. '25 Years to Life for the Arsonist at Happy Land'. *New York Times*, 20 September 1991.
- Tomasson, Robert. 'Shock Lingers as Happy Land Trial Starts'. *New York Times*, 9 July 1991.
- Velasco Luz, Adriana. 'Con polémica, finaliza temporada de "Nada más que la verdad"'. *El Tiempo*, 5 October 2007.
- Court Case: Details of the sentence as handed down by the Hon. Justice Bell (Neutral Citation Number: [2005] EWHC 2541 [QB] Case No: 2004/109/MTS) in the High Court of Justice Queen's Bench Division Royal Courts of Justice. 15 November 2005.

## CHAPTER TWENTY-ONE

- Ekman, Paul. 'Would You Lie to Me?' *The Observer*, 27 April 2003.
- Fleming, Rebecca B. 'Scanty Goatees and Palmer Tattoos: Cesare Lombroso's Influence on Science and Popular Opinion'. *The Concord Review*, 2001.
- Havelock, Ellis. *The Criminal*. Adamant Media Corporation, 2000.
- Lombroso, Cesare. *Criminal Man*. Duke University Press, 2006.
- Lombroso, Cesare; Guglielmo, Ferrero. *Criminal Woman, the Prostitute, and the Normal Woman*. Duke University Press, 2004.
- Rafter, Nicole. 'Apes, Men and Teeth: Earnest A. Hooton and Eugenic Decay'. *Popular Eugenics: National Efficiency and Mass Culture in the 1930s*. Currell, Sue; Cogdell, Christina, eds. Columbus, Ohio, Ohio University Press.
- Rafter, Nicole. 'Earnest A. Hooton and the Biological Tradition in American Criminology'. *Criminology*, Issue 42.
- Rafter, Nicole. 'The Murderous Dutch fiddler. Criminology, history and the problem of phrenology'. *Theoretical Criminology*, Vol. 9, 2005.
- Rafter, Nicole. 'The Unrepentant Horse Slasher: Moral Insanity And the Origins of Criminological Thought'. *Criminology* 42.
- Rafter, Nicole. 'Rethinking criminological tradition. Cesare Lombroso and the origins of Criminology'. *The Essential Criminology Reader*, Henry, Stuart; Lanier, Mark, eds. The Perseus Books Group, 2006.

- Ramey, Jessie. 'The Bloody Blonde and the Marble Woman: gender and power in the case of Ruth Snyder'. *Journal of Social History*, Spring edition, 2004.
- Staff. 'Pessimist'. *Time Magazine*, 7 January 1935.
- Staff. 'After Lombroso'. *Time Magazine*, 30 January 1939.